D0225375

HE
6371
.A54
1989

Adie, Douglas K.

Monopoly mail

$34.95

DATE			

BUSINESS/SCIENCE/TECHNOLOGY DIVISION

© THE BAKER & TAYLOR CO.

MONOPOLY MAIL

This book is sponsored by the Cato Institute

Founded in 1977, the Cato Institute is a public policy research organization dedicated to exploring policy options consistent with the traditional American principles of individual liberty, limited government, and peace.

MONOPOLY MAIL
PRIVATIZING
THE UNITED STATES
POSTAL SERVICE

Douglas K. Adie

Transaction Publishers
New Brunswick (U.S.A.) and Oxford (U.K.)

Copyright © 1989 by Transaction Publishers
New Brunswick, New Jersey 08903

All rights reserved under International and Pan-American Copyright Con-
ventions. No part of this book may be reproduced or transmitted in any
form or by any means, electronic or mechanical, including photocopy,
recording, or any information storage and retrieval system, without prior
permission in writing from the publisher. All inquiries should be addressed
to Transaction Publishers, Rutgers—The State University, New Brunswick,
New Jersey 08903.

Library of Congress Catalog Number: 88-14691
ISBN: 0-88738-203-7
Printed in the United States of America

Library of Congress Cataloging-in-Publication Data

Adie, Douglas K.
   Monopoly mail : the case for privatizing the United States Postal
Service / Douglas K. Adie
     p.   cm.
   Includes bibliographies and index.
   ISBN 0-88738-203-7
   1. United States Postal Service—Management. 2. Privatization-
-United States. 3. Postal service—United States—Management.
4. Government business enterprises—United States—Management.
I. Title.   1989
HE6371.A54 1988
353.0087'3——dc119   88-14691
                                       CIP

Contents

Acknowledgments

Research support and encouragement have been generously provided by the Cato Institute, Washington, D.C., the George F. Bennett Chair in Economics and Business at Wheaton College, and by Ohio University. I am grateful to Yale Brozen for first stimulating my interest in the U.S. Postal Service. It was Jim Dorn at Cato who approached me about doing this study and persevered through my initial reluctance, and has prodded me along from time to time. David Boaz, also at Cato, has offered counsel and made publication arrangements. Neither the Cato Institute nor Ohio University, however, is in any way implicated by the opinions or the conclusions expressed here. Linda Hayward, Lori Oeffner, Steve Folkerts, Tammy Thompson, and LaVerne Peterson have helped with research chores and typing and I am indeed grateful for their untiring service. Several of my friends and colleagues have read the manuscript and offered stylistic, strategic, and even substantive suggestions, many of which I have borrowed shamelessly. I am indeed grateful for their labors, which have improved this study immensely. They are James Rogers, John Crutcher, David Stover, William Niskanen, David Boaz, Barry Seldon, Catherine England, Katharin Foster, Ismail Ghazalah, Doug Bandow, James Bovard, Lynn Scarlett, Robert Poole, and James Dorn. My wife, Dolores, and my three teenage children have tolerated my absence from normal family responsibilities and given my isolation enough respect to allow me to carry on much of the research chores around the house in relative tranquility. I am indeed grateful to them for this.

1

Introduction

The Need for Reform

The United States Postal Service (USPS) deserves attention because it is the largest government-owned utility operating in the private sector. Also of concern is the fact that it receives huge subsidies out of general tax revenues while displaying gross inefficiencies. As the largest civilian employer in the nation, it employs 790,557 people (1987). It delivers over 154 billion pieces of mail per year along 156,000 routes to 91.2 million separate addresses. To move the mail, it operates 145,811 cars and trucks, the third-largest vehicle fleet after Hertz and Avis. It also commands considerable buying power, spending $1.3 billion annually for air, highway, and water transportation. In fiscal year 1987 the USPS spent $32.5 billion (about 1 percent of GNP), of which $25.6 billion was salaries and benefits. These facts make it clear that the USPS is a major player in the marketplace and deserves close examination. More important than its size, however, is its ability to raise excessive revenues from first class mailers as a result of its government-bestowed monopoly embodied in the private express statutes.

Furthermore and perhaps more important, the Postal Service is worthy of study because of its impact on personal freedom. Postal labor unions, which represent approximately 80 percent of postal employees, serve no productive function but enjoy support that is indirectly derived from government subsidies, favors, and recognition. In return for this, the unions make implicit threats of violence during illegal postal strikes that interfere with the rights of nonunion workers to compete in a free labor market. The postal monopoly in the delivery of first class mail also denies consumers freedom in their choice of a delivery service for their letters, and prevents entrepreneurs from offering letter mail service. It forces taxpayers to subsidize operations that are inefficient and workers who are often insensitive to patrons.

1

The power possessed by Congress involves the right to determine what shall be excluded from the mails. For instance, unsolicited contraceptives and advertisements for them are nonmailable except to specified individuals. Even though unsuccessful, members of Congress still introduce bills to make various things nonmailable, such as unsolicited advertisements, unsolicited credit cards, drug and cigarette samples, and mailing lists from "adult" magazines, businesses, or government agencies. The members have been interested most in obscenity. They have made "salacious advertisings" or offensive sex materials sent to youths under eighteen, nonmailable matter. The law, however, now puts the burden for enforcing these laws on parents rather than on the Post Office.[1]

Some attorneys have recently asked if the Postal Service and the IRS have colluded against tax shelter investors and tax protestors. They assert that in the past year the Postal Service has misdirected an abnormally high volume of mail addressed to tax shelter investors and tax protestors to the IRS centers, where IRS officials have opened them, stamped them "opened in error," and then forwarded them to their intended addresses. For instance, San Francisco attorney Bartholomew Lee says that the IRS office in Kansas City, Missouri, opened a letter from Vaughn Oil Production Company in Niles, Illinois, addressed to his client, Annie Lee Hudson, whom he was representing in litigation with the IRS over a tax shelter.[2] If this practice has any regularity, there is no sanctity to Postal Service mail delivery, and those desiring confidentiality in their correspondence need to turn to another deliverer.

Although much of this is of paramount importance, it has been true for many years without eliciting a policy outcry. A new ingredient is now present that greatly enhances the prospects for radically changing much of the above. This ingredient is the burgeoning new communications technology, which cries out for reforming the postal monopoly. Potentially, it may be the most important factor for precipitating change. For all of these reasons it is now appropriate to take a new look at the policy alternatives for the Postal Service.

Some Recent Opinions on Postal Reform

Numerous policymakers have recently discussed postal reform. For instance, John W. Crutcher, vice chairman of the Postal Rate Commission, has been an outspoken critic of inefficient and wasteful postal practices. He recommends a version of privatization that focuses exclusively on contracting out postal functions to private businesses while keeping the managerial functions of the postal corporation intact.[3]

Bert Ely, head of his own consulting firm, Ely & Company, has entered the discussion to privatize the Postal Service in a private memorandum entitled "Privatizing the Postal Service—How To Do It." Among other things, he suggests that the entire Postal Service be sold, rather than having the Postal Service make piecemeal arrangements with private businesses, as Crutcher suggests. His reason is that mail delivery is time sensitive and requires precise coordination, which is not possible under contracting of postal functions. Ely suggests that parcel post be sold separately, and the rest be sold as a unit to increase the revenue and leverage for gaining political support for the privatization policy.[4]

Rep. Bill Green (R-N.Y.) has introduced a bill, HR 1048, that would suspend the private express statutes and permit competition within any postal district where the USPS consistently fails to meet its own official standards of service, i.e. delivering 95 percent of the intracity first class mail overnight. Five Republican members of the House (David Dreier and Robert Dornan, Calif.; Philip Crane, Ill.; Richard Armey, Tex.; and Howard Neilson, Utah) are cosponsors. The purpose of the bill is to put pressure on the Postal Service to improve service. If the Postal Service fails to meet overnight delivery requirements, this bill would create opportunities for entrepreneurs. Green does not intend to relieve the government of all responsibilities for mail delivery but only gradually allow private firms to serve the public's interest in one area after another.[5]

Newspapers are also entering the discussion. A *New York Times* editorial noted that the benefits from reorganization had not been realized. It also noted that where legal alternatives exist, people and businesses eagerly grab them, even at premium prices. For instance, Federal Express and other firms have built a booming business in overnight mail, and United Parcel Service (UPS) continues to increase its share of package delivery. Ironically, the main success of the Postal Service, which Crutcher desires to enlarge upon, has been private subcontracting, including presort mail and 5,000 profit-making rural mail deliverers. With historical perspective, the *Times* notices that mail delivery has been most efficient where competition determines service standards and the government does least. In conclusion, the *Times* suggests, as does James C. Miller III, current director of the Office of Management and Budget (OMB), that the risks of jeopardizing a universal delivery service from repealing the private express statutes are grossly exaggerated. Also following Miller, the *Times* suggests that any diminution of service to rural customers could be remedied more cheaply with public subsidies than by continuing the inefficiencies of the Postal Service in its present organizational form. Rather than a drift toward an unplanned privatization, as would happen under the Green bill, the *Times* prefers a decisive disposition of the Postal Service. It asks, "Wouldn't it be better to consider all the alternatives and choose the best?"[6]

For at least ten years Miller has advocated repeal of the private express statutes, and in his job at OMB this policy is taking a higher priority. Under repeal, Miller predicts, existing private mail firms would expand, new ones would enter the market and the Postal Service would improve its performance.[7] Thomas Moore, a member of President Reagan's Council of Economic Advisers and head of the administration's interagency task force on privatization, is working on a plan for ending the Postal Service's monopoly on first class mail, initially by allowing anyone to stuff material in private mailboxes and then by gradually eliminating the laws that created the monopoly.[8]

Miller said recently that deregulating the Postal Service will probably be on President Reagan's agenda soon. The proposal may advocate selling all the assets or just allowing private companies to compete on an experimental basis in delivering mail to rural areas. The Board of Postal Governors, a majority of which are Reagan appointees, has authority to determine just what kind of mail only the Postal Service can deliver. Postal officials currently allow private companies to carry first class material but only under very tight restrictions. The board could narrow the definition of the private express statutes to reduce the Postal Service's monopoly by granting waivers from the statutes for certain geographical areas or even repeal the statutes. How far the proposals of the White House go will depend on how much capital will have to be spent on that issue versus other issues.[9]

In an op-ed piece in the *Los Angeles Times*, Doug Bandow, a senior fellow with the Cato Institute, challenged the Postal Service to suspend enforcement of the private express statutes, which bar private firms from carrying first class mail. To indicate the failure of the Postal Service to meet consumer needs, Bandow notes that many businesses illegally transport foreign-bound letters overseas, and mail them themselves rather than send them through the Postal Service. Bandow also points out that Harold O'Brien, owner of House and Senate Delivery Service, has gained favor with lobbyists and others who want to communicate quickly by delivering messages to members of Congress twice as fast for less than one-fourth the Postal Service charge. John McKean, a postal governor, admits that his public corporation is not serving consumers well. By suspending enforcement of its monopoly provisions, the Postal Service could prove that it sincerely wants to serve the interest of consumers. Otherwise, Bandow recommends that Congress repeal the private express statutes. He believes there is no doubt that private firms could do a better job delivering the mail and so should not be suppressed by government-sponsored suits, as they have been in Kansas and New York.[10]

International Resource Development (a research and consulting firm) predicts that by the mid-1990s the Postal Service will be restructured along the lines of the postdivestiture American Telephone & Telegraph and privatized like British Telecom.[11] The steady stream of comments and proposals on restructuring mail service, all pointing generally in the same direction, is another indicator that now is the time to discuss and recommend policy alternatives respecting the disposition of the Postal Service.

A Short Preview

On July 1, 1971, the Post Office, as it was then called, ceased operating as a department of the federal government and began operating as a public corporation called the U.S. Postal Service.[12] Since reorganization, new problems have combined with old ones to pose a threat to the Postal Service, its customers, and the general public. In this book I will discuss the problems and how they have arisen. I will explore the relationship of the problems to the present structure of the Postal Service and pose some possible solutions. These will range from the dissolution of the Postal Service to various restructuring possibilities aimed at meeting the challenges of the next fifty years.

At the root of the Postal Service's existing problems is an unsound organizational structure, particularly those features that distinguish it from a privately owned and operated business. The features are these:

1. A governmentally bestowed and supported monopoly on letter mail,[13] which yields 60 percent of its revenues.
2. Authority to interpret and administer its own monopoly powers.
3. Total exemption from federal, state, and local taxes.
4. Ability to borrow through the Treasury up to a maximum of $10 billion.

Behind these distinguishing characteristics are two questions that have plagued the Postal Service since its start:

1. Should a governmentally owned monopoly or private business provide mail service?
2. Should the Postal Service seek as its primary good to service its customers as faithfully and competently as possible, giving the best service at the lowest possible cost; or should it rather seek to fulfill some public-service-oriented goal related to the national purpose?

These questions are not mutually exclusive but interrelated. If we believe the Postal Service should serve the public by providing individual postal patrons the services they desire for the lowest cost, private business would best fulfill this goal. On the other hand, if the Postal Service should pursue as a first priority the public service goal designed to benefit the whole country rather than postal patrons, some form of government participation would be more compatible.[14] The historical consequences of choosing from these alternatives will form the content of chapters 2 and 3.

In subsequent chapters, I will apply lessons learned in private business to the Postal Service. In particular, AT&T will be singled out in chapter 4 for detailed attention because it is an analog to the Postal Service in many ways. For instance, it is in the communications business, was the largest utility before being divested, is approximately the same size, offers virtually universal service, and in many respects is a prototype for the deregulation and divestiture of the Postal Service. With respect to this last feature, AT&T has experienced a detailed and dramatic divestiture process that has resulted in a transformation that has great potential as a model for restructuring the Postal Service. If the Postal Service undergoes a similar restructuring, the present experience of AT&T can be exceedingly instructive.

In chapter 5 we look at the airline industry (and a few others) because they provide a mature picture of the effects of deregulation. The airline industry, although considerably short of equilibrium, nevertheless provides guidelines on some of the longer-run effects of deregulation that one might expect.

Chapter 6 examines labor relations in the Postal Service in the light of the Professional Air Traffic Controllers Organization (PATCO) affair, which the author regards as a watershed in labor relations for the entire country and, in particular, for federal employees. Compensation for labor services in the Postal Service are 84 percent of total costs and have come under considerable scrutiny by many economists. These economists, including me, have concluded that postal workers are overpaid by as much as 35 percent.[15] Although this conclusion rests upon methodologically sound research, to date few have listened to attempts to reduce this inequitable discrepancy.

A change in attitude toward the Postal Service salary structure now seems to be emerging, and because salary discrepancies are gaining visibility, the PATCO confrontation takes on unique significance for the Postal Service. Although the history of postal labor relations, pre- and post-reorganization, has been invariably on labor's side, during the post-PATCO period at least some sobriety is being introduced into the discussions. Chapter 6 will argue that arbitration, which will be utilized almost exclusively to resolve labor disputes in the Postal Service, is not designed to bear the strain of redressing the inequities of excessive wages.

Chapter 7 reviews the privatization experiences in Canada and England. These countries are chosen because their economies are most like the U.S.

economy and their experiences provide suggestions for privatizing the U.S. Postal Service.

Chapter 8 tackles the tough organizational choices of the future by examining Postal Service *divestiture* in light of AT&T; *privatization* in light of the Canadian and British experiences; and *deregulation* in light of AT&T and the airlines industry. The conclusion reached is that bold restructuring that includes divestiture, privatization, and deregulation is the only alternative that offers hope for the Postal Service as an organization, as well as longer-term security for postal employees. (Indeed, business will meet customers' needs in one way or another regardless of what happens to the Postal Service. If the Postal Service does not adapt, technology will enable the public to bypass it for most of its necessary functions.)

Restructuring that makes the Postal Service a competitive rather than a subsidized business will reduce the tax burden of private citizens. No longer will the public be forced to contribute to a postal system immune from marketplace realities. No longer will the government place its reputation on the line to guarantee Postal Service debt.[16]

Some Postal Problems

Businesspeople, federal administrators, and legislators were led to seek a reorganization of the postal function in the mid-1960s due mainly to mounting consumer complaints, insistent demands by postal unions, and annual deficits. President Lyndon Johnson appointed a commission in 1967 to study the matter. Headed by Frederick Kappel, retired board chairman of AT&T, the commission recommended that the Post Office be reorganized under a corporate model but with much less accountability than for a typical for-profit business.

The Kappel Commission asserted that outdated and inappropriate management techniques were the root causes of the postal problems. Poor management, it reported, had led to unresponsive service, antiquated personnel practices, unfavorable working conditions, limited career opportunities, a perverse redistributional rate system, and a growing deficit. The commission's major failure was in succumbing to the fallacy of misplaced concreteness and thereby leaving unearthed the deeper, more fundamental problem that had produced the symptomatic shortcomings listed above. It called that which in fact was a symptom of the problem, namely, unresponsive management, the root problem; at the same time it ignored the real problem, which was a lack of correct motivation stemming from the nature of the organization itself. What was true before reorganization is still true. The Postal Service lacks a bottom line and people to care about it. In effect, reorganization addressed symptoms only and failed to provide an organizational structure characterized by enough motivation to use resources efficiently.

The following list of current problems is indicative of a lack of proper motivation brought on by structural deficiencies that yet exist in the Postal Service:

1. the failures of Bulk Mail Processing, E-COM, INTELPOST, and possibly ZIP + 4;
2. unduly generous wage settlements;
3. increasing delivery times; and
4. an unhelpful attitude toward customer complaints.

Operational and Innovation Failures

To illustrate the first point, the volume of parcels handled by the Postal Service between 1951 and 1974 fell over 50 percent. A reason for this may be that the USPS, as reported by an internal survey, damaged half the packages marked "fragile." Instead of focusing on the problem of package handling, the Postal Service responded to the loss in package volume by spending a billion dollars to build twenty-one new bulk-mail centers to win back business. The result was a disaster. For example, the mechanical conveyor belts used in the USPS centers included a drop of up to four feet; the UPS had no drops. Fourteen years after the first USPS bulk-mail center was opened in Jersey Meadows in 1974, UPS was carrying almost 90 percent of all parcels. Originally promoted as a cost-cutter, the National Bulk Mail System has turned into a $1.5 billion albatross.

To date, the Postal Service's experience with E-COM runs parallel to its bulk mail experience. E-COM is an electronic computer-originated mail system that, despite legal prohibitions, was heavily subsidized. The customer paid only twenty-six cents per E-COM letter, but the Postal Service lost $5.25 on each E-COM letter the first year and continued to lose over one dollar per letter until E-COM's termination in the fall of 1985. The system required considerable volume just to break even, and actual volume consistently fell short of predicted volume. Though each message was beamed electronically to one of twenty-five post office receiving stations, once there it could still take two days or more to deliver. Communication expert Michael Cavanagh said, "There's just no way this can be characterized as anything else than an abysmal failure." Rep. Glenn English (D-OK.), chairman of the Government Operations Committee, concluded that E-COM "certainly looks like a turkey and it gobbles like a turkey."[17] Confirming this failure, the Postal Service announced in 1985 that it would shut down E-COM and was looking for a buyer.[18]

INTELPOST is another example of what appears on the surface to be a good idea but fails in execution at the hands of postal managers. INTELPOST is an electronic mail service that sends instantaneous facsimile copies between continents. The Postal Service seems to have misjudged the market, which has proven to be much lower than projected. One cannot rule out, however, unreliable service as the real culprit here too. In any event this venture, too, has failed.

ZIP + 4 is a nine-digit zip code system that permits a greater degree of mechanized sorting, and in the right hands potentially could cut labor costs dramatically. The Postal Service has requested $900 million to implement ZIP + 4, even though it is not clear that it would allocate enough funds to customers to encourage its use. The Postal Service has obscured the costs and perhaps exaggerated the benefits of the program as it is currently conceived. Whether the expanded zip code will succeed is an open question.[19]

To date, the Postal Service has not demonstrated competence in planning, carrying out, or marketing electronic services in a competitive and unregulated environment.[20] Indeed, the Postal Service has not learned much from its mistakes and apparently is plagued with the Midas touch in reverse.[21] A pattern of failures in innovations that should have succeeded does not bode well for the future of the Postal Service in its present organizational form as it faces competition in a communications industry that is developing rapidly. Experience to date should raise a warning flag to both postal management and employees that the Postal Service needs a new form of organization that can cope and respond in today's rapidly paced communications industry.

To highlight the gross inefficiencies of the Postal Service, President Ronald Reagan concocted the following illustration some time ago while campaigning in New York City. He said that farmers in Ghana grow cocoa beans and sell them to the marketing board, which then exports them to London. From there wholesalers ship them to New York and then to Hershey, Pennsylvania. Farmers in Jamaica grow sugarcane, refine it, and ship it to New York. From New York it, too, is shipped to Hershey, Pennsylvania. Farmers in Wisconsin produce milk products that they also ship to Hershey, Pennsylvania. Paper mills in Quebec, Canada, produce labels and ship them to Hershey, Pennsylvania. In Hershey, Pennsylvania, the Hershey Company processes all of these products and manufactures a chocolate bar, packs and sends it to New York and many other places around the country where it can be purchased for as little as fifteen cents. And it costs the Postal Service twenty cents just to send a letter from one coast to the other.

Labor Relations Failures

Since reorganization, postal wages have increased faster than both the consumer price index and the wages of civil service workers.[22] Between 1969 and 1981 the Consumer Price Index (CPI) rose 146 percent while postal wages rose 163 percent, or about twice that of civil service wages. From 1972 to 1981 federal government wages rose 70 percent while postal wages increased 123 percent.[23]

In July 1969, before reorganization and before the pay increases following the 1970 strike, an average postal worker earned $8,030 at level five, step ten. Level-five postal workers (PS-5) then were paid the same as level-five civil service workers on the General Schedule (GS-5). In 1981 workers at the same level and step were making the equivalent of a GS-9, and by 1983 were earning $22,849.[24] This trend is particularly disturbing because *before* reorganization postal workers were receiving disproportionately higher wages than their counterparts in the private sector. (From the postal worker's point of view this, of course, is a matter of pride and achievement.)

Although reorganization should have increased management's ability to conduct wage negotiations more favorable to the interest of patrons and taxpayers, that clearly did not happen. The experience prompts the question, "Does the existing organizational structure provide management with the tools and/or incentives to negotiate in the public's interest with postal workers and unions?" Throughout this book and especially in chapter 6 experience and logic answer with a resounding No.

The Kappel Commission estimated "at least twenty-five percent of the cost of postal operations could be saved by organizational changes giving postal managers authority to bargain with unions concerning mechanization and productivity increases." Naturally, to negotiate successfully, management must have the power and will to bargain hard with unions such as the American Postal Workers Union, which will predictably oppose such things as presorting programs, nine-digit zip codes, and other economies that would result in fewer clerk positions.[25] Since reorganization the postal managers have been no more successful in negotiating changes in inefficient work rules and the introduction of labor-saving innovations than before reorganization.

The Postal Service in its January 1979 Comprehensive Statement says: "This upgrading of compensation and benefits has prevented gross productivity gains from being reflected in lower postage rates in real dollars." From January 1971 to January 1982 the CPI rose 137 percent while first class postage shot up more than 200 percent. The discrepancy indicates that much of the increase in postal employee wages has come at the expense of first class mail customers.

Financial Failures

We will turn now to another problem area. In the twenty years before postal reorganization the postal deficit, defined as the difference between operating expense and operating income, averaged about $700 million a year. Since reorganization the deficit has been redefined as the difference between costs and total revenues, which now include appropriations from Congress. If the books were kept on the same basis as before reorganization, we would see, for example, that the Postal Service ran an annual deficit of between $1.5 and $2.8 billion per year from 1971 to 1978. From 1979 to 1986 the bottom line of the budget has fluctuated between a deficit of $1.9 billion in 1980 and a surplus of $95 million in 1982, with the most recent budget in 1986 showing a need for total government appropriations of $411 million (see table 1.1). In the 1976 Amendments to the Postal Reorganization Act the Postal Service received a one-time subsidy of $1 billion to offset the deficits of the prior two years. Since 1979 there has been a shift away from deficit financing as the Postal Service has relied more on funds generated through rate increases.[26] This shift in Postal Service revenues from monies taken out of tax revenues to monies paid for first class postage does not reflect savings to the general public through efficiencies in operations.

The 1977 Commission on the Postal Service, authorized in the 1976 Amendments and established in January 1977, recommended a doubling of the permanent public service subsidy over that established under reorganization.[27] (To their credit the postal managers resisted a permanent increase in the subsidy.) The commission attempted to raise the public service appropriations to $1.1 billion for fiscal year 1980, $1.2 billion for fiscal year 1981, and $1.3 billion for fiscal year 1982 and beyond. Although these payments (appropriations) were designed to compensate the Postal Service for providing public services and therefore are no longer called subsidies, they in fact amount to direct subsidizing out of tax revenues. While the H.R. 79 bill provided for increased public service funding—a euphemism for providing more revenues with which to compensate postal employees—incorporating the commission's recommendations on subsidies, no legislation has been passed since 1976. This record of inaction has spared the taxpayer but has placed a heavier burden on first class postal patrons.[28]

TABLE 1.1
Government Subsidies to the Postal Service
(Millions of Dollars)

Subsidy	1971	1972	1973	1974	1975	1976	1977	1978	1979	1980	1981	1982	1983	1984	1985	1986	1987
Public service appropriations							920	920	920	828	486	12	0	0	0	0	0
Revenue forgone appropriations							792	802	800	782	789	695	789	879	970	716	650
Total government subsidy	2,086	1,424	1,486	1,750	1,533	1,645	1,712	1,722	1,720	1,610	1,275	707	789	879	970	716	650
Loss (net income)	204	175	13	438	989	1,176	688	379	(470)	306	588	(802)	(616)	(117)	252	(305)	223
Total government appropriations	2,290	1,599	1,499	2,188	2,522	2,821	2,400	2,101	1,250	1,916	1,862	(95)	173	762	1,222	411	873

Source: *Annual Report of the Postmaster General,* 1971-1986.
Note: From 1977 on, the figures are for fiscal year ending September 30; before 1977, the figures are for fiscal year ending June 30.

Efficiency Failures

Efficient operations utilizing up-to-date equipment have been a hall-mark of private businesses that must survive in competitive markets. Instead of translating surpluses and appropriations into extravagant wages, the Postal Service should have used these funds to pursue mechanization, especially labor-saving devices. Apparently it has been reluctant to behave efficiently for fear of reducing the number of jobs available to union members, and has preferred the risk of precipitating public outcry through repeated increases in postal wages, now at an unconscionable level.

The Postal Service has available to it several key machines that are capable, with very few employees, of handling the mail quickly, efficiently, and in huge volumes. The multiposition letter-sorting machine (MPLSM) is probably the most important such machine. Forming the heart of the mechanization program, it is capable of sorting 36,000 pieces of mail an hour and, considering current labor costs, is well worth its $250,000 price. It moves a letter into the sight of one of its twelve operators, who types a ZIP code on a keyboard, sending the letter to one of 277 destination bins.

Although the MPLSM was introduced in 1955, the Postal Service had installed only 282 of these machines by 1971, partly because it required that the mail be ZIP coded. By 1981 only 800 MPLSMs and 440 single-position letter-sorting machines (SPLSMs) were in service. They have enabled some reduction in the total work force in spite of increasing volume. Unfortunately, the gains from these efficiency measures were not passed on to customers as lower postage rates or to the public by a cessation of all subsidies. Rather, they have been squandered on various inefficiencies and wage increases for existing employees. (Chapter 7 discusses the structural reason for this.)

As an example of how efficiencies from mechanization can be transformed into inefficiencies, 7 percent of outgoing mail processed on letter-sorting machines is misdirected by the machine operators. This lowers the average speed of service and causes mailhandlers to sort the same mail more than once. The Postal Service has experienced the same problem with parcel sorters. In the hands of the Postal Service the effects of labor-saving devices seem to be perverse. It appears as though the more sorting machines the Postal Service installs, the more mistakes operators and machines make and the longer it takes parcels to reach their destinations.

Chronic inefficiency in the Postal Service raises a series of questions. Is there consistent petty sabotage on the part of the employees in an attempt to protect jobs? Is there a laxity in management's demands for performance? Or is there just a jinx on the Postal Service that allows it to take a perfectly sound idea and see it fall way short of its potential? Whatever the reason, a restructuring of the Postal Service as a private profit-making business would introduce enough incentives for management to find out what the problems are and solve them—or else themselves be removed.

How Much Time Do We Have?

As the communications industry becomes increasingly dependent upon high technology, it will experience rapid and dramatic changes. The Postal Service is going to require aggressive, flexible management if it is to survive. More than anything else, competitive pressures will bring these qualities to the forefront. It will be necessary for managers to assume risks under conditions designed to encourage better decision making. It will take new and aggressive managers to contend with the fact that even with automated mail handling perfected (something not yet accomplished), there may still be little room for the Postal Service in the communications world of the future.

The Postal Service is confronted with a dilemma. Concentrating on conventional mail processing will result in lost business, but in its present organizational form, its forays into electronic transfers and other innovations have been for the most part disasters. Companies like AT&T are devoting great efforts to new communications opportunities. The Postal Service has failed in pursuing the status quo and its attempts at innovation. It had better organize itself in a way that meets society's changing communications needs or its usefulness will cease. For example, electronic transfers are faster, easier, and eventually will be cheaper than traditional correspondence, and will substantially change the way the United States communicates. Electronic transfers will spell disaster for the USPS as it is now organized and functioning. Unless one advocates the support of useless institutions with tax dollars, there is virtually no alternative but to change the organizational structure of the Postal Service.

James J. LaPenta, Jr., postal union leader, senses the problem for the Postal Service and says, "The third largest workforce in the United States . . . is going to be devastated by our emerging national policy on telecommunications."

The fulfillment of LaPenta's fears could provide one way in which private competitors in the communications industry achieve dominance. *The Postal Service may simply fall into disuse!* Of course another strategy is radically to restructure the Postal Service so it can become competitive. Postal workers and labor union leaders need to see this and ease the adjustment process. Otherwise they may find themselves presiding over the decline of the Postal Service in much the same way that John L. Lewis did over the coal industry some thirty years ago!

How much time can pass before the communications industry bypasses the Postal Service? When will electronic mail systems be cost effective? As it now stands, postal prices will continue to rise as electronic prices fall. Even at the time of this writing some electronic communications services are cost effective. For instance, direct-dialed, late night, or weekend transcontinental one-minute calls cost about thirty cents, the cost of postage and stationery for one letter. In one minute a computer can transmit a considerable amount of information to another computer. When the transformation to electronic communications becomes complete, the Postal System may well become an anachronism unless it adjusts.

Can We Reduce Today's Problems to Basics?

The economic issues are numerous, but there is an overriding political issue that all agree must be confronted. This issue centers on how to make the Postal Service accountable to the public without subjecting its policy-making and particular decisionmaking to political influences. Can we devise a method for bringing accountability to an institution that at present is almost autonomous?[29]

The accountability issue divides into two smaller fundamental problems with which Congress must wrestle: (1) the level of public service the Postal Service should provide coupled with the size of appropriations to the Postal Service out of general tax revenues, and (2) whether the Postal Service should be a nationalized industry run by the government, and if so, how competitive it should be with private business. These problems are interrelated, have been part of the discussion for many years, and are still at the heart of the matter.

In its infancy the Post Office became a governmentally owned and operated industry. The government was not asserting moral, political, or economic principles but only its desire to create a convenient medium for the subsidization of numerous educational, governmental, and developmental public service functions.[30] The desire to subsidize these public service functions explains why the government has always displayed ambivalence over how competitive the Post Office should be with private business. Sometimes it has restrained competitors and at other times it has ignored them altogether. The government's attitude at a given moment has often been a function of whether the Post Office needed to be pressured by the private sector to "get its house in order." Overall, the government's position has always been one of expediency in the pursuit of convenient and temporary objectives. Private competition has never been allowed to determine the character of the Postal Service but, rather, has been used manipulatively to interject some efficiency into the oftentimes lethargic postal enterprise when inefficiencies reached a crisis level. Legislators justified this manipulative, erratic, and unusual use of competition in the private sector because they were convinced that the Postal Service provided essential public services that were helpful to the public but not profitable for private business to undertake.

As noted, the government's original purpose for creating, as well as presumed reason for continuing, its support of the Post Office has been a perceived need for certain public service functions that would presumably benefit the nation. These services were seen as outside the scope of that which private business would provide. As long as the legislators viewed these functions—namely, to provide universal communications at a cost accessible to everyone, to diffuse important information to the nation, to provide postal service to every burg and hamlet in the nation, and to facilitate the transportation network of roads, rails, and airlines—the Post Office as a government-owned business was safe. However, these public service functions are now substantially complete and there is a growing interest among legislators to divest themselves of the perennial problems of dealing with postal matters.

Prompted by the growing realization that the three-hundred-year-old public service tasks of encouraging economic development were completed, the legislators, in the reorganization of the Post Office into the Postal Service, set in motion a course directed toward reducing if not eliminating the public service functions. Chapter 3 demonstrates the logical implication of this, which is for the government to divest itself completely of the Postal Service.

Because the need for the public service functions, which was the raison d'être for the government's ownership of the Postal Service, no longer exists, it is now consistent for the government to allow private businesses to compete with the Postal Service by repealing the private express statutes. In consideration of the interests of Postal Service employees, it is also humane for Congress to free the Postal Service to compete in all communications activities by divesting and privatizing it and thereby allowing it to have a fighting chance at survival.

Notes

1. See Dorothy Canfield Foster, *Unmailable* (Athens-University of Georgia Press, 1977), pp. 198-202.
2. See "IRS Accused of Opening Investor Mail," *Financial Product News* 2 (November 1986): 13.
3. See John W. Crutcher, "Privatizing the U.S. Postal Service," *Vital Speeches* 50 (October 15, 1983): 29-32; John W. Crutcher, "Remarks at the First National

Conference on Privatization Opportunities," New York City, June 29, 1986 (unpublished manuscript).

4. See Bert Ely, "Privatizing the Postal Service—How To Do It" (Alexandria, Va.: Ely and Co., 1986; unpublished manuscript).

5. See Bill Green, "Privatizing the Postal Service," *Journal of the Institute for Socioeconomic Studies* (Summer 1986): 74-85.

6. *New York Times*, editorial, "Move the Mail, or the Postal Service," June 16, 1986.

7. See James C. Miller III, "End The Postal Monopoly," *Cato Journal* 5 (Spring/ Summer 1985): 149-55; Douglas K. Adie, "Abolishing the Postal Monopoly: A Comment," *Cato Journal* 5 (Fall 1985): 657-61.

8. See Bill Neikirk, "Putting Government on the Auction Block," *Chicago Tribune*, March 23, 1986, sec. 1, pp. 1, 18; Charles Wheeler, "Reagan's Priest of Privatization," *Washington Times*, May 2, 1986, pp. 1B, 7B.

9. See Mark Tapscott, "Budget Chief Seeks Steady Deregulating of Postal Service," *Washington Times*, June 25, 1986, p. 7C.

10. See Doug Bandow, "Postal Service Doesn't Deserve Monopoly," *Los Angeles Times*, July 2, 1986, part 2.

11. See International Resource Development, Inc. (6 Prowitt St., Norwalk, CT 06855), "Tele-Printing and Electronic Mail," #65 IRD, May 15, 1985.

12. Here, as in other places in this book, the term *Postal Service* is used to refer to the government organization that has delivered the mail in the United States before and since reorganization, even though before reorganization it was called the Post Office. It should be clear from the context whether this generic term is being used or whether only the organization since the reorganization is being referred to.

13. Although the financial importance of the monopoly pertains to "first class" mail, the bulk of which is letter mail, there are some nonletter materials in "first class," i.e. parcels. The statutory monopoly is on letter mail and there are letters in third class mail to which the monopoly applies also. How is the third class mail covered by the monopoly distinguished from that which is not? Advertising materials may be delivered by private companies if they are not addressed. The U.S. District Court for the District of Columbia upheld Postal Service regulations defining addressed advertising matter as a letter for purposes of the Private Express Statutes. *Associated Third-Class Mail Users* v. *U.S. Postal Service*, 440 F. Supp. 1211 (1977). Thus, a third class piece, even one labeled "occupant" is covered if it is addressed to a particular place. Third class mail totals over 55 billion pieces per year.

14. In the context of the "public choice" literature it might be argued that to serve the national interest and actually achieve the positive public service goals sought, it would be best for the Postal Service to serve its customers in the best way possible. Any other solution will result in falling short of all goals whether public service or service to the public. For instance, if the pursuit of a public service goal involves subsidizing one group of customers at the expense of another, it is inequitable. Is it then equitable to allow union workers to harm nonunion workers and consumers, as is currently done? Is it equitable to force inner-city residents to subsidize rural families, some of whom are very wealthy?

15. See note 22, below.

16. The only subsidy currently being paid directly from tax revenues is that provided by 39 U.S.C. sec. 2401(c), for revenue forgone as a result of preferred

rates to nonprofit, within-country, and other statutorily favored groups of mailers. If the Postal Service were operating efficiently, it might be argued that these are not direct subsidies to the Postal Service but rather to the mailers (who do benefit to some degree), and that the Postal Service is a conduit only. This, however, is not the case. In addition to this subsidy the Postal Service enjoys eminent domain, is free from taxes, and can borrow at government-guaranteed interest rates.

17. *Washington Post*, December 4, 1983, quoted by James Bovard, "The Last Dinosaur: The U.S. Postal Service," *Policy Analysis* (Cato Institute), no. 47 (February 12, 1985): 7.

18. "Postal Service May Close Its Electronic Mail Service," *Wall Street Journal*, June 7, 1985, p. 14.

19. In dealing with the Postal Service, one quickly reaches a quandary and becomes exasperated. If ZIP + 4 is not cost effective at any volume, as it may appear, certainly the USPS's failure to provide incentives for using it is not grounds for criticism; but in this case its requesting $900 million is. However, if it would be cost effective at higher volume levels, failure to increase volume through the use of incentives is grounds for criticism.

20. House Government Operations Committee, *INTELPOST: A Postal Service Failure in International Electronic Mail*, April 11, 1984, p. 9.

21. The Midas touch in reverse refers to the Postal Service's uncanny ability to take what appears to be a perfectly good idea and under the most favorable circumstances destroy its effectiveness through incompetence and bungling.

22. See Joel L. Fleishman, ed., *The Future of the Postal Service* (New York: Praeger, with the Aspen Institute for Humanistic Studies, 1983), p. 12 n. 31. See Douglas K. Adie, "How Have Postal Workers Fared Since the 1970 Act?" in *Perspectives on Postal Service Issues*, ed. Roger Sherman (Washington, D.C.: American Enterprise Institute, 1980), pp. 74-93; commentary by Sharon P. Smith, pp. 94-98; and discussion, pp. 99-107. See Douglas K. Adie, *An Evaluation of Postal Service Wage Rates* (Washington, D.C.: American Enterprise Institute, 1977). See review of foregoing book by Sharon P. Smith in *Industrial and Labor Relations Review* (October 1978): 122-23, and her book *Equal Pay in the Public Sector: Fact or Fantasy?*, Research Report Series no. 122, Industrial Relations Section (Princeton University, 1977). For a study commissioned by the Postal Service, see Michael L. Wachter and Jeffrey M. Perloff, "An Evaluation of U.S. Postal Service Wages," report commissioned by U.S. Postal Service University of Pennsylvania Discussion Paper (July 15, 1981). Also Joel Popkin states that postal workers' wages have risen approximately .7 percent faster than those of private nonfarm workers, which with annual compounding quickly becomes a sizable number. For instance, in ten years, say from 1954-63, it would lead to a wage premium of 7.22 percent; in another ten years to 1973 the premium would grow to 15 percent; in another ten years to 1983, the premium would become 23 percent, which is only slightly smaller than the approximately 30 percent premium most researchers say the postal workers enjoy. (See Michael L. Wachter and Jeffrey M. Perloff, "U.S. Postal Service Economic Presentation," manuscript, July 15, 1981. A unanimity of conclusions was acknowledged by me and by Jeff Perloff in our testimony in congressional hearings; see Joint Economic Committee, Economic Goals and Intergovernmental Policy Subcommittee, *The Future of Mail Delivery in the United States*, 97th Cong., 2d sess., June 18, 21, 1982, pp. 282-99, 299-313, 323-24. For a general treatment

of the literature discussing and evaluating postal worker wages, see Alan L. Sorkin, *The Economics of the Postal System*, (Lexington, Mass.: Lexington Books, 1980), pp. 73-78, 85.

23. General Accounting Office, *Comparison of Collectively Bargained and Administratively Set Pay Rates for Federal Employees* (July 2, 1982), p. 6.

24. There has been some discussion lately that civil service workers are overpaid relative to their private sector equivalents. How much more does this criticism apply to postal wages? See U.S. Office of Personnel Management, *Reforming Federal Pay: An Evaluation of More Realistic Pay Alternatives* (December 1984), p. 80.

25. The American Postal Workers Union (APWU) opposes the concept of presort discounts but has supported the ZIP + 4 program; it sponsored testimony in Docket No. R84-1 favoring a 1.5-cent discount for all ZIP + mail, in contrast to the USPS's proposal to continue the 0.9-cent (nonpresort) and 0.5-cent (presort) discounts established in 1983. Postal Rate Commission (PRC) Op. R84-1, paras. 5157, 5160-62. On losing the issue, the APWU has pursued this issue in the Court of Appeals. The reason for this is that by 1984, 40 percent of the total mail stream sortation operation was handled by private contractors. The Zip + 4 program is not so much an innovation to improve efficiency of mail delivery as it is an alternative program to compete with the presort industry. See Green, "Privatizing Postal Service," p. 84.

26. First class rates are not the only rates that have been raised, but it is the rise in first class rates that generates the bulk of the increase in revenues. Each one-cent increase in first class rates raises approximately $750 million, with no discernible decrease in mail volume.

27. See Fleishman, *The Future of the Postal Service*, p. 78. The commission was chaired by Gaylord Freeman, honorary chairman of the First National Bank of Chicago.

28. See note 27, above.

29. For Congress's attempt to deal with this problem, see House, *Postal Reorganization Report, together with Supplemental and Additional Views*, 96th Cong., 1st sess., May 8, 1979, H. Rept. 96-126, pp. 3-4.

30. See Wayne E. Fuller, *The American Mail: Enlarger of the Common Life* (Chicago: University of Chicago Press, 1972), pp. 331-38. The public service functions that motivated the original decision to create a publicly owned post office have now been accomplished. This will be elaborated on in chapter 2. Suffice it to mention that educational objectives were among those the government desired to subsidize in the early days of the United States because the dissemination of information took place primarily through the mailing of papers, books, magazines, and letters. This was also viewed as contributing to the mission of binding the nation together. Although educational mail is still directly subsidized and favored in the rationalizing standards of the current law (39 U.S.C. secs. 3622(b)(8), 3626(a)), no one would argue that it is the indispensable or even the predominant means of communicating information. If the USPS were to disappear, it is unlikely that the educational system would even notice it. In chapter 2 it will be argued that all the "public service" functions have been one-time achievements of a more-or-less permanent infrastructure character whose completion at some time in the past has now made the governmental postal system obsolete.

2

Monopoly, Competition, and the Private Express Statutes

Historical Perspective

What has been the history of the Post Office monopoly in the carriage of first class mail? What has been the attitude of the government toward the Post Office monopoly, expressed most comprehensively in the private express statutes? What has been the attitude of the government toward private businesses that from time to time have encroached upon this monopoly? A consideration of the history of an institution can often provide the overall perspective for the recommendation of structural changes that have a good chance of succeeding. The postal monopoly is fortunate to have had several competent studies of its history, by Wayne Fuller, John Haldi, and George L. Priest.[1] With this policy purpose in mind, let us consider the historical record for answers to the above questions.

Early British Experience

The antecedent to the U.S. postal system was the British postal system. The Stuarts used the postal monopoly primarily to discover and suppress treason and sedition through mail inspection. Although in principle the crown had no objection to allowing private competition, those plotting treason were forced to use the expensive private messengers or risk detection. The postal monopoly also enabled Elizabeth and the Stuarts to economize on inspection costs because they did not need to monitor as many carriers.

Even though Charles I entrusted postal operations to his secretaries of state and declared all private carrier systems illegal, the postal monopoly failed in its objective of protecting him. In 1646 he was deposed in a civil war. When postal responsibilities fell to Parliament, instead of dropping the ineffective monopoly provisions, it merely tried to prevent the diversion of profits to private postal managers. It carried out this change by auctioning the contract rights to manage the postal monopoly after specifying frequency of delivery, routes, and other aspects of service quality. In exchange for the rent, in which the government captured the expected monopoly profits, the managers were permitted to collect and retain all postage revenues at stipulated rates. Contractors were motivated to operate efficiently because they could keep all residual profits.

When ownership of the postal monopoly passed from Parliament to the king, efficiency was greatly impaired. Instead of holding competitive bidding for the postal monopoly, Charles II gave it successively to his friends Bishop Daniel O'Neill and Baron Berkeley. Because each in his turn could have appropriated the profit, the incentive was present either to run the Post Office efficiently or hire managers who could. This did not happen. The Post Office, apparently, was such a low priority to both men that it did not receive careful attention. No new services were initiated; no new routes extended or delivery speeds increased. The successive owners were content to reap the monopoly profits from the natural growth in established markets. In 1677 when the government absorbed the Post Office into the government, postal operations were little affected because the bureaucratic mentality was already present.

Early American Experience

In the colonies the Massachusetts General Court appointed Fairbank's Tavern to be the first post office in November 1639. At a charge of a penny a letter it ordered that all incoming letters from overseas be deposited at the tavern. Despite this official endorsement of a private institution for the handling of incoming overseas mail, the arrangement did not constitute a monopoly, for the order was not obeyed. Numerous other private arrangements existed simultaneously.

The New York to Boston post road, established fifty years later in 1689, was the first permanent domestic route. Two years later in 1691 the British government, following the British precedent, gave to Thomas Neale a twenty-one year domestic postal monopoly for the colonies from Virginia to Canada, but only with the consent of the legislatures. Not all colonies expressed enthusiasm for this arrangement. Maryland and Virginia refused to join. New Hampshire, New York, Pennsylvania, and Massachusetts enacted the proposed legislation, but Massachusetts included a proviso that it would withdraw if service proved to be inefficient. Finally, the New York assembly refused to extend Neale's monopoly along the most densely populated Hudson River area where other private services operated.

A postal monopoly existed during our colonial period, but its character differed substantially from today's postal monopoly. For instance, it was bestowed on a private business by the British government but without the permission and enforcement of the colonies, many of which were unenthusiastic. By refusing to participate Maryland and Virginia indicated that the monopoly status was voluntary. By exempting densely populated areas from the monopoly so other delivery companies could service them, New York instructs us that the first monopoly was geographically limited. The fact that at least one colony reserved for itself the option of withdrawing from the monopoly arrangement if service was not satisfactory indicates that the monopoly was conditional. All these characteristics make the original postal system stand in stark contrast to today's postal organization, despite the common use of the term *monopoly* to describe both systems.

The Neale postal monopoly, which was a government-sanctioned private business, began operating in 1693. Its monopoly provision was never secure because many letters traveled by other means, resulting in losses of postage revenues. In attempting to correct this situation in 1699, Neale prevailed on Andrew Hamilton to join him in London to plead on his behalf for a strengthening of the postal monopoly in the colonies. Even at this early date we find the familiar scenario of a vested interest attempting to enlist the coercive power of government to defend its position. In this case the government, to its credit, rebuffed the overture.

In an early act of nationalization the British government bought back the American postal monopoly in 1707, hoping to make it work. However, as late as 1721, due to unsatisfactory service, Americans were still sending their letters via other systems. The public's business invariably gravitated toward private carriers because their service was cheaper and more dependable. The royal colonial officials refused to enforce the monopoly and to put private carriers out of business. The government could have marshalled its force to protect its monopoly but was content to treat it with benign neglect. The moral strength seemed to be more on the side of the monopoly breakers: quality communications were of obvious value to the government, and this fact was used to justify the existence of private systems. The service provided by the government monopoly was not satisfactory. Although the postal organization had a monopoly in actuality, it conferred only limited rights. This was understood and accepted by postal managers and patrons alike.

The historical facts show that the early postal service was a monopoly enterprise, sometimes privately sometimes publicly owned. Whether publicly or privately owned, an officially sanctioned postal service succeeded only if the public perceived the rapidity, dependability, and cost of its service favorably. The fact that the government sanctioned the monopoly was not sufficient to insure its success. In the background private express companies and individuals always stood ready, willing, and able to pick up the slack when the service of the officially sanctioned postal monopoly fell below acceptable standards as judged by average citizens. The right to engage alternative communications services, which were cheap and rapid, appears to have superseded the protection that governments gave to the monopoly. Courts did not regard violators of the monopoly with much culpability, for the monopoly was a prudential construction rather than a moral imperative. The necessity of communicating efficiently and at low cost was a moral imperative, rather than the desire to protect an officially sanctioned monopoly.

Alexander Spotswood, deputy postmaster general from 1730 to 1739, made improvements in postal service. He was an exception, however. A-part from him little was done during the postal service's early history to change what was generally considered to be poor service. Benjamin Franklin, appointed postmaster in 1753, changed this state of affairs. He brought his ingenuity to the job, sped up service, improved its regularity, and made it sufficiently attractive to gain the support of customers who were inclined to send their letters by other services. Franklin understood clearly that the key to success was not the legal enforcement of a monopoly but rather superior performance. Only through excellence of service could the postal service command the loyalty of its customers and look forward to a prosperous future.

Having achieved a position of strength through good service, Franklin subsequently moved to strengthen the monopoly of the Post Office. He did this by interpreting the legal restrictions of the postal monopoly in a way that was favorable to the Post Office. For instance, he ruled that one could legally avoid postage only when private messengers, who did not make regular trips from town to town, carried letters. Sending letters by stagecoach drivers who made regular trips would be a violation of the Post Office monopoly as he interpreted it. Although they admired the efficiency that he brought to the Post Office, the revolutionaries did not appreciate Franklin's efforts to enhance the monopoly status of a British post office. Rather, they viewed the high postage rates that he cooperated in levying as another form of tyrannical British taxation.

For those of us today who are more concerned about security than liberty, it is difficult to appreciate the vehemence with which the revolutionary founders of this country confronted situations they regarded as oppressive. Any impediment to communication was sufficient to justify a violation of a monopoly, which was highly suspect to begin with. Once this is understood, the historical foundations of the postal organization cannot be properly interpreted as supporting the continued existence of today's postal monopoly.

Shortly after Franklin's efforts, regular postriders developed large private businesses by charging low rates. The king's officials stood by helplessly while postriders carried an increasing volume of letters outside the official system. By 1776 the official Post Office's business had diminished to the point that it required government support. In 1782 Congress attempted to help the Post Office by affirming its monopoly on carrying letters. This, however, was to no avail because of high postage rates, a depression, and an apparent scarcity of currency. Citizens continued to send their letters by friends or other travelers to cut their costs. Congress was powerless to prevent this evasion of the law and the attendant loss of revenue. The early postal monopoly never had the unqualified support of the public. The public tolerated it and used its service when it offered satisfactory service at a reasonable price. Otherwise citizens thought nothing of circumventing the laws' provisions, and this was done with the knowledge if not the tacit approval of a helpless government.

The Constitution gave Congress the temporary and uncertain power "to establish Post Offices and post Roads," but it was not until the 1792 postal act became permanent in 1794 that carrying letters outside the mails was clearly against the law. During the years surrounding the founding of this country, the citizens regularly practiced evading high postage rates and substandard service by one device or another.

Beyond the practice of using private carriers, the public used other tactics within the official postal system to reduce the effective postage rates. Some of these tactics included writing messages on newspapers for which postage was considerably cheaper than for first class messages, or underlining words in newspapers, or making tiny pinholes in selected newspaper words to form a message. However, by the 1840s, instead of resorting to covert tactics, Americans were once again breaking the postal monopoly laws en masse, openly and with gusto.

Most of the evasion of the monopoly laws was in the densely populated East and resulted from years of frustrated efforts to reduce postal rates. A congressional report echoing the prevailing public sentiment excused the lawbreakers' behavior by saying, "Having demonstrated in vain against what they deem to be exorbitant and oppressive rates of postage, they have at last adopted the conclusion that it is right to oppose and evade laws which they consider unjust and oppressive."[2] This remark seems to give official sanction to those who evaded the monopoly law and seems to affirm the notion that the laws were convenient, prudential, and possibly temporary in nature rather than absolute, moral, and permanent.

Unlike the British and Europeans, Americans have had an ambivalent attitude toward their postal system. Given the tentative public acceptance of the U.S. Post Office, one might go so far as to characterize it as a stranger in its own country. The government restricted its activities and prevented it from developing to its full potential as a business. This mixed public reception was not without good reason in the American setting.

The United States was an experiment for many ideas, including some that were economic and political. The existence of a government-owned and -operated post office on U.S. soil conflicted with the political and economic presuppositions of those who founded this country. For instance, most nineteenth-century Americans believed that free political institutions could not exist without free enterprise and private property; that the government should never do what private enterprise could do; that competition was competent to regulate the economy; that monopoly, which the Post Office surely was, was bad; and that any extensions of the postal power that the Constitution had given Congress were dangerous. Given this set of beliefs emanating primarily from Adam Smith, it is a wonder that the public tolerated at all a government-owned and -operated Post Office. That it did stems from the public service functions (discussed in chapter 3) that various legislators put forth to justify the postal exception to the widely held antigovernment monopoly sentiment.

Another justification of an exception to the general principles on which this country was founded (which the government-owned postal monopoly surely was at this time) hinged on the Post Office's being a test case. It was readily admitted by all that the Post Office as a government monopoly functioned as such an exception. Champions of free enterprise found in the inadequacies of the Post Office arguments against socialistic experiments; those who railed against the abuses of laissez-faire capitalism pointed with pride to the Post Office as an example of the benefits of a government-owned business. In effect the Post Office served as a concrete demonstration of the strengths and weaknesses of these conflicting economic principles.

Although the government owned the Post Office, it was not a clear test case of economic principles because the government did not directly control all operations. As early as 1794 Congress authorized the postmaster general to utilize private contractors and hire private stagecoach lines to carry the mails. When some of these contractors colluded to raise bids, they artificially increased the cost of mail transportation. To combat this development, the postmaster general hired other private stagecoach operators to increase competition and thus check those attempting collusion. The existence of collusion was used by many not to argue for the government's control of all postal functions but, rather, as an argument for transferring the Post Office entirely to private hands.

In the 1840s the mood of the country was very receptive to having the mails carried by private express companies operating outside the government monopoly. In 1839 William F. Harnden, a Massachusetts Yankee, traveled the rails and steamboats with messages and packages that he conveyed personally. Viewing the efficiency, dependability, rates, and coordination of the private express companies, in 1840 William Leggett, editor of the *New York Post*, expressed the sentiments of many when he wrote, "We are ourselves inclined to the belief, that if the clause in the federal charter which gives Congress the control of the Post Office had never been inserted, a better system would have grown up under the mere laws of trade."

In 1843 Alvin Adams and fifteen express companies transported large numbers of letters outside the mails. In 1843 the Post Office sued the Adams Express Company for violating the postal monopoly *and lost*. Unlike today, the courts then regularly demonstrated respect for the principles on which this country was founded and recognized that the government postal monopoly was an exception that needed extraordinary justification to be continued. The burden of proof rested with the Post Office. Encouraged by their victory in court, express companies began to advertise openly that their services were cheaper, quicker, and superior. On the basis of the legal decision the express companies grew enormously in the 1840s.

Lysander Spooner's American Letter Mail Company was one of the private express companies in the 1840s. In 1844 he opened offices in New York, Philadelphia, Baltimore, and Boston, charging in advance 6.25 cents per half ounce. Spooner's business strategy was "to give the public the most extensive facilities for correspondence that can be afforded at a uniform rate" and "to thoroughly agitate the question, and test the Constitutional right of competition in the business of carrying letters."[3] This statement is indicative of the attitude and the spirit of a growing number of private express companies intent on challenging the Post Office. They desired not only to provide superior service at less cost to their customers and a profit to themselves but also to use the Post Office to test the country's founding principles. Given the opportunity to compete fairly, they believed they would drive the Post Office out of business.

During this period the Post Office was understandably threatened with the possibility of financial collapse by reason of competition from private express companies and a series of increases in rail rates that raised their costs. In 1845 Congress intervened. It lowered postage to five cents for moving a half-ounce letter three hundred miles and passed a law providing stiffer penalties for those who violated the postal monopoly. Spooner responded by lowering his rate, too, but in 1851 Congress put Spooner out of business by once again lowering rates and strengthening the monopoly provisions. Specifically, Congress made all streets post roads and thereby ruined the intracity delivery business critical to the survival of many private companies. (The Post Office's reestablishment of free city delivery also contributed to this result.)

Due to financial pressure brought by congressional protectionism, private carriers were forced to abandon much of their intercity mail delivery. Some well-established carriers continued to operate in a few selected cities where their own delivery systems were well established, but eventually these too failed. The attrition of private express companies was completed by 1860 when the successor to D. O. Blood and Company's delivery system in Philadelphia was ended by court action.[4] By 1890 only a handful of private express companies were left, including Wells Fargo, American Express, and Adams' Express. They carved up the nation and were acting as private monopolies in their own sections. Nevertheless, even this limited and somewhat self-serving invasion of the government's postal monopoly by private business (they took the most profitable business of carrying mail between cities and left the rest to the Post Office) was a boon to mail service because it forced the government to improve its postal system.

While in an expansionary mood in 1866, the Post Office considered operating savings banks and the telegraph. These were likely candidates because both had been nationalized in Europe, and the United States still thought of itself as a follower rather than a leader in the world community. The proposal, however, was crushed when it was argued that such a plan was contrary to the principles of free enterprise and therefore encroached on the domain of private business. The founding principles of the country still had enough support to quench attempts at an expansionary policy.

More Recent American Experience

It was not until 1918 that the postmaster general, in compliance with a congressional resolution but in flagrant violation of free enterprise principles, took control of the operation of the telegraph and telephone companies. The government justified the action on the basis of national security considerations, which, it was asserted, required that the government take control of the operations to assure the secrecy of government messages during wartime. Preventing a national emergency during wartime in the face of a threatened strike in the telephone and telegraph industries was also mentioned as a justification. Under the management of the Post Office for one year, inefficiencies multiplied to such an extent that it became necessary to increase the cost of telegrams. In 1919, after the war ended,

Congress quickly denationalized the companies by selling them to their previous owners.

The denationalization was generally popular. Indiana's Republican senator James Watson captured the prevailing sentiment when he commented on the government's experience running the telegraph service, "It is exceedingly gratifying to those of us who have always opposed the policy of government ownership to know that it has been a failure."

This brief historical recap, based primarily on the work of Wayne Fuller, indicates that the Post Office monopoly was not intended to be permanent but expedient. The government reluctantly supported the monopoly from time to time, often without conviction. Private businesses that violated the monopoly laws were not regarded as criminals but as supporters of the tradition of free enterprise. It is clear that historically competition tended to appear more when the Post Office was offering defective service at exorbitant rates, and that the presence of private companies helped to correct the situation.

Bullying Tactics

As in the past, so in recent years the U.S. Postal Service (USPS) has been faced with repeated challenges from private companies. The modern response of the Postal Service has not been in the best tradition of this country. Rather than increasing efforts to provide superior service at reduced rates the Postal Service has responded with legal maneuvers. For instance, in 1971 a federal district court prohibited the Independent Postal System of America from carrying Christmas cards in Oklahoma on the basis that the plaintiffs, a postal employees' union, suffered "significant loss of work time, overtime employment benefits . . . and morale."[5]

The response does not mention free market principles or even attempt to balance them with the need to provide important public service functions. In contrast, the rationale underlying this decision broke new ground. In this instance the court concluded that private delivery of Christmas cards would be a "widespread public nuisance" (hardly the case!) and imposed significantly higher costs and slower service on postal customers. The court ruled against the private firm to support something as vague as postal workers' morale.[6]

Unfortunately, this attitude does not exist in isolation. In 1976 a New York Cub Scout pack tried to raise money by delivering Christmas cards. Postal Service lawyers ordered them to stop and threatened the ten-year-olds with a $76,500 fine. The Postal Service seems now to be acting on no higher principle than protecting its own self-interest. Apparently the Postal Service is intent on using its power to crush the competition rather than to provide better service or even to earn its own way. A recent *New York Times* editorial bemoaned this unfortunate disposition when it expressed regret that the Postal Service's carriers were not as fast as its lawyers.

A further example of how the Postal Service deals with competition in this modern era occurred in Rochester, New York, where the P. H. Brennan Hand Delivery Service offered same-day delivery in 1978 for ten cents while the Postal Service could not guarantee overnight delivery for fifteen cents. The Brennans operated during snowstorms and never lost a letter or had a complaint, while the Postal Service did not even attempt delivery in bad weather. When the Postal Service attorneys took action against the Brennans, Rochester lawyers, reflecting public sentiment, provided them free legal defense services. The Postal Service, however, persuaded a judge to issue a cease-and-desist order because they were a "threat to postal revenues."[7]

Although these actions are out of character in a country based upon the principles of free trade, they are symptomatic of the self-justification in which the Postal Service now wallows. In rhetoric only has the Postal Service pursued excellence of service at low rates. Moving beyond the mere preservation of its monopoly, the USPS apparently now wants to put small companies out of business if they even dare cross its self-defined service boundaries. Ironically, this territorialism can result in legal costs that exceed the loss of revenue, much to the detriment of taxpayers and postal patrons.

Is the Postal Service not unique as a U.S. organization in having the right to interpret its own monopoly powers? For example, in 1974 the Postal Service unilaterally expanded its definition of a letter to include intracorporate communication, blueprints, computer tapes, credit cards, and fishing licenses. In the proposed changes it asserted that when a delivery person drops off unaddressed advertising circulars from a memorized list, each circular becomes magically addressed and transformed into first class mail falling under the private express statutes. This proposal is simply ludicrous.[8] The Postal Rate Commission's (PRC) public counsel concluded that the Postal Service's goal was actually to "gather under its exclusive domain nearly all mailable material."[9] The definition of a letter now reads: "a message directed to a specific person or address and recorded in or on a tangible object."[10] As James Bovard has comically suggested, under this definition the USPS could assess postage on a belly dancer sent to a congressional party with someone's name inked on her abdomen.

In addition to defining the nature of a first class letter, the Postal Service continually harasses both customers and competition with its interpretations of the private express statutes. The interpretation that a homeowner's mailbox, purchased by the homeowner, attached to the house and clearly the homeowner's property, is Postal Service property is pernicious and self-serving. The intention behind this definition, which clearly amounts to theft, is that the Postal Service can then prohibit access to its customers' mail receptacles by private carriers (or anybody else) and seize letters, notices, or paraphernalia found in them. This practice is indefensible and should be stopped, regardless of whatever other structural actions are taken in the future.[11]

As an example of the Postal Service's harassment of its competition, the USPS tried throughout the 1970s to levy postage charges against the United Parcel Service (UPS) because it included *its own* advertising material in the parcels it delivered. Also, after initiating its own Express Service, the Postal Service attempted to intimidate the customers of other express services by threatening frivolous legal actions. The simple truth is that aggressive behavior such as this has nothing to do with offering superior mail service at reasonable rates. If anything, these bullying tactics force us to take seriously the arguments of the Postal Service's competitors against allowing the Postal Service to enter the market for electronic mail. Their assertion among others, is that even if the Postal Service's operations were grossly inefficient, the Postal Service would still be able, by virtue of its size and power, to use predatory pricing and other forms of intimidation to drive them out of business.

Current Competition

When faced with economic rather than legal competition the Postal Service has not fared well against competitors of much smaller size. An inspection of the distribution of revenues to the Postal Service from dif-

TABLE 2.1
Distribution of Mail and Revenues by Class of Mail

Class	No. of Pieces (bil.)	% of Total	Revenues (bil.)	% of Total Revenues	Weight (mil.lbs.)	% of Total Weight
First	68.4	52.0	$15.2	62.3	2.5	15.5
Second	9.5	7.2	1.0	4.1	3.9	24.2
Third	48.3	36.7	4.2	17.2	5.8	36.0
Fourth	.6	.5	.8	3.3	2.3	14.3
Other	3.6	3.6	3.2	13.1	1.6	10.0
Total	131.5	100.0	24.4	100.0	16.1	100.0

Source: *Annual Report of the Postmaster General, 1984,*
pp. 28-29.

ferent classes of mail described in table 2.1 shows this. For classes two and four, for which postal revenues receive no protection whatever, postal revenues are only 8 percent of the total. For third class mail, much of which falls under the private express statutes because it consists of letters, the Postal Service receives 17.2 percent of its revenues.[12] Despite the Postal Service's subsidizing of these classes, much smaller postal competitors have still made substantial inroads.

In fact, table 2.1 indicates that fourth class mail is no longer very important to the Postal Service. The UPS, a much smaller company, has built an immensely successful enterprise out of what was once Post Office business. It has provided better quality service at a lower price. Fortunately for the public and UPS, court rulings requiring that postal rates reflect direct and indirect costs for each class of mail have prevented the Postal Service from engaging in gross predatory pricing tactics and driving the UPS out of business. In this economic competition the UPS has consequently decimated the parcel business of the USPS until now the Postal Service carries less than 12 percent of the packages that UPS carries.

Alternative delivery is also growing for third class advertising and second class magazines and newspapers, which from table 2.1 constitute 21.3 percent of the Postal Service's revenues. Innovatively, newspaper publishers have recently inserted third class advertising circulars and brochures in their papers. Further, at least twenty-seven major publishers, including the publishers of *Better Homes and Gardens*, *Business Week*, *Newsweek*, *Reader's Digest*, *Sports Illustrated*, the *Wall Street Journal*, and a few book and record firms, use private delivery to send out part of their second class mailings.[13] One estimate indicates that 5,000 to 7,000 private carriers delivered 10 to 12 billion advertising pieces in 1977.[14] Since then activity in this area has undoubtedly increased.

It is first and third class letter mail that receives monopoly protection. The private express statutes, however, provide only limited protection for the USPS against the forces of competition for these mails. Table 2.1 indicates that first class mail constitutes only 52.0 percent of the pieces but generates 62.3 percent of postal revenues. As a testimony to the free enterprise system, neither the private express statutes, the Postal Service's interpretation of them, nor congressional attempts to restrict competition have been able to stop competitors from eroding postal business, even first class mail.

A 1981 estimate suggested that private delivery firms deliver more than 25 billion pieces of mail a year.[15] For example, some utility companies deliver their own bills when reading meters and thereby reduce the quantity of first class mail passing through the Postal Service. Alongside telegraph service by Western Union, overnight delivery firms such as Airborne

Freight Corporation, Emery WorldWide Air Freight, Purolator Courier, and Federal Express offer both package and letter delivery of time-sensitive material and thereby avoid the monopoly provisions for first class mail. Federal Express, the largest of these private carriers, which began in 1972, delivered 178.9 million pieces in fiscal year 1987, an increase of 28 percent over 1986. The firm's volume continues to grow at about 25 percent a year, and it expects to deliver about 225 million pieces in 1988.[16] This business has been facilitated by the USPS's suspension of the monopoly as to some types of letter mail—principally the "extremely urgent" letters carried by Federal Express and other similar firms.[17]

About 50 percent of today's mail, most of which is first class, is potentially divertable to electronic communications. Firms offering electronic funds transfers, telephone service, and data and voice transmission, in addition to firms using facsimile machines, store and forward systems, word processing systems, TWX/Telex systems, interactive cable television systems, and in-home computers pose a substantial threat to the USPS's monopoly on first class mail. Electronic transmission potentially could erode the Postal Service monopoly as surely as the repeal of the private express statutes. This potential moves closer to realization day by day as postal rates continue to increase relative to telephone rates.

New electronic forms of communication, such as video text and two-way cable, are already established and growing. With this equipment users can write letters, pay bills, send greetings, and communicate almost instantaneously via telephone lines and satellites. Such systems, including pay-by-phone and electronic publishing, are even termed "electronic mail" and will almost certainly work against the private express statutes as they become cheaper and more accessible. Electronic funds transfer (EFT) alone could absorb enough first class volume to cripple the Postal Service. For example, the Treasury Department is electronically depositing 15 million checks a month that used to go through the mail.[18]

Many experts foresee the commonplace use of electronic mail within twenty years. Some believe the changeover will come sooner. Should private computers deliver most of the mail, the volume of mail delivered by the Postal Service will decline and the remaining letters will be more expensive. When this happens, revenues will decline and the number of jobs in the Postal Service will decrease. The residual effect on employment could be greater than any automation the Postal Service has installed. Many postal employees and their unions refuse to acknowledge this scenario.

The Postal Service is being threatened by a variety of forms of competition. Two strategies are possible to confront this situation. One is to preside over a shrinking Postal Service and supervise its orderly demise. The second is to plan to counter the competition with new services to replace revenues in declining markets. This latter strategy, however, would require managerial skills and entrepreneurial abilities that do not normally surface in nationalized businesses and certainly have not surfaced in the Postal Service to date. The postal employees should not be held responsible for this deficiency. The motivational system that exists under the current organization makes any other result unlikely. These qualities, however, which are necessary to engage in risk-taking activities, are honed under conditions in which those who are responsible for making decisions suffer the losses from their mistakes or enjoy the gains from their successes. In short, it requires that the Postal Service be a private business. Protectionism, a poor substitute for managerial effort, is the direction the Postal Service has invariably taken in the past when faced with difficulties. If experience has any predictive value, it also suggests how the Postal Service will react to difficulties in the future under its present organizational form.

Legislators with this in mind have heeded the pleas of telecommunications companies that quite properly have argued to prevent the Postal Service from building or leasing its own transmission system and thereby making a commitment to electronic mail. Some other reasons for opposing the Postal Service's entrance into the telecommunications business are the following:

1. The Postal Service might apply the private express statutes to electronic mail to gain monopoly control.
2. The Postal Service could subsidize electronic mail with revenue from other classes of mail.
3. The Postal Service has an unfair competitive advantage because it pays no taxes, receives subsidies from Congress, and has access to low interest funds through U.S. Treasury bond sales.
4. The Postal Service will bungle its activities and waste taxpayers' money because it has no comparative advantage in electronic communications.[19]

The behavior of the Postal Service, which we have examined in this chapter, especially since reorganization, certainly does suggest that these reasons are not without foundation.

Some Prevailing Attitudes

Critics of the private express statutes have advocated their repeal since their enactment in 1792, but in recent years, accompanying the bullying tactics of the Postal Service and its deteriorating service and rising rates, this opposition has grown stronger. In 1976 James C. Miller III, then assistant director for governmental operations and research of President Gerald Ford's Council on Wage and Price Stability, testified before the PRC that the statutes should be repealed.[20]

In January 1977 the U.S. Department of Justice declared that the USPS did not compete in its market, which is now the largest utility service. Even if there was justification in the past for this monopoly position, which the Justice Department doubted, it is not justifiable today and should be terminated unless very compelling public policy reasons could be assembled.[21] The report goes on to make a compelling case for eliminating the postal monopoly.[22] The essential argument, not unlike that posed here, is that the historical record has shown that competition is the only reliable way of forcing the Postal Service to be efficient. Firms exercising monopoly power tend to preserve costly inefficiencies, especially if there are no owners to appropriate profits. For the Postal Service to act like a business and not like a government agency, it needs to face full competition for first class mail.[23]

The Heritage Foundation, in *Mandate for Leadership*, called for repeal of the statutes and suggested "the Attorney General . . . issue a pro-competitive opinion on the scope of the postal monopoly."[24] In June 1982, James C. Miller III, now director of the Office of Management and Budget, urged Congress to end the Postal Service's monopoly of the delivery of first class mail.[25] Assistant Secretary of Commerce Bernard J. Wunder, Jr., Reagan's top communications adviser, seconded Miller by saying, "Minimal government involvement, and maximum possible competition will best serve the public's interest."[26] Miller says,

> The burden of proof that the postal monopoly's benefits outweigh its costs should be on those who support maintaining the private express statutes. . . . In my view the USPS should be required to produce a detailed empirical study of whether the economic justification exists, if it ever did, for continuing the statutory monopoly over first class mail. . . . Should such an investigation fail to provide strong economic justification for a continuation of the postal monopoly, I would urge Congress to repeal the private express statutes.[27]

John Ryan, a Reagan appointee who headed the transition team for the Postal Service and a current postal governor, has advocated repealing the postal monopoly for a long time.[28] Reagan has not yet taken a stand on the Postal Service, although his formal budget proposals to Congress call for elimination of most congressional appropriations to the Postal Service. If the Reagan administration heeds the Heritage Foundation report on the Postal Service as it has on other matters, it may stop at nothing short of shutting it down.[29]

Some Brief Arguments for and against the Postal Monopoly

The argument favoring repeal of the postal monopoly is economic. I will consider it in detail in connection with the divestiture of AT&T in chapter 4 and the deregulation of the airlines in chapter 5. Chapters 4 and 5 assert that there is no evidence that AT&T, the airlines, or the Postal Service are natural monopolies experiencing declining average costs per unit of service, so there is no economic justification for imposing a statutory monopoly on any of them.

One of the principal arguments supporting the private express statutes is that the new entrants, which repeal would encourage, would skim the cream off Postal Service business by serving only the most profitable markets, mainly urban ones, and leaving high-cost rural delivery areas to the Postal Service. This was the argument used by the Board of Governors in a 1973 report to Congress in which it rejected the idea of repealing the private express statutes. It argued that competition combined with uniform rates would lead to cream-skimming and declining service revenues.

Several commissions, task forces, and review boards have later argued that the Postal Service should continue to charge uniform rates for first class mail.[30] Supporters of the postal monopoly rejected repeal of the statutes, which would permit competition, because it would jeopardize the principle of uniform pricing. Nonuniform rates are most probably a concomitant of repeal.

Advertisers' Distribution, a firm in Cambridge, Minnesota, that makes a profit delivering third class advertising to rural homes underscores the falseness of the cream-skimming arguments. If a new entrant can skim off cream in the delivery of low-rate third class advertising mail in a sparsely populated rural area, then there must be gross inefficiencies in the Postal Service's operations.[31] Also in response to those who are concerned about rates for rural delivery, it seems foolish to let a relatively small percentage of the business ($1 billion for rural delivery out of a $29 billion annual budget) determine the organizational direction of such a large enterprise as the Postal Service.[32]

The second argument favoring the Postal Service monopoly is that the public would suffer a reduction in service from universal six-day doorstep delivery at a uniform price. Repealing the private express statutes, however, will open up first class mail to competition, and lead to lower postage rates overall and greater responsiveness to customer needs. Maintenance of the Private Express Statutes, it is alleged, is imperative for uniform postage rates and service, especially to thinly populated areas.

To devise an appropriate policy, it is necessary to compare the benefits with the costs of keeping the Postal Service monopoly. The desire to provide public service functions, as described above, has been one of the strongest arguments used to support the monopoly over the years, especially on the part of those who espoused free market principles. The next chapter examines these arguments.

Notes

1. See Wayne E. Fuller, *The American Mail: Enlarger of the Common Life* (Chicago: University of Chicago Press, 1972); John Haldi, *Postal Monopoly: An Assessment of the Private Express Statutes* (Washington, D.C.: American Enterprise Institute, 1974); George L. Priest, "The History of the Postal Monopoly in the United States," *Journal of Law and Economics* 18 (April 1975): 33-80. These are the sources I have relied on for the review of the historical record. If more detail is desired, they should be consulted.
2. See Fuller, *The American Mail*, p. 62.
3. See Lysander Spooner, *The Unconstitutionality of the Laws of Congress Prohibiting Private Mails* (1844). For a short biography of Lysander Spooner, see Dumas Malone, ed., *Dictionary of American Biography* (New York: Charles Scribner & Sons, 1935).
4. William H. Russell, Alexander Majors, and William Waddell in 1860 established the Pony Express, a private company to carry mail from St. Joseph, Mo., to Sacramento. After it failed, the Post Office used the Pony Express rider as its identifying symbol.
5. *National Association of Letter Carriers* v. *Independent Postal System of America Inc.*, 470 F, 2d 265 (10th Circuit, 1972).
6. See James Bovard, "Postal Monopoly Only Fuels Inflation," *Chicago Tribune*, April 28, 1980, p. 4, for this example and the subsequent one.
7. See statement of Patricia H. Brennan in Subcommittee on Economic Goals and Intergovernmental Policy of the Joint Economic Committee, *The Future of Mail Delivery in the United States*, 97th Cong., 2d sess., June 18, 21, 1982, pp. 135-39.
8. It should be noted that in *Associated Third Class Mail Users* v. *U.S. Postal Service*, 440 F. Supp. 1211 (D.D.C. 1977) and appeal D.C. Cir. no. 78-1065, the Court of Appeals approved the USPS rule.
9. U.S. Postal Rate Commission, docket R78-1, p. 56.
10. "Private Express Statutes—Exclusive Right of the USPS to Deliver Letters," Postal Service press release. See James Bovard, "The Last Dinosaur: The U.S. Postal Service," *Policy Analysis* (Cato Institute), no 47 (February 12, 1985): 14.
11. The Supreme Court, led by Justice Rehnquist in *U.S. Postal Service* v. *Council of Greenburgh Civic Associations*, 453 U.S. 114 (1981), upheld the prohibition against First Amendment challenges brought by plaintiffs who wished to deposit notices and other messages in home mailboxes without using the mails. Justices Marshall and Stevens dissented.
12. In docket R84-1, Appendix G, the Postal Rate Commission estimated the per piece attributable cost of first class letters to be twice that of third class regular bulk mail (14.9 vs. 7.3 cents). If average revenues for third class mail were about half those for first class mail, they would be 22.2 * .5 = 11.1 cents instead of the 9.7 cents (i.e. 4.7/48.3) that they are. This suggests that third class mail is being subsidized by 14.4 percent.

13. Kathleen Conkey, *The Postal Precipice, Can the U.S. Postal Service be Saved?* (Washington, D.C.: Center for the Study of Responsive Laws, 1983), p. 491. See also Alan L. Sorkin, *The Economics of the Postal System* (Lexington, Mass.: Lexington Books, 1980), pp. 139-41. I have found many of the details discussed in Conkey's book helpful as examples to illustrate principles discussed in this book and have used them at numerous points.

14. U.S. Postal Service, Research and Analysis Branch, Office of Commercial Marketing, Customer Services Department, *Competitors and Competition of the U.S. Postal Service*, 15 (December 1981): 3.

15. Association of Private Postal Systems, "*Planned Postal Deficits*," press release, (Cambridge, Mass., 1981), unpaginated (6).

16. Telephone conversation with Ed Clark, investor relations division, Federal Express Corp., February 11, 1988.

17. See *Federal Register*, 132, 44 (July 9, 1979): 40076.

18. U.S. Postal Service, *Competitors and Competition of the U.S. Postal Service*, p. 5.

19. See Conkey, *The Postal Precipice*, pp. 436-38.

20. U.S. Postal Rate Commission, *Comments of the Council on Wage and Price Stability Concerning the Private Express Statutes*, Docket RM76-4, January 16, 1976.

21. U.S. Department of Justice, *Changing the Private Express Statutes: Competitive Alternatives and the U. S. Postal Service*, (Washington, D.C.: Government Printing Office, January, 1977), p. 31.

22. *New York Times*, January 20, 1977, p. 21:5. See also U.S. Department of Justice, *Changing the Private Express Statutes*.

23. See Joel L. Fleishman, ed., *The Future of the Postal Service* (New York: Praeger, with the Aspen Institute for Humanistic Studies, 1983), p. 76.

24. Heritage Foundation, "U.S. Postal Service and Postal Rate Commission," *Mandate for Leadership* (Washington, D.C., 1980, draft), pp. 2-3.

25. See Joint Economic Committee, Economic Goals and Intergovernmental Policy Subcommittee, *The Future of Mail Delivery in the United States*, 97th Cong., 2d sess., June 18, 21, 1982, p. 240.

26. Ibid., pp. 177-78.

27. This approach to the question is in the style of the late G. Warren Nutter; see his *Political Economy and Freedom* (Indianapolis: Liberty Press, 1983), and my review of his book, "Freedom First, Last and Always," *Modern Age* 30 (Winter 1986): 56.

28. House Post Office and Civil Service Committee, Postal Service Subcommittee, *Operation and Organization of the Postal Rate Commission Hearings*, January 29 and 30, 1974, serial no. 93-43, pp. 2, 6.

29. Conkey, *The Postal Precipice*, p. 447.

30. See Fleishman, *The Future of the Postal Service*, p. 198. If it costs more to phone across country than across town why should it not cost more to send a letter across country? There is no moral imperative for charging equal rates for unequal service. Rural residents could pay a surcharge for home delivery the same way urban residents pay a surcharge for firewood and fresh vegetables.

31. In surprise testimony before the President's Commission on Privatization, January 28, 1988. Dr. Gene A. Del Polito, executive director of the Third Class Mail Association, requested that third class mail be exempted from the private express statutes. He believes private mailers can deliver this "junk mail" faster,

more reliably, and cheaply. Most of this mail is low rate subsidized mail. If private mailers are successful in handling this class of mail, what will come next?

32. Joint Economic Committee, Economic Goals and Intergovernmental Policy Subcommittee, *The Future of Mail Delivery in the United States. Hearings*, p. 39.

3

Public Service or Service to the Public?

The intention of public service activities is to serve the entire country; serving the public refers to services given to individual postal patrons in exchange for a fee. This chapter first discusses public service, then service to the public. I distinguish these frequently confused types of service because they have considerably different emphases. Public service depends on one's readiness to attribute to it "public goods" characteristics and is frequently the target of political exploitation. Service to the public concerns an agreement between parties that, in a competitive atmosphere, results in benefits mutually agreeable to each side. Unfortunately, many use the term *public service* in a blanket sense without respecting the distinctions.

History of the Postal Service Public Service Function

In the previous chapter we saw how crucial the public service function was to the official justification of the government-owned and -operated postal monopoly, especially in a country whose guiding principles included reliance on a free enterprise economy.[1] The public service function has been used almost exclusively to justify the government's involvement in postal matters in the United States, but this has not been the case elsewhere in the world. We will examine the historical record to compare the justifications for the government postal monopoly in Europe and the United States and to identify the role that the public service function played in the United States but not in Europe.

In the Middle Ages the mail service in Europe was exclusively private. Franz and Johann von Taxis organized the most famous private postal system, which operated for more than four hundred years beginning in the late fifteenth century. This indicates the durability and dependability of a private mail service. In the sixteenth and seventeenth centuries there were many private posts, which sometimes competed with and sometimes complemented one another. By the time of Henry VIII private posts were relied on to carry all mail, including that of the government.

In England national security concerns on the part of an insecure government were used to justify the entrance of the government into the mail delivery business. Henry VIII appointed Sir Brian Tuke to establish a royal post to protect and convey sensitive government messages on matters concerning the crown's security. At first private posts were not prohibited but allowed to exist alongside the government's postal service. A short time later, the all-too-familiar pattern of government encroachment on private business arose.

New restrictions were placed on private posts by James I, Cromwell, and Charles II to control communications and prevent subversion. Once again it was "national security" considerations that were relied on to justify the government's continued intervention in the mail delivery business. For instance, in 1609 James I ordered his subjects to send all letters through the royal mail; in 1657 Cromwell strengthened the government's monopoly to prevent subversion; and Charles II opened and resealed suspicious-looking letters.

Many private posts continued to exist to meet the communications needs of private citizens because the royal mail service was expensive and unreliable. These are basically the same reasons that private mail services did not respect the government's attempts to curtail their service and why they flourished throughout periods of United States history. Illegal private services forced the British government to expand its service to meet private competition. This scenario, too, was an antecedent of the pattern experienced later in the United States.

In contrast to England, in the United States national security played only a minor role in justifying a government-run mail service. From earliest times, the U.S. Post Office justified its nationalized character because it was the vital and sometimes only link that bound Americans together over vast and sparsely populated areas. Benjamin Franklin articulated this when he defined the postal mission as binding society together through a reliable communications system. This idea developed into the mission of a universal postal system that states that mail delivery should be available to everyone in the United States at the same postage rate. Under this policy the Post Office helped to bind the Union together, support incumbent politicians, and subsidize a variety of activities that affected many groups. For example, it diffused knowledge, subsidized the delivery of newspapers and magazines, underwrote the building of the stagecoach, railroad, steamship and airplane lines, and promoted business with cheap postage rates for advertising. Some argue that these activities benefited the whole nation.

The government desired to encourage and foster these activities with subsidies. For instance, for over a century after Congress established postal rates in the 1790s and reduced them substantially in 1851, it steadily reduced postage on reading material to encourage the diffusion of knowledge. The purpose of this policy was to bind the nation together. The Post Office became a convenient low-visibility vehicle for doing this, despite the fact that these activities ran contrary to the country's calling, which included heralding and demonstrating the benefits of the free enterprise system to the world.

Specific activities conducted by the Post Office to bind the nation together were not necessarily permanent but were, rather, subject to periodic review, examination, and even termination. For instance, in 1901 President Theodore Roosevelt directed Congress to examine what he regarded as abuses of the second class privilege. He noticed that it composed 60 percent of the weight, but its revenues contributed only 3.6 percent of the costs of running the postal service. (To compare this with the present situation see table 2.1.) In effect, Roosevelt was asking whether diffusing knowledge was costing the government more than it wanted to pay. He was confronting the possibility that this policy, although nobly conceived, ultimately was being selfishly used and defended with specious arguments.

Extending regular delivery to remote rural areas was another public service function that found shelter under the Post Office's mission of universality of service. Beginning in 1845 contractors brought mail to tiny rural post offices once or twice a week, along "star" or contract routes. Rural free delivery, approved by Postmaster General John Wanamaker in 1891, became postal policy in 1902. The purpose of the policy was to link rural Americans to their country and stimulate road improvements and the development of highways. The development of highways was stimulated because the Post Office offered rural free delivery only where roads were good. The provision of rural delivery service at no extra cost has continued to this day because it has strong advocates.

The arguments in support of rural free delivery are similar to the concerns expressed by those who were apprehensive of the effects on rural service of deregulating the airlines. I will examine the arguments in chapter 5. It is still argued by some that those who do not send letters, such as the elderly and the isolated, benefit from the reassuring sight of a letter carrier visiting the neighborhood six days a week and that this federal government presence is a vital connection that binds the nation together.

Suffice it to say at this point that not all Americans were convinced that the public service function of subsidized rural delivery justified the government's intervention into the private free market. As early as 1840 there were those who spoke against the public service function of the Post Office. For instance, a writer in *Hunt's Magazine* noted that if the Post Office were privately owned, "the solitary squatter in the wilderness might not . . . hear the forest echoes daily awakened by the postman's horn, and his annual letter might reach him charged with greater expense than he is now required to pay. But there is no place on the map which could not be supplied with mail facilities by paying a just equivalent; and if they are now supplied for less, it is because the burden of post office taxation is imposed with disproportional weight on the populous sections of the land."

The Post Office had accomplished the postal mission by the end of World War I, when the American people had received all the principal mail services they needed. With the development of the telephone and radio, and later television, the urgency of the mission and the importance of the provision of its services was greatly diminished. Post roads to new settlements were no longer needed and it was only necessary to improve the services and keep the postal system functioning efficiently and cheaply with the use of up-to-date technology. (The Post Office, oddly enough, has not met this less dramatic challenge.)

New communications and transportation technologies not only have undercut the Postal Service public service function as a mission but also have raised questions about the longevity of the Postal Service itself. Congress has become less interested in the Post Office, has abandoned the public service mission as a policy guide, and has focused increasingly on alternative uses for the appropriated dollars.[2] Postal executives seem to have grasped this radical change in policy, but the rank-and-file employees, their unions, and even the postmasters are still functioning under the mythical concept of mission rather than in the reality of present circumstances. Some of the oral and written reactions to a recent speech presented to the members of the National Association of Postmasters of the United States indicate that they are, for the most part, still functioning under this concept of mission.[3]

The following two questions indicate this. The first questioner asked, "Many of us are from small or rural areas and a lot of us are the only government official in the town. Not only do we deliver the letters, but for people who cannot see or cannot read, we even read them to them on occasion and help them answer questionnaires from the government, etc., so we really do a lot larger service in the rural area than just deliver the mail. Don't you think there's a need for the government to provide that kind of service to the people?" The second questioner asked, "I have an Indian reservation that borders my community in rural America. [Big business] mail is being delivered on one Indian reservation where I make out every single one of the light bills when they come in because many cannot read or write. This is an additional service. Are they going to get this in private enterprise?"

Certainly we must applaud the display of personal compassion on the part of people who serve others on their own time and at their own expense. Such unselfishness is one of the reasons for the greatness of this country. However, for each such act of concern there exist many accounts of smug and secure postal workers who ignore their customers' needs. Postal policy cannot rest on anecdotal incidents of either type. Postal workers need to practice being good neighbors in general at their own inconvenience rather than at the taxpayers' expense. The Postal Service exists to deliver, not read or write, the mail; to perform a limited task efficiently, not for supererogation. Delivering the mail courteously and efficiently should form the backbone of postal policy.

During the periods of history when the public service mission was an effective policy guide, postmasters did not use it to evade fiscal responsibility. Alexander W. Randall, who became postmaster general on July 25, 1966, however, was an exception. He believed that it was not necessary for the Post Office to pay all its expenses from service-generated revenue. It must be noted that this relatively recent point of view contrasts sharply with attitudes historically displayed by government officials and the people. William Bolger, a more recent postmaster general, reflects the typical attitude. In his desire to make the Postal Service more financially independent, he consistently refused to fight postal appropriations cuts, saying such decisions are political and the Postal Service can absorb whatever cuts Congress and the president want. He said increased productivity, service cuts, or postage increases could make up the difference.

The Kappel Commission recently expressed its opinion on whether the Postal Service should be a *business* providing service to the public or a politically responsive institution providing a *public service*. It effectively pronounced the benediction on the postal mission philosophy when it declared that the Post Office was no longer needed as an instrument of government to support U.S. politicians, newspaper and magazine publishers, and the transportation system. The new postal corporation resulting from the Kappel Commission's work is a victory for all who believed that the Post Office should be self-supporting even at the sacrifice of public service functions. At the time of reorganization the Post Office ceased to be an instrument of government policy for public purposes, and public service was no longer to take priority over a balanced budget. The Post Office, the commission made clear, was a business, and like all businesses should be supported by its customers and be subject to the market. The bald eagle, new symbol of the Postal Service, marked not only the reorganization of the postal system but also a change from a postal policy that was almost two centuries old.

Attitudes toward Public Service

The romanticized myth of public service is exemplified in the inscription in the Main Post Office in Washington, D.C.:

> Binding Together a Nation
> Messenger of Sympathy and Love
> Servant of Parted Friends
> Consoler of the Lonely
> Bond of the Scattered Family
> Enlarger of the Common Life
> Carrier of News and Knowledge
> Instrument of Trade and Industry
> Promoter of Mutual Acquaintance
> Of Peace and Good Will
> Among Men and Nations

Although emotionally appealing, the inscription embodies what may always have been but certainly now is a myth: that a universal postal system with uniform rates binds the nation together and fosters democracy. It is impossible to subscribe to this myth with anything more than detached nostalgia when we are, with telephone in hand, able to "reach out and touch someone" instantly, day or night. The advent of the telephone undermined the need for a universal Post Office. Because the Postal Service is no longer exclusive in its universality of communication, it is no longer an essential component of our democracy. To grasp this fact and work out its policy implications is part of the task of this book. The Postal Service should now forsake its somewhat pretentious mission of "binding the nation together" and concentrate its efforts on the humbler task of just providing the best service it can at the lowest possible cost.

James H. Rademacher, president of the National Association of Letter Carriers, and many others whose lives have been bound up in postal activities do not want to admit that the Postal Service is undergoing demythologizing.[4] On July 17, 1969, Rademacher exemplified this stubborn attitude of refusing to face reality when he testified,

> The Post Office is and always must be, a service to all the American people. It is not a money-making scheme; it is not a public utility. The postal service is far too essential to the social, economic, industrial, mercantile and political life of the American people ever to permit it to be removed from the ultimate control of the people. We cannot turn it over to a band of corporate strangers.[5]

While some view the Postal Service's public service functions in a poetic glow, they attach a social stigma to a private profit-making business. While they view the government mission-oriented enterprise as functioning with a kind of idealism on a higher moral plane, they denigrate the humbler provision of services by private businesspeople operating in a free market and motivated in part by the pursuit of profit.

This attitude is by no means universal. With equal facility others assert that the postal functions are too essential to be left in the hands of the government or to be allowed to drift aimlessly in the accountability wasteland of a public corporation. Postal functions need, rather, to be undertaken by a vested interest operating in a competitive environment to be performed responsibly. These alternative attitudes are only noted and not analyzed here. Suffice it to say that when a vision blatantly conflicts with reality it must at least be laid aside, if not discarded altogether. Such is the case with the postal myth of the priority of public service.

Once the myth of the postal mission has been unmasked, the public service philosophy stands vacuous. Some public service functions now performed by the Postal Service could probably be performed by some other organization. These include the posting of FBI wanted-posters, stocking and distributing tax and draft registration forms, as well as forms for Treasury Department medallions, and providing a place to get a passport or to buy a money order. Also of importance are certain functions that supplement the efforts of other government departments. For example, the Postal Service segregates plant and food materials for the Department of Agriculture; handles export claims and forms for the Department of Commerce; and locates relatives of dead soldiers and stores burial flags for the Defense Department.

Other government departments and agencies or private businesses could provide all of these functions just as well as the Postal Service. It would be a good policy to take all the above functions away from the Postal Service with whatever tax revenues, tax breaks, and financing privileges it receives and contract for these services with others on a bidding basis, whether the Postal Service is privately or publicly owned. This would provide the Postal Service with a clean break with the government and make possible a straightforward evaluation of how well the Postal Service delivers the mail.

Public Service and Rate-Making: The Discussion Degenerates

Rate-making in the past has functioned under the direction of the public service aspect of income redistribution. Who should pay for postal service and in what shares: senders of mail, recipients of mail, or taxpayers? From the standpoint of economic efficiency, senders should pay the full costs with no appropriations from tax revenues. If uniform rates prevail, some customers will pay less than the cost of service while others will pay more, thus redistributing benefits from one group to another. Viewed from a public welfare standpoint this redistribution is morally defensible only if the implicit subsidy in this scheme goes to those who are needy or worthy, while those we desire to penalize or those who can easily afford to pay the extra, pay the excessive rates. As we will see in chapter 8, even on this criterion the outcome resulting from a governmentally directed process is as apt to be perverse as beneficial.

Instead of addressing the aforementioned problem inherent in a redistributional scheme, the guiding principles in the rate-setting process for the Postal Service have shifted from redistributional concerns to attempts to attribute costs of Postal Service activities among the different classes of mail. In response to a congressional mandate the Postal Service has abandoned the welfare justification of subsidizing one group of mailers with revenues from another group. This shift to a revenue-maximizing calculus ignores the underlying problem with redistribution and is much more in accord with the expectation of standard bureaucratic behavior. The public-choice theory of revenue maximizing, which will be further examined in chapter 8, is selectively explored below.

According to this revenue-maximizing calculus, the Postal Service charges first class mailers more because they will bear more without deserting the Postal Service for alternative mail delivery systems. The Postal Service charges users of other classes less because they are more flexible in their choices. That is, the Postal Service values its business customers more than individual consumers because it holds no monopoly on most categories of second and fourth class mail that businesses use and fears that if these rates rise too high, mailers will use cheaper alternatives. The unavoidable conclusion is that individual consumers receive less consideration because they have less attractive alternatives.

A further consideration of the existing regulatory mechanism reinforces these conclusions. Competitors of the Postal Service are regulated by other agencies, such as the Interstate Commerce Commission for United Parcel Service (UPS) or Federal Communications Commission for AT&T. The Postal Rate Commission (PRC) has no responsibilities other than to monitor and regulate the activities of the Postal Service. The PRC conducts administrative hearings on requests by the Postal Service for changes in postal rates, fees, and mail classifications, then issues its decisions based on the hearings. The PRC is also empowered to issue advisory opinions regarding proposed national mail service changes, and may also review appeals on proposed post office closings and entertain complaints by mail users.

However, the main charge given to the PRC is to survey the rate-making process to ensure that rates for different categories of mail represent their costs. This is an important function for private competitors of non-first-class mail because they constantly feel threatened that the Postal Service will subsidize a service that competes with them and drive them out of business. Such fears are not without reason. The Postal Service invariably is tempted to resolve its financial problems by charging the bulk of its operational costs to first class mail because it can raise revenues easier this way. The strategy is to bury excessive costs in first class mail delivery. If the Postal Service is successful, two things happen: first, a form of predatory pricing is inflicted on competitors of the Postal Service for second, third, and fourth class mail; second, first class mailers, who include individual postal customers, pick up the tab for cross-subsidies between classes of mail but in the absence of any defensible welfare reason.

The PRC and the court that hears administrative law cases concerning the Postal Service have unsuccessfully opposed the power of the Postal Service to influence rates in the above manner. A. Lee Fritschler, former chairman of the PRC, said in response to the perversity of cross-subsidization, "The private express statutes which grant the Service a legal monopoly in first class must not be used to exploit captive customers who have no legal alternatives."[6] Addressing this same issue, Chief Administrative Law Judge Seymour Wenner said, "If somebody gets something for nothing, somebody else has to pay for it."[7]

From the start the PRC has had the responsibility of monitoring and regulating the setting of postal rates for different classes of mail from their costs. This process, while sound for making relative judgments in rates between different classes of services, has failed in assessing and monitoring the absolute level of rates. Unfortunately, it is in this latter situation that we find the grossest inefficiencies, which harm the public most. This is the case because the cost of gross inefficiencies is buried in small amounts across multiple layers of the Postal Service bureaucracy, thus going largely unnoticed while nevertheless amounting to a substantial amount when summed over the entire institution.

Further complicating the picture, the PRC will likely make errors for other reasons both in relative and absolute judgments concerning Postal Service costs. This will occur because the true costs for the respective classes of mail and levels of service are unknown due to faulty data, the presence of remaining public service functions, and the use of the same facility and workers for many different kinds of services. This is not so much a criticism of the PRC as it is an indictment of the regulatory process. As with AT&T and the airline industry, this problem is pervasive in the regulatory process. Until there is a rigorous, full-scale study of postal costs, there will not be a solid basis for judging what the public service function is, what its costs are, and what the Postal Service pricing policy should be for each class of mail. Given the experience in regulating other industries, it is most unlikely that these data will be available as long as the Postal Service remains in its present organizational structure.

In the first rate case the Postal Service used a standard for attributing costs among classes of mail based upon the variability in volume found in each class.[8] It divided all costs into twenty segments; then it divided the segments or cost category into costs that varied with mail volume and costs that were fixed. The volume-variable costs were attributed to the different classes of mail. The remaining fixed costs were divided up using the controversial Inverse Elasticity Rule (IER) that, in a maze of technicality, apportions fixed costs to the classes of mail according to the reciprocal of their elasticities. This results in the assignment of most of the fixed costs to first class mail, where the elasticity is lower.

To indicate how this method works, the costs of the bulk mail centers (used only for bulk mail) were considered fixed, and so assigned predominately to first class letter mail. This procedure, by assigning the costs of fourth class mail to first class mail, is an affront to common sense but conveniently serves the purposes of the Postal Service. The court has since objected to the IER Rule,[9] but the Postal Service and the PRC continue implicitly to use it.[10] The use of this rule is consistent with the Postal Service's desire to use the rate structure to maximize revenues regardless of the welfare effects.

Even from its own self-interested perspective it is foolish for the Postal Service to ignore that substitutes exist to divert all classes of mail including first class away from the Postal Service. For this reason, the strategy of raising revenues through raising first class rates does not have unlimited potential. Although the higher second, third, and fourth class mail rates required by the *Greeting Card* decision[11] are likely to divert more mail from the Postal Service in the short run, the Postal Service alternative of higher first class rates poses a greater danger to the longer-run survival of the Postal Service. The game of trying to juggle rates between classes of mail to maximize short-term revenues is more like a war of attrition when the Postal Service ignores the fact that for first class mail, first class postage will eventually exceed the cost of sending a hard-copy electronically. This will occur first in densely populated areas, where electronic message services will find their markets. So it appears that no matter which way the Postal Service turns with its rate policy, it will lose.

Service to the Public

Service to customers will be satisfactory when the Postal Service gives them the benefits they want at the lowest possible price. This requires that the Postal Service identify customer needs through market research and data analysis, respond to these needs with appropriate services, and continuously monitor the situation to discover changing needs and better forms of service. Such an approach, unfortunately, is alien to the *modus operandi* of the Postal Service. Instead of taking a market-oriented approach, the Postal Service has engaged in a mammoth public relations campaign of image building that has its genesis in communications techniques. It is an approach, again unfortunately, that seeks to deal with serious problems in consumer and employee relations with denials of their existence, cosmetic public relations modifications, and an imposition of the gag rule on employees.[12]

Despite upbeat policy pronouncements, media blitzes, and commercials, the Postal Service has been cutting back on its service to the public. It has become more lax in providing service, unresponsive to individual users, and more expensive to use. These developments are often irritating to postal customers and taxpayers and have brought renewed and vigorous calls for the abolition of the private express statutes.

Speed of Service

The speed of service in the USPS has not changed much from the first postal system in ancient Persia, of which Herodotus, the Greek historian, said, "Nothing mortal travels so fast as these Persian messengers."[13] The reason for his amazement was that the Persian postal workers delivered mail between points fifteen hundred miles apart in close to seven days—not much slower than today's USPS standard.

The Post Office's 1960 *Annual Report* raised the hopes of postal customers when it announced "the ultimate objective of next-day delivery of first class mail everywhere in the United States." Behind the scenes, however, official standards for overnight delivery in the late 1960s were lowered, not raised, by trimming the target zone for overnight delivery from a state to convenient local areas covered by local mail-sorting routes. A further slowdown stemmed from a secret cost-cutting policy that reduced the number of night shifts preparing incoming mail for next day delivery. Avoiding payment to some postal employees of a 10 percent night pay bonus meant that many letters required an extra day for delivery. Except for its expensive express service, the Postal Service no longer advertises overnight mail delivery.[14]

Mail service has become slower, more expensive, and less reliable since reorganization. According to Postal Service records, it took 10 percent longer to deliver a first class letter in 1982 than it did in 1969: 1.69 days in 1982 as opposed to 1.5 days in 1969.[15]

Former postmaster general William Bolger conceded in 1978 that delivery may have been more reliable in the 1920s than it was then.[16] Unfortunately, in 1986 stamped first class mail delivery was slower than it was in 1982. For instance, while local mail was delivered overnight 95.5 percent of the time in both 1982 and 1986, two-day delivery within a 600-mile radius was achieved for only 88.0 percent of the mail in 1982 and 87.5 percent of the mail in 1986. Cross-country delivery was achieved in three days for 89.8 percent in 1982 and for only 88.8 percent in 1986.[17]

Current Postal Service standards accept two-day delivery of mail traveling less than 600 miles and three-day delivery of cross-country mail. To paraphrase James Bovard, Why should mail move slower than people? Or, why should not a letter mailed in the morning on the East Coast arrive on the West Coast the next day?[18] According to Bovard, in 1981 Sen. Steven D. Symms (R-Idaho) compared the Postal Service with the Pony Express. He said a woman on horseback delivered a letter from Washington, D.C., to Harper's Ferry, West Virginia, in less than nine hours, and the Postal Service took three days.[19] As noted in chapter 1, it was possible for the Postal Service to beam a message electronically, using the modern (but nearly defunct) E-COM system and still take two or more days to deliver the message once it had been received.[20] A final example illustrates how the USPS deals with its problems. It considered cutting its total costs by relaxing its delivery speed standards and at the same time by using public relations techniques to educate the public *not* to expect "prompt service."[21]

Verification

Even using the Postal Service's own criteria, the speed of delivery has slowed down. Making matters worse, private studies record the speed of delivery as substantially slower than the Postal Service's self-reports. It is therefore possible that these Postal Service-sponsored studies may be grossly understating the slowdown. For instance, the results of a study independently conducted by Rep. Bill Green found in his New York district that in 1978 the Postal Service delivered only 33 percent of intra-Manhattan mail overnight, and in 1986, about 68 percent.[22] The Society of Association Executives in 1983 also conducted a test mailing of 363 letters within Manhattan: 42 percent arrived the next day; 21 percent took two days; and 37 percent took three days or longer.[23] Bovard cites the *Miami News*, which conducted a mail test in November 1983 and found that 35 percent of letters mailed arrived late, with a letter on average taking seven days to get from New York or Washington, D.C., to Miami.[24] A 1983 Doubleday test, also cited by Bovard, found that 10 percent of Spiegel catalogs and almost 20 percent of a discount coupon were lost in transit.[25]

Although these private tests are highly selective, they do suggest deficiencies in speed and dependability of service that grossly exceed standards of service claimed by the Postal Service.

The Postal Service, on the other hand, spends tens of millions of dollars each year to deceive the public about the quality of mail service by publishing misleading information on productivity increases, nine-digit zip codes, and delivery times. It does this to convince the public that poor service is really good service and that the problems and errors that many people apparently experience are statistically insignificant aberrations. The Postal Service spent over $4 million a year on biased tests purporting to measure the speed of delivery and boasts that it delivers 95 percent of local mail the next day.[26]

James Bovard reviewed Postal Service testing procedures that were in order in 1970. According to Bovard, test letters were clearly marked before entering the mail stream. Postal clerks were then given advance warning and ordered to look out for the test letters and rush them.[27] A 1975 General Accounting Office (GAO) report found that even after use of this seriously biased procedure the test scores were altered further by postal supervisors who knew their promotions depended on "good" scores. On random checks the GAO found that in Detroit postal employees deliberately removed late mail from the delivery stream before the test began, thus inflating overnight delivery scores.[28] The *Washington Post* reported that postal clerks were told by their supervisors to alter the reports if they showed a high percentage of "late" mail.[29]

The U.S. Postal Service now uses a different testing procedure, which, unfortunately, is seriously flawed, too. Postal employees now check postmarks on randomly chosen letters in designated post offices. This procedure underestimates delivery times because the designated post offices that are to be checked receive notification of the test day a month in advance so they can "get their office in order." Additionally, this system measures only the time between the postmark and the arrival at the destination post office bin. Obviously, if a postal employee picks up a letter at a drop box but does not postmark it until the following day, its actual delivery time is one day more than that recorded for test purposes. Also, if the carrier fails to deliver the letter on the day it arrives in the destination bin, the actual delivery time is greater than the recorded time. There is little doubt that the current testing procedure biases the speed of delivery measurements as recorded and publicized by the Postal Service.

Handling

The U.S. Postal Service has lost most of its package business to the UPS due to high rates, slow and unreliable delivery, and careless handling. As noted by Bovard, a 1974 internal survey found that the USPS damaged half the parcels marked "fragile."[30] Clerks in the New York City Post Office were told not to throw fragile packages more than five feet![31] Making matters worse, postal clerks, when responding to charges that they are unnecessarily rough when handling packages, often exhibit a certain defensiveness rather than improved performance. A newspaper reported "the case of a woman who reacted strongly when a postal clerk slammed a stamp on her fragile cookies, whereupon the clerk had the woman arrested and the cookies sent to the bomb squad."[32] Postal patrons generally agree that postal employees handle packages roughly. Even former postmaster general E. T. Klassen conceded that the Postal Service damaged five times as many packages as UPS.[33]

Postal employees should not shoulder all the blame for the rough handling of packages. The physical specifications of the new bulk mail centers, built to compete with UPS for parcel business, also have been "unfriendly" to packages. The mechanical conveyor belts have drops of up to four feet for packages. Ridiculous design blunders such as this tend to destroy whatever employee morale may exist. For example, the self-proclaimed motto of employees at the Washington bulk-mail center in 1978, as quoted by Bovard was, "You mail 'em, we maul 'em."[34]

Pride and esprit de corps of this nature is unfortunate. A GAO spot check in Chicago found over 3 million mangled, misplaced, or incapacitated packages and letters, and the New York bulk-mail center had twenty-six employees working full time rewrapping packages torn or damaged by the machines. When morale breaks down entirely, you get the kind of wholesale error that happened in Memphis, where it was reported that parcels got mixed with the trash and were delivered to the dump.[35]

Other Reductions in Service

Not only is the mail moving slower, it is not being delivered as often nor as directly. For instance, until 1950 mail was delivered to residences twice a day. In 1978 the USPS terminated home delivery for new homes and began phasing it out for older homes, too. "Cluster boxes" at central locations, sometimes requiring a trip from home of a half mile or more, is replacing home delivery. As James Bovard notes, the cluster boxes themselves are too small, located inconveniently, freeze shut in cold climates, provide little privacy, and are easily vandalized.[36]

The Postal Service asserts that participation in the cluster-box program is voluntary, but signs of coercion are clear. The Postal Service communicated the details of its cluster box program to prospective customers as follows: "Your Postal Service is upgrading the mail delivery in your area.

. . . Your area is one of the first . . . to receive this service. . . . Each customer involved will benefit" (Dickinson, N.D.). Or "It's a new concept, whereby neighborhoods can have beautiful, attractive boxes, free of charge. . . . It's one of the new innovative ways that the Post Office has of serving the American people with better Postal Service" (Eugene, Ore.).[37]

In reality, the Postal Service is arrogantly and aggressively using its power to implement the cluster-box program, especially in rural areas. Bovard notes that when the residents in Maryville, Tennessee, refused to surrender home delivery and sign up for cluster boxes, they were told that the Postal Service would temporarily hold their mail at the Post Office until they could collect it.[38] It should also be noted that a disproportionate number of cluster-box conversions occur in housing projects where the poor who pay full cost for postage are singled out for service cuts.[39]

Up to 1950, residences received mail delivery twice a day. In the past fifteen years the USPS has reduced business and residential deliveries, slowed mail delivery, cut back on collection pickups, reduced target zones for overnight delivery, imposed strict size requirements on the letters it will accept, began the abolition of home delivery, and along with Congress contemplates ending Saturday mail delivery.

More recently, French Johnson, assistant postmaster general for communications, announced that the Postal Service would close many of the 39,000 post offices on Wednesday afternoons and stop Sunday mail collections, thereby reducing the amount of mail processed on Sundays and delivered on Mondays. This will slow down the speed of delivery further.[40]

Rep. Thomas Daschle (D-S.D.) and postal union leader James LaPenta seem to agree that the service reductions spell the end for the private express statutes. Daschle says, "Many [private] carriers believe that if a cut in service does take place, their right to take up the slack and in the process to throw out the Private Express Statutes would be sustained in court. The danger and threat is clear. Once the Postal Service cuts back its entire base of operations, its subsequent reasons for existing become extremely vulnerable to successful challenge."[41]

In slightly different words LaPenta says the same thing: "The budget cutters don't care about reductions in service. They know service reductions will effectively deregulate the Postal Service and quietly kill the monopoly. . . . As we have seen happen in mass transit, obsolescence leads to reduced use and reduced service, which leads to higher rates and even less use. It is a vicious circle."[42]

In light of the gradual decay of the Postal Service in its present form, does the existing mail service provide enough benefits to the entire nation to warrant propping it up? Is its importance in the dissemination of information any longer crucial for the perpetuation of democracy, if it ever was?

Are the "public good" aspects of postal services of such compelling importance that we cannot permit the USPS to fold? The answer to these questions is a resounding No. There is no convincing evidence that postal rate increases have significantly hampered the flow of information. Nor is it clear that the postal subsidy is the most efficient way of promoting the government's concerns for democracy, information flow, and other public service concerns.

Notes

1. This recap of the historical details depends heavily on the original historical work, Wayne E. Fuller, *The American Mail: Enlarger of the Common Life* (Chicago: University of Chicago Press, 1972). The opinions, however, are my own.
2. The general public service (public-good-providing) function of the USPS has been declining in parallel with the public service appropriation. This is the economic reality; the statute has not been changed. See 39 U.S.C. secs. 101(a),(b); 402(a),(b).
3. See "Privatizing, Divesting and Deregulating the Postal Service," remarks by Douglas K. Adie, George F. Bennett Professor of Economics, Wheaton College, and Professor of Economics, Ohio University, before the Annual Chapter Officers' Conference, National Association of Postmasters of the United States, Washington, D.C., February 20, 1984. Excerpts from my speech, and questions and answers were reported by Leonard J. Doerhoff, "The Shape of Things to Come?" *Postmasters Gazette* (April 1984): 5-7. For some comments on this speech, see Bob Williams, Postal Scene, "Expectations Too Great," *Federal Times*, April 9, 1984, p. 6; Fritzie Miller, "Fritzie's Bits and Pieces," *Badger Postmaster* (March 1984): 3; "Napus Officers/Legislative Conference," *Sooner Postmaster* (Oklahoma Chapter, No. 41, National Association of Postmasters of the United States) 17 (April 1984): 1.
4. If postal workers relied on this myth to give their lives meaning, this change might not be possible without deep personal and psychological pain.
5. Kathleen Conkey, *The Postal Precipice, Can the U.S. Postal Service Be Saved?* (Washington, D.C.: Center for the Study of Responsive Laws, 1983), pp. 54-55.
6. U.S. Postal Rate Commission, "Concurring Opinion of Commissioner A. Lee Fritschler," in *Opinion and Recommended Decision upon Reconsideration*, June 4, 1981.
7. Chief Administrative Law Judge Seymour Wenner, in U.S. Postal Rate Commission, *Chief Examiner's Initial Decision on Postal Rate and Fee Increases*, February 3, 1972. Postal Rate and Fees Increase, 1971, Docket No. R 71-1, p. 97.
8. U.S. Postal Rate Commission, *Postal Rate and Fee Increases: Opinion and Recommended Decision*, Docket R71-1 (Washington, D.C.: Postal Rate Commission, 1971).
9. "Distributing billions of dollars on the basis of thinly supported judgments is not an acceptable method and it is an invitation to pressures which Congress ought to avoid." More precisely, the court was objecting to the failure to attribute more costs on the basis of causal relationships, and to the use of arbi-

trary methods to assign the excessive pool of institutional costs left over. The IER, however, is not an arbitrary method but essentially a mechanical one. See *Association of American Publishers, Inc.* v. *Governors, U.S. Postal Service*, 485 F.2d 768 (Washington, D.C., 1973), at 777-78. The D.C. Circuit Court expressed its objections to the IER more forcefully in *National Association of Greeting Card Publishers* v. *U.S. Postal Service*, 569 F.2d 570 (1976) (NAGCP I). The Supreme Court overturned NAGCP I, and so higher second, third, and fourth class rates cannot be required. The immediate result of this 1976 court decision, as indicated by Docket R77-1 and NAGCP III, was the Service-Related Cost Theory, which tends to increase first class costs and rates and lower those of nonpreferential third, fourth, and some second class mails.

10. See Alan L. Sorkin, *The Economics of the Postal System* (Lexington, Mass.: Lexington Books, 1980), p. 161.

11. *National Association of Greeting Card Publishers* v. *U.S. Postal Service*, 569 F.2d 570 (1976).

12. The gag rule prevents employees of the Postal Service from complaining to politicians about internal postal matters. It even prevents communications to the Board of Governors or politicians except through normal administrative channels. Violation of this rule can be a cause for discipline. I will leave it to the reader to discover the beneficiary of this rule.

13. For a description of the first postal system in the Western world, in ancient Persia, see Fuller, *The American Mail*, p. 3.

14. Ronald Kessler, "47 Chances for Delay," *Washington Post*, June 10, 1974, pp. A1, A16. For instance, Winton M. Blount, President Nixon's appointee for postmaster general, told officials, "I don't give a damn if ninety percent of my mail doesn't get there for a week or three or four days."

15. U.S. Postal Service, *Origin—Destination Information System Quarterly Report* (Washington, D.C., Fall 1969; Summer 1982). In compiling the material for this section and the two following sections, I have heavily utilized James Bovard's "The Last Dinosaur: The U.S. Postal Service," *Policy Analysis* (Cato Institute), no. 47 (February 12, 1985). Many of the sources to which I refer were mentioned first in his paper.

16. American Enterprise Institute, *The U.S. Postal Service: Can It Deliver?* (Washington, D.C., 1978), p. 19.

17. See *Annual Report of the Postmaster General 1986*, p. 3.

18. In a nondescript publication addressed to letter carriers, probably by their union, an explanation is suggested why some of the mail is late and some never delivered. For instance, this publication says, "A local resident observed a carrier throw mail into a garbage can. He notified a Postal Inspector who retrieved the mail. An interview with the carrier disclosed he had delivered the flats associated with the cards but 'didn't have time' to deliver the cards. ... In another instance, a carrier took approximately 1500 pieces of third class mail 'for a ride.' He intended to 'work the mail in' later, but had an accident and was off work for two months. When he returned to work, the mail, some consisting of income tax forms, was too old to deliver. The mail was later found in his trunk." The common thread running through these and other cases is that the employees first intended only to take the mail "for a ride," but either time or volume accumulated made it necessary to throw the mail away.

19. Bovard, "The Last Dinosaur," p. 9.

20. "Postal Service May Close Its Electronic Mail Service," *Wall Street Journal*, June 7, 1985, p. 14.

21. *Washington Post*, June 10, 1974.
22. See Bill Green, "Privatizing Postal Service," *Journal of the Institute for Socioeconomic Studies* 9 (Summer 1986): 77-78.
23. Ralph Blumenthal, "Officials Call Postal Delays Worst Since 1980," *New York Times*, December 24, 1983, pp. 1, 11.
24. *Miami News*, November 17, 1983.
25. Doubleday & Company, "Bulk-Third Class Delivery Test," March-April, 1983.
26. For less than $100,000 a methodologically sound, statistically reliable test could be devised and executed privately to measure the speeds of the delivery between major areas of the United States.
27. *Washington Post*, June 12, 1974.
28. General Accounting Office, *System for Measuring Mail Delivery Performance—Its Accuracy and Limits* (Washington, D.C., October 17, 1975).
29. *Washington Post*, June 11, 1974.
30. Ibid., June 10, 1974.
31. Ibid., June 11, 1974.
32. See Bovard, "The Last Dinosaur," p. 6.
33. "Chances for Better Mail Service," interview with Postmaster General Elmer T. Klassen, *U.S. News & World Report*, June 25, 1973, p. 43.
34. *Washington Post*, February 27, 1979, cited by Bovard in "The Last Dinosaur," p. 6.
35. *Washington Post*, June 11, 1974, cited by Bovard in "The Last Dinosaur," p. 6.
36. See Bovard, "The Last Dinosaur," pp. 11-12.
37. House Government Operations Committee, *Postal Service Moves Toward Centralized Mail Delivery* (Washington; March 15, 1983), p. 3, as cited by Bovard, "The Last Dinosaur," p. 11.
38. See Bovard, "The Last Dinosaur," p. 12.
39. House Government Operations Committee, *Postal Service Moves Toward Centralized Mail Delivery*, p. 68, as cited by Bovard, "The Last Dinosaur," p. 12.
40. "Postal Service to Close Offices a Half Day a Week," *Wall Street Journal*, January 19, 1988, p. 1.
41. See Conkey, *The Postal Precipice*, pp. 322-23.
42. Ibid., p. 480. For a discussion of a case in mass transit, see Douglas K. Adie, *An Evaluation of Postal Service Wage Rates* (Washington, D.C.: American Enterprise Institute, 1977), pp. 60-62.

4

Deregulation: The Transportation and Steel Industries

Regulation and Deregulation: A Brief History

For more than one hundred years consumers, government, and business supported regulation because they believed it could deal with problems in markets. Economists justified it for "natural monopolies"; industries thus classified were required to submit to regulation in return for a government-granted monopoly. Such notable figures as George J. Stigler,[1] parting company with his mentor and teacher at the University of Chicago, Henry Simons, have argued that government regulatory bodies eventually become captives of the industries they regulate. Ultimately, Stigler contends, regulatory bodies subvert the workings of the market, which results in inefficient operations. Following Stigler, it is increasingly argued that for most industries, the cost of government regulation far outweighs whatever benefits the public allegedly receives in return. Further, the current conditions of technological innovation make the concept of natural monopolies virtually obsolete. Innovation plus competition, not regulated monopolies, afford the best possibility for providing goods and services to the public.[2]

Although some may disagree with the above position, most would at least agree that without a competitive market to give the regulators signals and good data on costs to increase the efficiency of monopolies, the price-setting function of regulation proves to be at best illusory. Regulation, by definition, substitutes the judgment of the regulator for that of the market. Regulators, finding themselves in the uncomfortable position of having to rely on *ad hoc* methods of making price decisions, will eventually lose credibility. After some serious soul-searching even regulators themselves will realize that their well-intentioned and orderly views can cause enormous distortions in productivity and service.[3]

Deregulation: The Airlines

Dramatic technological advances in aerospace coupled with a rapid growth in air travel hid some of the inefficiencies that were sheltered by regulation in the airline industry. Nonetheless, many people in the mid-1970s noticed that the intrastate markets in Texas and California operated successfully with a minimum of regulation. There emerged a consensus that the intrastate benefits that were enjoyed under newly deregulated conditions could prevail nationally. Changing economies of the industry and certain political events, along with a series of detailed economic studies described in note 3, eventually led to a restructuring of the industry in a deregulatory direction. The Civil Aeronautics Board (CAB) began relaxing its regulatory hold late in 1976. The results were positive and confirmed the Texas and California experience. Congress passed the Airline Deregulation Act two years later in 1978.

It is helpful to cite some of the longer-run effects of deregulation in the airline industry and extrapolate them to a hypothetically deregulated mail delivery industry. Most economists applaud airline deregulation as a significant positive reform despite the impression that the industry still seems far from equilibrium. The economists who have been close to the airline industry believe that competition, for all its imperfections, is superior to regulation as a means of serving the public interest. We must then ask, would this be true of the Postal Service as well?

Before the Airline Deregulation Act of 1978, opponents of deregulation claimed that free entry would result in airlines tearing up their timetables in the pursuit of profits, disregarding their route certificates, and forgetting they had franchises and public convenience responsibilities. In the midst of such chaos many thought the industry would abandon service to 500 of the cities it serviced in favor of operating between the fifty most profitable points. Of course, the adjustment to deregulation did not follow this bleak scenario.[4]

Before deregulation the established airlines declared that cream-skimming by new entrants would force them to abandon service to remote and sparsely populated areas. After deregulation it was not cream-skimming on the part of the new entrants that led the established airlines to drop commuter routes but the lure of profitable opportunities in serving routes between major population centers. Taking the place of the established airlines, which had reluctantly serviced sparsely populated areas, were new entrants that surfaced voluntarily. These companies have been able to provide better service at about the same price but with fewer government subsidies.

Dismantling the CAB freed the airlines to compete, and as a result, long distance airfares have declined by more than 50 percent in real terms in the past seven years while the industry provided 19 percent more output with 1 percent fewer employees. Some dislocation of course resulted. Braniff and a number of smaller airlines failed (Continental operated under chapter 11; Eastern, Republic, and others have struggled to survive) and fourteen new airlines entered the competitive arena.

During forty years of regulation in the airlines industry the watchword was "all for one and one for all." Until 1978 most airlines had minimal competition and offered the same fares and service. Government regulators protected airline managers from some of the risks of competition by automatically approving fare increases when their costs went up.[5] If a carrier experienced financial problems, the CAB supervised a merger with a stronger airline. Institutional arrangements between the regulators and the airlines affected the relationship between management and labor and placed the airline unions in a strong bargaining position. Because of this, the pilots succeeded in capturing much of the cost savings resulting from the technological advances that increased passenger miles of service per employee hour.[6]

Under deregulation new low-cost airlines, motor carriers, and intercity bus competitors are doing to the airlines industry what foreign competitors did to the steel and auto industries. The industry has divided into two tiers: the first being the large, established, and heavily unionized carriers with high, fixed labor costs; and the second being small, nonunionized new-entrant carriers. Vast wage differences exist between these two tiers. The large carriers did not worry excessively about labor costs under regulation because they could always pass along higher union salaries in higher fares. Predictably, wages grew steadily over forty years of regulation as carriers shifted most of their costs to consumers. Under deregulation established airlines can no longer do this and so they share the undesirable commonality of high labor costs. Labor costs amount to 33 to 37 percent of total operating costs for unionized carriers, compared to 19 to 27 percent at new nonunionized companies. (Eighty-four percent of Postal Service costs are for labor.) It should be particularly interesting to watch the process by which the airlines adjust to their excessive wages because it might suggest many techniques that would be applicable to adjustment by a divested, privatized, and deregulated Postal Service that would begin with the same problem.

Deregulation made it possible for new competitors to set their own fares. The nonunionized carriers now offer inexpensive fares and are experiencing rapidly increasing market shares. Larger, unionized carriers have responded. Fares have dropped in this sector, too. Labor costs, the largest controllable outlay for the larger unionized carriers, are being slashed in what Marvin H. Kosters of the American Enterprise Institute calls "disinflation in the labor market." These cost-reducing measures, though not popular with the unions, have been inevitable. For instance, a pilot in a new airline earns a maximum of $52,000, compared with over $100,000 for a pilot flying for a large carrier. Further, pilots flying for new airlines also dispatch and sell tickets, and their flight attendants often work as reservation and ticket clerks, baggage loaders, and plane cleaners. Cut-rate carriers, such as Southwest and the former People Express, resemble flying bus lines, making frequent flights with high-density seating over relatively simple routes. Cut-rate airlines have motivated their workers by offering them a sizable stake in their companies. By working hard, airline workers help themselves, other stockholders, and the flying public.

A number of creative solutions have emerged among unionized carriers in response to competition from cut-rate airlines. Continental, for instance, has confronted its workers with the tough choice of less pay for more work or no jobs at all. Stronger companies offer job security for wage concessions, and while others are forming nonunion subsidiaries to offer equity participation in exchange for labor concessions, Continental and others have used the bankruptcy law to abrogate labor contracts.

Republic received a 15 percent pay cut for nine months, on which it expected to save $100 million; five unions at Western agreed to a 10 percent pay cut in exchange for a 25 percent stake in the company. At Continental, in addition to cutting pay by half for pilots and flight attendants, Chief Executive Officer Frank Lorenzo shortened vacations, suspended the pension plan, and imposed tightened work rules that would raise productivity. Pat Austin, vice chairman of the Airline Pilots Association (ALPA), said, "People are scared to death." In addition to pay cuts and deferrals of raises, pilots at many airlines have agreed to fly more hours a month.

The Pilots Association at American Airlines accepted a two-tier salary structure, as well as new personnel policies that placed costs on a level with new-entrant airlines and reorganized established carriers. American's two-tier pilot wage structure permits hiring of new pilots at 50 percent less than current levels after 1986. These developments will pressure flight attendants to follow the same pattern. Negotiations with union leaders for work rule and wage concessions continue.

As a cost-cutting measure, American is flying McDonell Douglas MD-80s, which require two cockpit crew members rather than the three required in the Boeing 727s. Also at American, in November of 1983 the pilots agreed to forgo a 7 percent raise and extend the number of years an employee needs to work before receiving a one-week increase in vacation time. Also to reduce costs, Delta and United delayed general pay increases through dates in 1984. Pilots at United who were interested in preserving jobs instead of working conditions exchanged employment guarantees for productivity improvements and a lower salary scale for recalled pilots. At United, one of several proposals under consideration was an early retirement program for more highly paid senior employees that would grant a retiring employee a year's salary, pension benefits, and pass privileges.

The most dramatic example of creative cost-cutting has been Continental's wage reduction engineered by temporarily going out of business on September 24, 1984. Lorenzo said that Continental had filed for protection from creditors under chapter 11 of the Bankruptcy Code of 1978 because it was unable to win $100 million of cost savings from its unions. He said the airline would shut down for two days and then begin flying a truncated schedule at sharply reduced fares with a third of its former employees working at half their former wages. The airline did close down and reopened as a smaller carrier with lower costs. Within fifty-four hours of filing petitions for reorganization under bankruptcy, it had fired 12,000 employees, invited 4,000 back at half their former wages, and reestablished service to a third of the cities formerly serviced.

Within forty-eight hours of Continental's move Frank Borman, chairman of Eastern Airlines, said that unless Eastern workers accepted a 15 percent wage reduction, he would shut the airline down completely or follow Continental in filing chapter 11 and reopen under new rules and wage scales. George Stigler, the Nobel Prize-winning economist from the University of Chicago, thinks that bankruptcy as used by Continental has become "a standard method of breaking a union," and indeed, a recent Supreme Court decision seems to support this. Failing companies filing for bankruptcy have the right to void collective bargaining agreements and repudiate union contracts.

Airline deregulation has pressured all airlines to have costs similar to those of the low-cost carriers. Not everyone is enthusiastic about these changes. An official of ALPA said, "Deregulation is ripping the guts out of this industry." The flying public, however, is benefiting from the cost-cutting.

Employees do not understand the function of profits and the need for lowering costs to remain competitive. People Express, whose pilots make up to $50,000 a year supplemented with profit sharing, started the trend to lower labor costs, which it asserted results more because of productivity increases than low salaries. Its labor costs, however, are only 20 percent of total costs.

"We've had a lot of cannonball entries into the airline market who just want to do the job as cheaply as they can and skim off the profits," said Allied Executive administrator Ralph L. Harkenrider. "Every fly-by-night fast-buck operator who wants to start an airline can," says the resentful president of Republic, Daniel May. Some worry that cost-cutting will jeopardize safety, but former CAB chairman Dan McKinnon says that is unlikely because maximum workload is still set by the FAA.[7]

Even though the hard-pressed airline unions talk about a return to regulation, higher profits, and greater job security, Congress shows little interest. Perhaps Congress is taking the lead from workers who are beginning to understand that companies must make a profit or there will be no jobs. The International Association of Machinists lost its strike at Continental because 600 union members crossed the picket line. It is doubtful whether such a walkout, or even another airline bankruptcy or two, would cause Congress to consider re-regulation. The Reagan administration will almost certainly continue to support deregulation. In 1978 Alfred Kahn, chairman of the CAB and patriarch of deregulation in the airline industry, said, "The purpose of deregulation was not to make life easy for the airlines. Survival is part of the discipline of the competitive process." "The only people calling for re-regulation are the ones whose monopoly rents are being squeezed," says William A. Niskanen, a former member of the president's Council of Economic Advisers.

In conclusion, it must be noted that the circumstances justifying deregulation in the airlines industry are even more prevalent in the Postal Service. The moves to improve efficiency and service in the airlines pale into insignificance when compared with probable results from competition under deregulation in the Postal Service. Experience in the airline industry also suggests the changes that will occur under the pressure of competition. Although a maximum amount of freedom needs to exist for the Postal Service, its workers, and their union representatives to work out suitable arrangements in changing circumstances, the patterns set in the airline industry are suggestive of trends that could also develop in the Postal Service when deregulation occurs.

Reverberations at Greyhound

The effects of deregulation in the airline industry brought about direct repercussions in intercity bus transportation. For instance, Greyhound lost 45 percent of its New York-Buffalo business to People Express, which charged half Greyhound's fare. Southwest Airlines has offered a fare from Phoenix to Denver of $65 vs. $99 by Greyhound. With these fares, who is going to ride the bus and pay more for the privilege?

After being hurt by cut-rate airlines, intercity bus companies were given freedom to raise or lower fares. This triggered a price war between the two big carriers, Greyhound and Trailways. Greyhound planned to take on the airlines squarely by slashing fares but believed it must cut costs first, of which labor was 62 percent. Lower costs would enable lower fares, and lower fares would attract more bus customers from among those who might otherwise drive their cars. Although energy conservation may be a matter of fashion, this adjustment could lead to a saving of energy.

In an attempt to trim costs, Greyhound provoked a strike by asking unionized drivers to take a pay cut. The company argued that it had to reduce high labor costs to compete effectively following deregulation of intercity busing. The decision to resume operations during the strike prompted the worst outbreak of labor-related violence since the 1974 truckers' strike. After five strike days, Greyhound had 53,000 job applicants, many of whom were truck drivers and airline employees. (This compares to the 980,000 people who in 1982 applied for one of the 27,000 open positions in the Postal Service.) Greyhound restored partial service by hiring nonunion replacements, thus weakening the union. Union leaders reluctantly (and wisely) agreed to submit a new proposal for wage and benefit cuts to the rank and file for a vote and settled quickly.

This illustrates how deregulation in one industry, namely, the airline industry, has brought competitive responses in another industry, namely, intercity bus transportation. The lesson here is that the Postal Service is not immune to this same threat from developments in other communications industries. Changes such as these can overtake the Postal Service even if it tries to maintain the status quo, and when this happens, it will be in a much weaker position to face the future. Indeed, it is an open question whether there will even be a future for the Postal Service.

Competition in the Steel Industry

Tariffs and other trade barriers have protected the steel industry from foreign competition. In an industry thus protected, even though not completely regulated, lowering or removing tariffs produces many of the same effects that deregulation produces, through the introduction of more competition. The domestic steel companies view their problem as one of keeping competition from cheap foreign steelmakers out of United States markets.[8] Government subsidies and low wages, they assert, enable foreign makers to undersell them in this country by as much as $300 per ton. Although Japanese and European producers have agreed to limit exports to the United States, Brazil and other developing countries have not.[9]

The Reagan administration has not been as receptive to the domestic steelmakers' pleas for higher tariffs as have past governments. A cabinet-level official illustrated this with the following remark: "The industry's always crying wolf. If the industry had done tough, smart things instead of whining after government handouts, they wouldn't be in such trouble today. I've never seen such a bunch of bureaucrats in business suits as the steel chairmen."

Under the threat of competition, transformations are taking place in the steel industry, which previously had secure domestic markets protected by tariffs. Until recently the secure position of the U.S. steel industry allowed it to pay its workers as much as $25 an hour in wages and benefits. Things have changed. Many industry executives, because they have not been enterprising and efficient, view the new competition as tumultuous and disastrous. A company does not have to be efficient if it is not in a competitive industry. Under the present turmoil in the steel industry, many changes have been taking place that will almost certainly improve the efficiency of operations. Bethlehem Steel Corporation closed its Lackawanna plant and laid off 10,000 employees, thus reducing labor costs by more than $25 a ton. This has, in turn, provided greater security for the employees who remained. National Steel Corporation sold its Weirton, West Virginia, plant to its employees after they had accepted a 32 percent pay cut. In the contract negotiated in 1983, employees at Wheeling-Pittsburgh agreed to wage and benefit concessions worth as much as $2 billion a year in return for company stock. The union at Wheeling-Pittsburgh agreed to an immediate wage and benefit reduction of about $3.65 an hour, and the union at Laclede Steel Company in St. Louis agreed to a 14 percent reduction in pay in June 1982.

U.S. Steel reduced pay and benefits and froze cost of living allowances for 28,000 nonunion management, salaried, and hourly workers. The Co-ordinating Committee steel companies and the Steelworkers' union negotiated cuts in labor costs in return for improved job security and more aid for laid-off workers. The major concession was a pay cut of $1.31 an hour that included elimination of a 6 percent cost of living allowance. In addition, the premium rate for regularly scheduled nonovertime work on Sunday was reduced to time and a quarter from time and a half. The Extended Vacation Plan expired, under which employees in the top half of the seniority roll, in addition to their regular annual vacation, received thirteen weeks off every five years, and junior employees received three weeks. All employees eligible for at least two weeks of annual vacation lost one week in 1983. The Savings and Vacation Plan, which had been established to provide retirement, savings, and supplemental vacation benefits, was also eliminated. Finally, the Coordinating Committee steel companies dropped United Nations Day as an annual paid holiday.

At U.S. Steel, Vice Chairman Thomas Graham retired or furloughed 4,000 more managers in addition to the 8,900 salaried workers already let go in 1982. He shut down major plants in Cleveland, Trenton, New Jersey, and Johnstown, Pennsylvania, and sharply curtailed operations at a dozen other locations, including the South Works facility in Chicago. To improve overall efficiency, he is trying to reduce U.S. Steel's break-even point from 75 percent to 60 percent of capacity through better coordination of facilities. U.S. Steel (now USX) still has inefficient factories, but this may be changing. It is doing this by producing 55 percent of its steel with continuous casters (used exclusively by the more efficient minimills rather than the larger integrated steel mills).

Although the number of big steel mills is shrinking in the high-labor-cost area of the industrial Northeast and Midwest, the number of minimills continues to grow in the lower-labor-cost areas of Utah, South Carolina, and Nebraska. This has forced USS (the steel division of USX) to eliminate outmoded equipment and unprofitable mines, ceding its markets in steel wire, bar, and rope products to foreign competitors and the more efficient minimills. Graham said USS was abandoning a product strategy of supplying everything to everyone and stressing the needs of the oil and gas, construction, and auto industries.

When Graham first came to U.S. Steel, he was appalled at the "civil service mentality" he found there, namely, the attitude that if the world wanted to get along with Big Steel, let the world change. In the past the steel companies said, "We make steel. If you want it, you buy it." Graham must now change these unhelpful attitudes if he wants to compete. He hopes to make cautious plant managers more aggressive by meeting with them monthly and encouraging them to talk about their problems. Some doubt that Graham can transform the company because they doubt he can overcome the lethargy of USS's managers. On the other hand, some managers in response to Graham's urging have zealously cut costs, indiscriminately cut essential functions, jeopardized product quality, ignored labor contracts, and spawned grievances. For USS to be profitable, it will be necessary for its managers to strike a balance.

General Motors (GM), sensing the new competitive atmosphere in the steel industry and feeling pressures itself from foreign competition, announced in 1983 for the first time that it would require steel suppliers to bid against one another for its orders, forcing steelmakers to pay more attention to its needs. Besides price concessions, Armco offered GM volume discounts, a delayed payment plan, and a shipment guarantee. Republic Steel developed a high-strength, low-alloy, and lightweight steel for wheels. Bethlehem and U.S. Steel lost volume because they were not willing to give enough of a discount, but GM's savings are substantial. In addition to price concessions, lower rejection rates, and lower inventories, GM has gained manufacturing efficiencies from greater reliability of quality.

Not just in steel but in plants all across the country efficiency is increasing and labor is agreeing to concessions as company after company is forced to adapt to deregulation and competitive threats from abroad. With survival at stake, industries are transforming themselves with little if any guidance from Washington and demonstrating that given some patience, market forces work. The hope is that Congress will release the postal industry so that it, too, can break free from regulatory bondage and win back the support of the American people. We will now turn more specifically to the above-described developments and the Postal Service.

Lessons for the Postal Service

The lesson that experience in the airline, transportation, steel and auto industries teaches us is that the decisions needed to revitalize an industry and make it efficient result only under the threat of extinction that occurs under full-fledged competition. The competitive marketplace is the only effective regulator of economic activity. Through a process of trial and error, the market determines the most efficient way for producers to provide goods and services to consumers. The developments in the deregulated airline industry vividly demonstrate this view. It is futile to keep haranguing postal managers to be innovative, hard-nosed, and enterprising in their decisions. This does not happen in the private sector in the absence of competition, so why should a government-owned corporation with many more obstacles be expected to respond any better?

Of course, the forces of competition have to some extent already been unleashed in the telecommunications sector of the communications industry. Just as the effects of competition in the airlines industry ultimately impacted bus transporation, so will these competitive forces spread from telecommunications to mail delivery. Although the effects of electronic mail and cheaper long-distance telephone service are working more slowly than the competitive forces cited above (the Postal Service enjoys the privileges of a government-sanctioned monopoly), they are working just as surely and will eventually force the Postal Service to respond just as Greyhound and Trailways did. The experience in the airline industry also indicates that it is impossible to predict precisely all the effects of injecting competition into an industry. Determining in advance the full consequences of deregulation is an impossible task.

The internal decisions made by firms were many. The established airlines have been forced to reduce wages one way or another. Methods to increase the productivity of work forces are beginning to include new concepts of risk sharing between labor and management, as well as efforts to arrive at productive work rules and fair salary packages. The Postal Service will have to do likewise. For the Postal Service, 84 percent of its total costs are for wages and salaries, so it is inevitable that postal labor costs will fall.

Many of the arguments, techniques, and strategies used by the airlines, Greyhound, and the steel companies may be instructive to postal executives when they find themselves in a position of having to deal with this problem. Many other changes made by these companies, such as abandoning plants, moving operations, opening up new lines, specializing in some products, creating a new corporate mentality more conducive to efficiency, and changing work rules, might also be instructive to the deregulated Postal Service.

The strong fears that the reform of airline deregulation would adversely affect service to small rural communities are similarly present in discussions of postal reform. This makes the experience with the airlines a helpful example to guide policy in the case of the Postal Service. An evaluation of service in the airline industry indicates that travelers from many small communities now have better access to the air transportation system than before deregulation. As commuter carriers have replaced local-service airlines, service has improved. Local service has become more efficient as indicated by reductions in subsidies. For instance, when Congress passed the airline deregulation bill, many in Ft. Wayne, Indiana, worried that curtailment of air service by major carriers, particularly United, would leave their city without regular service to Chicago and Cleveland. In the two years following deregulation the number of seats not only recovered but had increased by 12 percent over the preregulation level. United Airlines left the market, but Delta stayed and American entered. It was a regional airline, Air Wisconsin, however, that really grew and has since become very important to Ft. Wayne.

Dayton, Ohio, is another example. It also found that immediately after deregulation the number of daily flights plummeted from one hundred to fifty. Soon after, Emery WorldWide Air Freight expanded, and began using Dayton as its major hub. Piedmont also made Dayton its midwest hub. Now Dayton has 140 flights a day. The same story can be repeated for the Quad Cities, Illinois area, where jet service to Chicago ceased after deregulation. Eventually, however, these cities gained service when three commuter airlines, Britt, Mississippi Valley, and Air Midwest, expanded the number of flights to Chicago and St. Louis.

One hundred fifty communities serviced by the smallest air fields will experience a phaseout of regularly scheduled airline service under the essential air service program [EAP]. In 1980 these communities received $109 million per year in subsidies; in 1986 they received $45 million; and in 1988 the subsidy ends. It was thought that when this happened, some small towns, such as Williston, North Dakota, Ft. Dodge, Iowa, and Hayes, Kansas, might lose their local service. This however had not happened as of February, 1988.[10] This illustrates the fact that no system is most convenient for everyone, but the number of individuals and families that now find it possible to travel long distances due to lower fares surely outweighs these relatively minor inconveniences. It is hardly efficient for society to spend tens of millions of dollars to provide air transportation for such a small number of people.

The pattern of development displayed in the above examples concerning the servicing of smaller communities with air transportation after deregulation is suggestive and instructive. The pattern of development in servicing rural or remote areas with postal service is likely to follow a similar pattern should the Postal Service be deregulated. From experience in other industries, there is no reason to believe that the effects of competition will be less beneficial for rural and remote mail delivery service than for small community air service.[11]

The fear of rural residents that competition will raise their rates and reduce their service is exaggerated. First, if competition reduces the overall level of postal costs by 50 percent (not at all unlikely), all consumers will benefit, including rural ones. Second, experience from deregulating trucking and airlines suggests that fears of significant reductions in rural service as a result of competition are probably unfounded.[12]

I have tried to describe the adjustments in other industries openly and honestly. Exposure to competition, after a long period of protection, can be a frightening and painful experience but is necessary to the maturation of a business organization. Despite the inevitable difficulties, courage can turn a negative and defensive reaction into a positive adventure. When deregulation began in the airline industry, policy changes followed one another very rapidly. Those in charge at the CAB from 1977 on, including Alfred Kahn, had the determination to use their authority to ease reforms and had some positive responses from the airlines to a lessening of regulation. In the time period just ahead, the Postal Service will require this same kind of leadership. We may want to recall the Biblical account of Joshua and Caleb who entered the promised land and spied it out. While other spies had negative reports, they said, "Let us go in and take the land, despite the size of the giants which inhabit it."

Notes

1. Former Walgreen Distinguished Professor of Economics and Business at the University of Chicago and Nobel Prize winner in economics.
2. See appendix.
3. The assumption underlying airline regulation was that competition divided up a fixed-size market among many small carriers, leading to wasteful duplication of services and facilities. Some monopoly power over routes, it was thought, would promote better resource utilization. As the larger routes became self-

sufficient, subsidies were provided to expand routes to smaller communities under the universality-of-service mission. Empirical research gradually undermined this view. Lucille Keyes could find no public benefit from the government's restriction on entry. See L. S. Keyes, *Federal Control of Entry into Air Transportation* (Cambridge: Harvard University Press, 1951). Richard Caves found no appreciable difference between the average costs of large and smaller airlines. See R. Caves, *Air Transport and Its Regulators: An Industry Study* (Cambridge: Harvard University Press, 1962). This indicated that there were few if any economies of scale and that route choices could be determined by competition. Michael Levine and William Jordon described the success of unregulated airlines in California, where low-fare airlines were capable of successfully competing with established airlines. See M. Levine, "Is Regulation Necessary? California Air Transportation and National Regulatory Policy," *Yale Law Review* 74 (July 1965): 1416-47, and W. A. Jordon, *Airline Regulation in America: Effects and Imperfections* (Baltimore: Johns Hopkins University Press, 1970). George Douglas and James Miller showed that regulation resulted in higher prices, excessive service competition, and more empty seats. See G. W. Douglas and J. C. Miller III, *Economic Regulation of Domestic Air Transportation: Theory and Policy* (Washington, D.C.: Brookings Institution, 1974). George Eads even questioned whether regulation encouraged airline service to smaller communities. See G. C. Eads, "Competition in the Domestic Trunk Airline Industry: Too Much or Too Little," in *Promoting Competition in Regulated Markets*, ed., A. Phillips, (Washington, D.C.: Brookings Institution, 1975), pp. 13-54. Sen. Edward Kennedy's hearings, orchestrated and documented by Stephen Breyer, launched the legislative actions culminating in the Airline Deregulation Act of 1978. See Senate Committee on the Judiciary, *Oversight of Civil Aeronautics Board Practices and Procedures* (Washington, D.C.: Government Printing Office, 1975).

4. For a full discussion of the adjustment of the airlines industry to deregulation, see Elizabeth E. Bailey, David R. Graham, and Daniel P. Kaplan, *Deregulating the Airlines* (Cambridge: MIT Press, 1985), and John R. Meyer and Clinton V. Oster, Jr., *Deregulation and the New Airline Entrepreneurs* (Cambridge: MIT Press, 1984).

5. Government regulators did not protect managers from the risks of competition by guaranteeing them positive profits. After allowing high wages for its workers, the airlines would compete away much of their other profits through frills such as "free" meals, drinks, playing cards, and so on.

6. It is somewhat ironic that when the airline industry was in its infancy the Post Office Department established the original formula for pilots' pay. When contracting replaced the Post Office's service in 1927, the same formula and rates were adopted. Pilots for the major airlines before the recent negotiations earned substantially more than either military or corporate pilots. Now, as a result of deregulation, some hard bargaining is taking place to bring airline pilots' pay back into line. In May 1985, United Airlines took a hard line in its negotiations with its pilots, threatening to replace all striking pilots at substantially lower wages. This trend may very well set the stage for the much-needed readjustments in postal workers' wages when the Postal Service is deregulated, divested, and privatized. Among other occupations, aircraft mechanics earn 28 percent more than the average for motor vehicle mechanics; aircraft inspectors earn about 48 percent more than the average for other blue-collar supervisors. Flight attendants earn about the same salary as school teachers or nurses.

7. See Meyer and Oster, "Commuter Airline Safety," *Deregulation and the New Airline Entrepreneurs*, pp. 88-89. For the period 1975 to 1980 commuters, which are the most recent entrants into the airline industry, had an average fatality rate of 1.1 per 100,000 aircraft departures, compared with 3.4 for the certified jet airlines. Proregulators such as the ubiquitous Frederick Thayer, a political scientist at the University of Pittsburgh's Graduate School of Public and International Affairs, argue that when deregulation went into effect more planes began flying and the FAA was not able to do a satisfactory job of maintaining safety, leading to an increased number of accidents. So far this view has not been substantiated by the evidence. Even if it should, however, it is questionable whether the structure of the industry should be altered to suit the size of the regulatory agency rather than the other way around.

8. The steel companies spent money on advertising and public relations rather than in modernizing their plants by purchasing and installing state of the art equipment. Newer and more efficient foreign companies were able to underprice them easily.

9. When foreign countries "agree" to limit their exports to the United States, this in effect prolongs the injurious course of industrial decline due to lack of competition.

10. See Michael Edgerton, "Regional Airlines Help Keep Small Cities on the Wing," *Chicago Tribune*, June 2, 1985, sec. 7, p. 23. The matter of scale in dealing with the airline industry is quite different from scale in dealing with postal services. Fort Wayne is a small community for airline service, a large community for postal services. Even the small towns of Williston, Ft. Dodge, and Hayes, which might lose direct air service because they are small in the airline industry, are not small for postal service communities because they have populations between 13,000 and 29,000. There would be virtually no possibility of their losing local postal service.

11. Two specific questions on this same subject were addressed to me after I spoke to the postmasters: One, "What bothers me is that once upon a time United Parcel delivered parcels in Alaska and then they found out it wasn't profitable and they had problems. Since it wasn't profitable they ceased that delivery. We still deliver parcels in Alaska. How would you handle a situation like that?" Northwest Airlines Air Cargo will take packages to Anchorage for $1.41 per pound and to Fairbanks for $1.30 per pound; the Postal Service charges $2.40 for up to two pounds, $4.40 for up to three pounds, and $1.00 per pound for each pound thereafter.

Another postmaster, concerned about the airlines, said, "Then you talk about deregulation. I live near Bismarck, North Dakota, 100 miles northwest. Before deregulation, I flew into Washington, D.C., for $219 and now pay $606. We've lost our major airlines. They're no longer there." For reservations made thirty days in advance and including travel on at least one Saturday, the round trip fare between Bismarck and Washington is $258 on either Republic or Northwest Orient; otherwise the round trip fare in $442. If you live 100 miles from the airport there would be a two-hour car ride to the airport. See Leonard J. Doerhoff, "The Shape of Things to Come?" *Postmasters Gazette* (April 1984), pp. 5-7.

In my discussions with the postmasters I detected a posture resembling that of other businesses that are very large and able to exercise power. A former GM president who became secretary of defense said, "What is good for General

Motors is good for America." Lee Iaccoca is attempting to do this today with Chrysler. The postmasters combined patriotism, national security, and their own self-preservation to justify their privilege and their exercise of power. I believe this is a dangerous infringement on freedom. People such as the Brennans of Rochester were run out of business because they ran afoul of the public express statutes.

12. See James C. Miller III, "End the Postal Monopoly," *Cato Journal* 5 (Spring/ Summer 1985): 154; and Douglas K. Adie, "Abolishing the Postal Monopoly: A Comment," *Cato Journal* 5 (Fall 1985): 657-61. Competition in the airline and trucking industries resulting from deregulation has been substantial and beneficial, but all regulatory experience has not been so favorable. The railroads, for instance, have been substantially deregulated since passage of the Staggers Rail Act in 1980, which reduced the Interstate Commerce Commission's authority over freight rates and services. Unlike the trucking and airline industries, which have spawned many competitor firms, the railroads have consolidated from twelve to seven major interstate lines and could shrink further to five. See *National Journal*, October 5, 1985, p. 2243.

5

Learning from Experience in Other Industries: Divestiture and Deregulation in AT&T

During testimony before the Subcommittee on Economic Goals and Intergovernmental Policy of the Joint Economic Committee of Congress, I sketched a brief scenario for privatizing, divesting, and deregulating the Postal Service.[1] Privatizing involves changing the ownership of the Postal Service; divesting involves dividing the Postal Service into a number of smaller regional companies along the lines of the division of AT&T; and deregulating means repealing the private express statutes and abolishing many other rules, regulations, and privileges applicable to the Postal Service.

These three words, *privatizing*, *divesting*, and *deregulating*, simple enough to understand superficially, denote complex processes that do not occur without considerable effort. Policymakers have successfully promoted these processes, and the results have been favorably received by the public because of their beneficial effects. For this reason the pioneer experiences in deregulating the airline industry, deregulating and divesting AT&T, and privatizing companies in Canada and Great Britain can instruct us on at least three points while we oversee the structural and organizational changes in the Postal Service.

First, the arguments made for and against deregulating, divesting, and privatizing are useful because of their applicability to the Postal Service. For example, we can compare the Postal Service with the airline industry and AT&T to determine whether arguments leading to their deregulation imply the same course of action for the Postal Service.

The second point of instruction centers on how various policy decisions made during the process of deregulation have actually worked out in other industries. A successful policy change requires a knowledge of motivations and an ability to anticipate the consequences of ideas. In the absence of concrete experience, ideology usually dictates policy in a hit-or-miss fashion. The experience of working out similar processes in other industries is of immense value and affords many practical suggestions.[2]

The third point of instruction comes from a continuous examination and monitoring of the deregulation of the various deregulated industries. In this regard, the deregulation of the airline industry is perhaps most instructive because it has been in the process of development for a longer period of time and the effects have had much more time to surface. Other industries have different points of comparison. For example, the Postal Service and AT&T are both in the communications industry, are approximately the same size, and have been regularly compared by policy analysts. Also the AT&T breakup constitutes the only example of a recent large-scale divestiture. The privatizations in Canada and Great Britain are instructive because their economies are similar to that of the United States and their experiences are successful examples of this process.[3]

The postal system has many similarities with the telephone system. Both have functioned under the same kinds of regulations: protecting their monopoly position and restraining competition. AT&T, in pursuing its privileges a little more aggressively, precipitated a host of problems over the years, not unlike the problems in which the Postal Service is enmeshed. AT&T and the Postal Service used the same arguments to defend their monopolies. A serious examination in a lengthy court review showed the arguments defending the telephone monopoly to be specious, and the monopoly to be a public nuisance. In the telephone industry this led to relief by the divestiture of AT&T (breaking up the then-largest utility into smaller companies) and removing its monopoly in many areas. The same arguments for divesting the telephone industry are relevant to the postal industry. In this chapter I consider the same type of remedy for the Postal Service, the largest existing utility.

Up to this point there has been insufficient experience to make a definitive judgment on the effects of the AT&T breakup on public welfare. Many people are still very skeptical concerning the effects of this deregulation and organizational change on the cost and quality of their phone service and are waiting to see the helpful effects before espousing the policy change.[4] If Judge Greene made a good decision, then the same reasoning applies equally or perhaps even more forcefully to the Postal Service.

All the arguments for retaining the Postal Service's monopoly have analogue in the telephone service industry. For instance, AT&T justified its monopoly primarily from universal availability of service at affordable rates. To justify the prohibition of competition, some people argued that competition would result in "cream-skimming," "service degradation," and service reductions, especially in remote areas. Since the introduction of competition, however, none of these adverse consequences have surfaced.

At this point we have the experience in other industries and the verdict in the AT&T case. Although my understanding of economics also predisposes me toward the deregulatory solution, the arguments for the Postal Service must stand the same test of experience. The lessons from experience in the AT&T case are instructive for making Postal Service policy. The case for the optimal disposition of the Postal Service depends on the outcome of the deregulation and divestiture of AT&T.

The AT&T Policy Reversal and the U.S. Postal Service

Developments leading up to the divestiture of AT&T go back to the consolidation of the Bell System.[5] The need for universal service has been a key justification for the monopolies of both the Bell System and the Postal Service. The founding father of AT&T, Theodore Vail, called for a system that was "universal, interdependent and intercommunicating, affording opportunity for any subscriber of any exchange to communicate with any other subscriber of any other exchange." He envisioned a telephone system "as universal and extensive as the highway system of the country which extends from every man's door to every other man's door." Vail, like many in the Post Office, did not believe that universal service could be "accomplished by separately controlled or distinct systems nor that there can be competition in the accepted sense of competition."

In 1913 Vail set forth a new strategy that greatly strengthened the Bell System. In his view regulation was better than both nationalization and extensive competition. In effect, Vail avoided both nationalization and competition by promising a universal system and acceding to public regulation. Further, by embracing regulation, AT&T was able to promote a relatively favorable regulatory climate for itself. Armed with these reasons, AT&T began successfully persuading state regulators to endorse and encourage its consolidation. At the same time all attempts to nationalize AT&T were rebuffed until the war in 1918, even though the telephone industries in most European countries had been nationalized by 1912. Even when President Woodrow Wilson decided in 1918 to take control of the telephone and telegraph system and put it under the postmaster general as a wartime measure, Vail's concept of universality of service in exchange for regulation was being pursued. The telephone system was returned to AT&T a year later. Subsequent legislation gave the ICC expanded regulatory authority.[6]

By 1934, AT&T had reestablished its dominance in the telephone market, was serving nearly every major city, and owned 80 percent of the telephones in the United States. During this period the mission concept led to a "spirit of service" that was epitomized by the lineman working outside during a storm or the operator staying at the switchboard during a flood. This tradition continues in a much weakened form in Bell Laboratories (now a part of the divested AT&T) as it works to reduce costs and improve the reliability of communications systems.

On April 1, 1938, Commissioner Paul A. Walker, chairman of the FCC's Telephone Division, made some startling allegations in his "Proposed Report" (called the Walker Report) that Western Electric unnecessarily drove up prices for consumers by overcharging the Bell System for its equipment, the cost of which was passed on to telephone customers through rate increases.[7] A suit followed this report, contending, "The absence of effective competition has tended to defeat effective public regulation of rates charged to subscribers for telephone service, since the higher the price charged by Western Electric for telephone apparatus and equipment, the higher the plant investment on which the operating companies are entitled to earn a reasonable rate of return." Walker urged direct regulation of Western's prices and called for legislation to force AT&T to purchase its equipment through competitive bidding. The Walker Report also recommended government ownership in the event that regulation failed.

AT&T, because it was large and powerful, responded to the suit by saying that the relationship between Western's prices and Bell System rates was subject to review by the FCC and by state agencies, which could disallow any costs that were found to be unreasonable or excessive. Although procedurally correct, the statement merely made obvious how ineffective state regulatory boards were when faced with the resources of a gigantic corporation. Unsuccessful in bringing any changes in AT&T, the Walker Report nevertheless raised for the first time questions concerning the structure of the Bell System. The questions led to the government's first antitrust suit against AT&T, which argued for the divestiture of Western Electric from the rest of the company. This suit led to the 1956 consent decree that preserved AT&T's monopoly.[8] It also confined the Bell System to the provision of regulated telecommunications services; its competitors were not so confined.[9] It appeared that the 1956 consent decree was a victory for AT&T because it was not required to divest itself of Western Electric nor to disturb its regulated monopoly. The U.S. Court of Appeals for the District of Columbia also ruled that customers had the right to use telephone equipment obtained from sources other than the telephone company. In other words, the high prices charged by Western Electric for customer premise equipment led eventually to competition in the provision of telephones and business office switchboards (PBXs). In addition, competitive forces were unleashed by this development that led to the deregulated telephone peripherals market.

Adding to this turn of events was the *Above 890* decision, a ruling in 1950 stating there were enough microwave frequencies above 890 megacycles for the development of private point-to-point microwave communications systems. This opened the door for new companies to transmit messages over long distances by microwave.

The 1968 *Carterfone* decision followed. Thomas Carter was an entrepreneur who began marketing a device called the Carterfone, which acoustically and inductively interconnected mobile radio systems with the wireline telephone system. AT&T quickly recognized that the device represented the possibility of a competing telephone network. When the telephone companies prohibited the use of this device, Carter asked the FCC for relief. In March 1968 the FCC concluded that AT&T's policy of prohibiting the use of the Carterfone was unreasonable and unlawful. The *Carterfone* case therefore firmly established the consumer's right to connect noncarrier equipment to the public telephone network, provided it was technically compatible.[10]

In 1969 Microwave Communications, Inc. (MCI), filed an application with the FCC for authority to construct a limited common carrier microwave system between Chicago and St. Louis. Subscribers needed to obtain their own links (or "local loop") from their premises to MCI's offices. MCI's proposed rates were lower than AT&T's. AT&T accused MCI of "cream-skimming," i.e. operating only high-density routes where lower fixed costs permit lower rates. It argued that MCI's proposed activities were not in the public interest because established carriers were required to serve all geographical areas. Competing with MCI, it claimed, would force it to drop the policy of a uniform average rate structure.

AT&T did not know MCI's costs and so did not know that MCI was an efficient, innovative entrant. This did not deter AT&T from charging MCI with being a cream-skimmer. The FCC did not accept the cream-skimming argument. Instead it estimated that the revenue diversion away from AT&T, resulting from competitive entry into the designated markets, would be insignificant. MCI was applying for permission to offer services that were not then being offered. This was an important basis for the decision. Subsequent developments have shown that the FCC was right and the cream-skimming argument of AT&T was inappropriate. The Postal Service's charges of cream-skimming by would-be competitors are just as rash and on careful examination are similarly inappropriate.

The FCC, not deterred by the threat of losing a universal rate structure, voted 4-3 that the competition proposed by MCI was not cream-skimming and so granted its application. Shortly after, the FCC was deluged by hundreds of applications from other businesses desiring to construct microwave facilities to provide specialized common carrier services between various parts of the country.

On November 20, 1974, the Justice Department filed its antitrust suit against AT&T, Western Electric, and Bell Telephone Laboratories, complaining that AT&T had monopolized telecommunications services and products. The Justice Department sought the divestiture of Western Electric, as well as the division of local telephone services into at least two Bell Operating Companies (BOCs). The proposed restructuring made possible the total dismemberment of the Bell System.

With the possibility of defeat hanging over its head, Bell agreed on January 8, 1982, to end its control of twenty-two local operating companies that constituted the bulk of the traditional telephone industry. In exchange for its cooperation in this divestiture and deregulation Bell received an end to the prohibition on its entry into the unregulated part of the telecommunications market. The Justice Department announced the agreement in a nineteen-page document, which, with some modifications, has become not only the blueprint for the largest corporate divestiture in U.S. history but also the foundation for the future development of the telecommunications industry.

Competition was to be the key instrument for governing the telecommunications industry. To compete in new markets and retain access to existing markets, the Bell System had to agree to restructuring.[11] The Justice Department forced the Bell System to cooperate with the divestiture solution or face continuing legal uncertainties that would make capitalizing on future market opportunities difficult. The solution called for AT&T to separate its local exchange services from all other operations, such as long-distance service, customer equipment, manufacturing, and research. It was also necessary to divide up the well-functioning, nationwide partnership of companies providing local communications service. This would prevent Bell from using revenues from monopoly services to subsidize other services and at the same time remove its incentive to prevent competitors' equal access to local networks. Breaking up the Bell system offers the prospect of resolving many of the problems of a regulated monopoly by transforming the telephone service market into a competitive industry. AT&T is, in many respects, a new industry.

It must be noted that court decisions and administrative rulings leading up to the AT&T divestiture were more favorable in creating a competitive environment in the telecommunications industry than court decisions have been in affecting the provision of postal services along similar lines. As discussed in chapter 2, the courts in recent years have almost unanimously defended the Postal Service's monopoly and even extended it for the grossest of self-interested reasons.[12]

The process leading to divestiture of the Postal Service has only recently become a part of the public discussion. Many of the same influences, however, that encouraged an agreement culminating in divestiture of AT&T are present in the Postal Service too. Many of the same benefits accruing to the telephone industry as a result of the breakup of AT&T would be available in the mail-handling industry also. However, much work remains to focus the public issues in a constructive way and to prompt a public dialogue that would culminate in legislation or court action designed to bring about restructuring in the Postal Service. An objective of this book is to prompt just such a process.

The series of legal actions taken by the FCC and the Justice Department against AT&T that ended in divestiture and deregulation began with the Walker Report in 1938 and continued with many other decisions. The only comparable action undertaken toward the Postal Service was the reorganization of 1971. The further restructuring advocated in this book is a continuation of work that began in the 1971 reorganization but was not finished at that time because the climate of public opinion was not sufficiently favorable.

The individuals who were active in regard to the divestiture and deregulation of AT&T could be important resource persons during a restructuring of the Postal Service. Many of the same questions addressed with AT&T will appear in the process of restructuring the Postal Service. Also, because AT&T has been divested and effects of this are currently being monitored, it should be possible to learn from the mistakes made, thus making the divestiture of the United States Postal Service less troublesome.

The Courtroom Controversy: AT&T Loses

The arguments put forth in the AT&T suit are relatively few in number and would appear in much the same form should there be a hearing or court case involving the Postal Service. From the outset it should be recognized that the possession of a monopoly is not in itself illegal. AT&T enjoyed and the Postal Service continues to enjoy an officially sanctioned monopoly over a lengthy time period. The acquisition and maintenance of a monopoly by illegal means, however, incurs antitrust liability. The government does not seem to be as ready to sue the Postal Service as the Department of Justice was to sue AT&T, perhaps because an arm of the federal government sets the pricing policies for the Postal Service. To win its liability case, the government needed to prove that AT&T engaged in exclusionary pricing, that is, a pricing policy that tends to keep potential competitors out of its business. The government also had to show the link between any such illegal acts and AT&T's structure, indeed a formidable task. Structural changes, such as divestiture, could be required and legally justified if and only if AT&T engaged in a *pattern* of illegal activity, the incentive and opportunity for which arose from its structure.

AT&T defended itself against charges raised by the Justice Department by denying it had committed many of the illegal acts and/or by denying that the acts were illegal. It asserted that monopoly was the best structure for the telecommunications industry and that its actions to preserve its monopoly were therefore justified. In defense of its monopoly position, it claimed economies of scale, high rates of productivity growth, and contributions to the national security.

The following is a synopsis of the arguments in the case. Asserting that it was a natural monopoly entitled AT&T, according to the accepted theory of utilities, to exploit its cost advantage for its own and the public's benefit. The Justice Department, however, noticed certain types of anticompetitive behavior from AT&T that were inconsistent with the position of a natural monopolist. For example, it used provisions of the regulatory process to increase the cost of entry for competitors; it deterred entry of competitors by precommitting investment funds;[13] it charged exorbitant fees to independent exchanges to interconnect with its local exchanges and for each call; and it used exclusionary pricing policies such as Telpak, Hi-Lo, MPL, and DDS tariffs.[14] The Justice Department asked, "If AT&T is a natural monopolist with over 80 percent of the market and the efficiencies of a declining average cost curve, why should it have to resort to such tactics?"

In answer to the charge of predatory pricing with tariffs and differential rates, AT&T declared that its mission to provide universal service required it to offer rates below marginal cost to some customers and rates above marginal cost to others. New entrants could take advantage of this strategy to profit by pricing their services slightly below the rates that are above marginal costs. "Skimming the cream" is the term applied to this practice because it supposedly left AT&T with the customers that cost the most to serve. AT&T stated that its various lower-cost tariffs constituted its response to these new entrants, both real and potential.

AT&T also said that because it was a natural monopoly, all competitive entrants were inefficient, and hence all tactics to keep them out of business were justified. It maintained that breaking up Bell would lead to gross inefficiencies in the provision of telephone services, for it would operate at a higher cost, smaller scale of operation. At a smaller scale of operation, it contended, the efficiency resulting from the coordination and vertical integration of services within one large company such as AT&T would no longer be available. Also, AT&T said that competition in the telephone services market would lead to chaos.[15]

The Justice Department countered by distinguishing the competitive behavior of new entrants from the activity of cream-skimming. The new entrant firms were low-cost, innovative firms using new technologies and supplying services not offered before. In the department's opinion, revenue would not be diverted from AT&T to MCI or other new entrants; instead the entrance of new firms would encourage coordination between firms in competitive markets because they all needed to become compatible with one another to earn profits. The argument that ultimately undermined the AT&T position was a recitation of the historical evidence that suggested that local telephone exchanges were really not "natural monopolies" at all.[16] Consider the background and details of this argument below.

The Communications Act of 1934 embodied the belief that the telephone industry was a "natural monopoly," in which competition would lead to waste and public inconvenience. At that time many thought that the competition arising with the advent of many firms resulted in wasted resources and capital due to such things as duplicate wires, terminal instruments, rights-of-way, and buildings. A consensus emerged that only one company should serve a particular geographic location. So AT&T became the sole supplier of local telephone service to over 80 percent of the nation's population, while local independent monopoly companies served the remainder. In opposing the breakup of the Bell System, AT&T stated that because the telecommunications network was a natural monopoly, an integrated enterprise like itself could construct and manage the network most efficiently.

In the 1950s advances such as microwave technology began to eliminate many of the "natural monopoly" elements of a cable-based intercity transmission service, if they ever existed, and widespread development and use of computers increased the need for high-speed digital communications services. Fearing the loss of business that would occur if its largest customers decided to construct their own private communications networks, AT&T filed its first Telpak tariff in 1961. It consisted of bulk quantities of private line circuits offered at substantial "volume discounts" from the individual private-line rate. The move delayed for a while a concerted effort by would-be entrants.

Eventually the new competitors were allowed to operate but were met with a series of price responses by AT&T: the Telpak tariff (in effect well before 1970), the Hi-Lo tariff, the MPL tariff, and the DDS tariff. Each of these price reductions excluded new entrants, or in the case of the earlier Telpak tariff, prevented customers from buying their own communications facilities.[17]

The government, however, did not have evidence showing that the discount prices were below AT&T's cost. The evidence did not exist because neither the government nor AT&T had any clear idea of what the costs were. There was no practical basis for establishing the actual costs of the various categories of service, much less what AT&T's costs should have been if they were operating efficiently. The scenario surrounding the timing of the rate changes raised the suspicions of predatory pricing. (This same problem has plagued the Postal Rate Commission, which attempts to regulate postal rates with the insufficient or inaccurate cost information provided by the Postal Service.[18])

The government's fundamental complaint was that Bell had used control of its bottleneck facilities at local telephone exchanges to shut out long-distance competitors of AT&T Long Lines, and equipment competitors of Western Electric. It was easy to prove that AT&T local exchange monopolies foreclosed competition or placed competitors at a disadvantage. Sometimes AT&T shut out long-distance competitors by simply refusing to interconnect with them, as in the case of MCI. Equipment competitors were discriminated against when AT&T refused to supply service to customers who purchased non-Bell equipment. As late as the early 1970s the FCC needed to authorize competition by MCI and the other specialized and domestic satellite carriers to open up the market.

The Justice Department presented a persuasive case that AT&T tried to deter entry into the market for intercity telecommunications services by erecting barriers to entry. First, AT&T used legal details and processes of the regulatory apparatus to impose high legal and regulatory costs on the entrants. Second, AT&T made interconnection with the local exchanges artificially expensive, thereby raising the entrants' fixed costs of operating. Third, AT&T charged entrants high rates for each call that passed through its exchanges. Fourth, AT&T precommitted investment funds for telephone exchanges as another strategy to deter entry by other telephone systems more efficient than itself. By announcing well in advance large planned capital expenditures for selected exchanges, it could deter would-be entrants from making investment commitments. Fifth, if independents did set up independent local telephone exchanges, AT&T used a combination of threats and actions to force them to merge or interconnect with the Bell System. Sixth, these independent firms, which developed relationships with the Bell System because of difficulties in interconnecting as independents, were not allowed to interconnect with other independents. If they did, the Bell System could revoke their licenses.[19] The accumulated force of these arguments was irresistible to Judge Harold Greene. AT&T assessed the judge's disposition toward it as unfavorable, which led it to cooperate with the Justice Department in drawing up the settlement underlying Judge Greene's decision.

(The Postal Service's corresponding ploy to deter competitors is less complex. It has simply defined a letter and expanded the interpretation of the private express statutes to cover the customers' mail receptacles. It is illegal to use these mail receptacles for any materials without paying U.S. Postal Service postage. This is blatantly anticompetitive but has not as yet aroused a public outcry. Other steps in the handling of the Postal Service's monopoly, discussed in chapter 2, are also instructive at this point.)

Beyond the Court's Decision: Two Key Issues

AT&T was unable to raise convincing specific defenses against the six specific charges of illegality outlined above. Instead it discussed the two broader issues it had used to defend its specific illegal monopoly practices. From the beginning the Bell System had said its goal was to make telephone service available to everyone in the nation. The Bell System adopted this policy from Alexander Graham Bell, who desired to see universal telephone service extended to the poorest families. Historically, two arguments defended universal service as a public policy: the first involves an externality argument that the aggregate value of communications services to society is greater than the sum of what individual customers would pay; the second is an equity argument of entitlement. These arguments, regardless of the direction that a given court decision might take, must be sifted and weighed by the American public in light of subsequent experience. We now turn to these arguments and their applicability to both Bell and the postal monopoly.

The externality argument states that the availability of phone service, even to a poor person, affects the value of phone service to others who may occasionally wish to phone the poor person. Social workers, salesmen, relatives, and employers get more value from their phones when they can reach everyone. (The Postal Service uses a form of this argument when it asserts that the universality of services binds the nation together.)[20]

Before the 1982 consent decree, AT&T handled the externality problem by cross-subsidization: it charged more than marginal cost for long-distance service used by business and affluent customers and charged less than marginal cost for local home service. It said that it used cross-subsidization of rates only for redistributional welfare concerns, where subsidies ran from lower-cost urban, business, and long-distance customers to high-cost rural, residential, and local service customers. (Despite congressional intent to subsidize some mailers, the Postal Service seems to have given up most references to redistributional rationales for its pricing decisions. Although a redistributional rationale is still referred to by others in discussions and not denied by the Postal Service, a revenue-maximizing calculus is the prime motive in setting postal rates.)

Those defending AT&T's monopoly say that if the telephone market were competitive, homeowners would pay the full cost of their service, and universal service as a public policy would have been impossible. However, by the mid-1960s the national policy objectives of affordable, universal telephone service and construction of the most rapid and efficient system possible were essentially fulfilled, and so supporting the monopoly was no longer necessary, if it ever was. This is precisely the situation in which the mail delivery industry finds itself, as discussed in chapter 2. It is at least not inconceivable to begin talking about a resolution of the Postal Service's problem similar to that employed in the AT&T case.

The problem with AT&T, as with the Postal Service, is that cross-subsidization to meet public service objectives typically harms competitors. The FCC's concern has been to detect and prevent just such occurrences, but it has failed. If not prevented, AT&T's practice of setting low rates for competitive services that it subsidizes with revenues from the provision of its monopoly services is unfair behavior, which will tend eventually to drive competitors out of the market. The PRC and the courts have been sensitive to the same problem with the Postal Service, which charges lower rates for its competitive services (second through fourth class mail) and a higher rate for its monopoly first class mail. When allowed, this behavior would permit the Postal Service to maximize its revenues unfairly and drive its competitors out of business.

In arguing against competitive entry into their markets, regulated public utilities often assert that their competitors are inefficient businesses seizing profit opportunities created by the discriminatory rate-making of a natural monopolist. The argument runs that if public utilities are natural monopolies, then a single firm can theoretically provide service more cheaply than several firms. Therefore the entrance of new firms can theoretically lead to wasteful duplication.

The Postal Service assumes that it is an efficient "natural monopoly" but nevertheless complains about cream-skimmers. This is ludicrous. If it were an efficient natural monopoly, its costs would be so low that no entrant firm would be able to undercut its rates. In fact, however, its price not only exceeds its average cost for first class mail but exceeds also the costs of beginning entrants operating at low volume. Under the "natural monopoly" assumption, the average cost of these new entrants—because they operate at low volume—should be much higher than the average cost of the monopolist. The Postal Service has impaled itself on the horns of a dilemma: either it is not much of a "natural monopolist" or it is in violation of the terms of reorganization because its price is above its average cost. If we note that Advertisers' Distribution Service, a Minnesota firm, delivers third class mail, already a low-rate mail, in rural areas at a price below that charged by the Postal Service and still earns a profit, it is not difficult to conclude that the Postal Service is extremely inefficient.

In addition to the externality argument, the policy of redistribution also uses the equity argument of entitlement to justify itself. In the case of AT&T, this argument asserts that telephone service, like education, medical care, housing, and postal service, belongs to everyone no matter how poor as an attribute of citizenship. For instance, some regard a home phone a necessity so the poor are within easy reach of potential employers with job offers or to obtain help if there is a medical emergency. The analogous application of the argument to the Postal Service is clear.

It is, then, these two arguments that ultimately are put forth in one form or another to justify the redistribution inherent in discriminatory pricing.[21] It is because of these arguments that prices might exceed marginal cost for some services or customers and be less than marginal cost for others.

It is the practice of discriminatory pricing, if not between classes then between groups of customers within the same class, that supposedly allows entering firms to cream-skim the public utility's markets. Under this practice, AT&T and the Postal Service contend that competing firms skim the cream—the profitable business—and leave the unprofitable business for the public utility. The response to this line of reasoning is to distinguish competition from cream-skimming. Competition exists where a new entrant competes with the existing business because (1) the existing business is making greater than normal profits because its price is above average cost, or (2) the existing firm uses inefficient production techniques or does not operate at the least-cost scale of production. The competitive process that takes place under these circumstances is very important to the vitality of the economy. It is through this process that the "invisible hand" of competition forces businesses to serve the greater good.

The Problem with Monopoly

The significance of this discussion is that the Postal Service's arguments defending its monopoly are not even as strong as those of AT&T. After a lengthy review and a close inspection, the courts were unable to justify monopoly in the case of AT&T. In claiming status as a natural monopolist, AT&T argued that (1) its competitors in intercity service were less efficient than it was, and were able to survive only because rate averaging made AT&T's rates exceed cost for some services, (2) in lowering rates, it was merely exploiting its inherent scale economies and not engaging in predatory pricing, and (3) breaking up the Bell System would eliminate efficiencies realized from common ownership and control of the telephone system. If pressed, the Postal Service would have a much more difficult time than AT&T convincing an unbiased court of the validity of any of the above arguments.

In arguing that it had economies of scale, AT&T discussed how the vertical integration of its services within one management organization allowed for central direction and coordination of services, which, it said, would be chaotic in a competitive environment. This argument demonstrates a total lack of appreciation for how a competitive economy produces coordination: coordination does not result from common ownership and control but from each party's realizing that it can make a profit by becoming more compatible with other parties. The problems of coordination that AT&T's economists identified and contended would impede progress if AT&T were divested do not seem likely to materialize in the telephone system created by Judge Greene. Furthermore, common ownership and central planning as practiced within the huge AT&T monopoly, create their own coordination problems, which are not unlike those of a socialist state.

Executives of large corporations such as AT&T and the Postal Service plan for their businesses just as owners of smaller businesses do. Which of these businesses will be more efficient? It depends on which system generates and uses knowledge best.[22] With multiple smaller businesses there are more people engaged in profit-and-loss accounting, which is the economic calculation underlying the bidding process. Although each entrepreneur possesses only bits of knowledge, the spontaneous interaction of bidders in the market brings about a state of affairs in which prices correspond to costs, resources are efficiently allocated, and welfare is maximized.[23] The combination of knowledge generated and utilized by the different entrepreneurs in the market brings about results that a directing individual in a single large corporation could match only if possessed of all the knowledge himself or herself.

It is not that individual entrepreneurs are smarter than managers or bureaucrats but that persons embedded in the competitive process by virtue of their rivalry with one another impart information about relative prices that in the absence of competition would not exist.[24] In a large business such as AT&T or the Postal Service that encompasses most if not all of a particular market, all the participants are on the same team and the competitive process does not exist. It is in the process of competition that the participants discover knowledge of prices they would otherwise have no way of obtaining. It is the judicious use of this knowledge that is crucial for profit and loss calculations that produces the efficient use of resources.

The success of planning in a large corporation such as AT&T or the Postal Service depends on whether enough information on prices exists and can be put at the disposal of a single authority who operates under sufficient motivation to make effective decisions for efficiency reasons.[25] The alternative form of business organization to a single large firm, which has been implemented in the divestiture of AT&T and could be implemented in a divestiture of the Postal Service also, is to allow individual entrepreneurs access to markets and the opportunity to generate and use the additional knowledge they need to dovetail their plans with others. In the telecommunications industry before the breakup, knowledge and information expanded so rapidly it could not be assembled, contained, and utilized within AT&T. Also, despite the fact that AT&T was a profit-making business, there was not enough motivation to implement existing technology as rapidly as it was developing. Instead, planning within AT&T became devoted to the preservation of capital values and took the harmful form of retarding innovations. Much of this description applies with equal force to the Postal Service under existing circumstances.

As a frontal attack on AT&T's position, historical evidence suggests that local telephone exchange monopolies that are still protected may never have been "natural" and that competition may improve service, reduce price, and encourage technological improvements. Melvyn Fuss and Leonard Waverman found, for instance, that Bell Canada did not have aggregate scale economies and so could not have had a natural monopoly over local, toll, and private line service.[26] This most recent and most comprehensive study of Bell Canada rejects the hypothesis that the telecommunications industry is a natural monopoly. The point is that the provision of service by a single firm, even in markets that resemble natural monopolies, may not be the most efficient arrangement available to society. There is no credible evidence that a single firm can provide any or all telecommunications services more efficiently than several firms. The Postal Service would have a difficult time convincing anyone that the quality of its services is superior to private companies already competing with it for second, third, and fourth class and express mail or that the service of potential competitors for first class mail would be inferior or more expensive.

Rationale and Prospects for AT&T's Divestiture

AT&T tied Americans together with a communications network unparalleled in the world. It became too large, pervasive, and powerful, however, for state or federal agencies to be able to regulate it adequately. For instance, the FCC was unable to discover a way to measure AT&T's cost that would permit it effectively to regulate interstate rates or the terms of access to local facilities so as not to eliminate the competition unfairly.

Many of these same problems of discovery of information and difficulties of regulating are present in the mail service industry, where the Postal Service dominates.[27]

Terms of Divestiture

Under the terms of divestiture, AT&T retained its long-distance business (the Long Lines Department), its equipment-manufacturing capability (Western Electric), and its research arm (Bell Laboratories), but surrendered its twenty-two operating companies, which have been organized into seven regional companies.[28] The divested local operating companies were required to provide the service and access to their "bottleneck" facilities to all long-distance carriers on a basis "equal in type, quality, and price" to that provided to AT&T.

The settlement barred the divested telephone companies from manufacturing customer-premise equipment, from providing long-distance service, and from offering service where they controlled the information content. As a result of Judge Greene's intervention, the local telephone companies retained their control of directory advertising, including Yellow Pages. The local companies were also permitted to market telephone equipment as long they did not manufacture it themselves.

In the Modified Final Judgment (MFJ), Judge Greene supervised the drawing of geographical boundaries around territories (called Local Access and Transportation Areas, or LATAs) into which the BOCs were permitted to offer services. Because a particular BOC provided all telephone calls within a LATA and long-distance carriers provided long-distance calls between LATAs, the boundaries functioned to divide the services functionally between those offered by the local exchanges and those offered by the interexchange services. Because each operating company operated only within contiguous LATAs, the boundaries also function to divide the operating companies geographically. AT&T proposed to organize divested operating companies into seven regional holding companies to provide local exchange service in 161 proposed LATAs, each the size of a large city and its surrounding areas. Some of the proposed LATAs are quite large, at times covering an entire state. For instance, Nevada is a LATA, and Delaware is part of a LATA that includes Philadelphia. Large LATAs provide greater revenue potential for the divested operating companies by offering them an opportunity to continue to monopolize a significant portion of what would otherwise be inter-LATA toll service. Small LATAs, on the other hand, produce more interexchange calls not available to the operating companies.

Judge Greene desired to construct the size of the LATAs according to an optimally efficient scale for the provision of local exchange service. If the LATAs were too small, the operating companies would not receive or be able to utilize AT&T's advanced switching equipment effectively. If they were too large, more calls would take place within them and there would be less opportunity for competition in long-distance service. There is no final answer to the optimal size of the LATAs and even if there were, it would probably change over time. Eventually open entry, which threatens to bypass the overpriced local exchange service, should prevail in intra-LATA service and limit the potential for anticompetitive behavior.

Should the Postal Service be divested into Postal Operating Companies (POCs) having LATAs? The decision-making criterion used in drawing the boundaries for AT&T can be instructive in drawing the boundaries for the separate companies in the divestiture of the Postal Service. The decree issued by Judge Greene in *United States* v. *AT&T* is the most significant achievement in the ninety-three-year history of section 2 of the Sherman Act.

Justification for Divestiture

An objective of the settlement was to separate markets that had a tendency toward a natural monopoly from those that had potential to be competitive and to prevent any telecommunications vendor from operating in both. The sole remaining domain of monopoly was the local exchange, so these companies were separated from all competitive activities. There is reason for believing that even after a few years local services might still have some monopoly power even with the existence of cable systems, cellular radio, and other alternatives operating side by side.[29] This period will be prolonged if the costs of implementing the new technology remain relatively high and most prospective customers are not willing to pay the increased cost for the quality and convenience of the new services.

The divestiture of Western Electric prevented BOCs from helping Western Electric monopolize equipment, prevented AT&T from using regulation to shelter Western's inefficient manufacturing operations, and prevented AT&T from avoiding rate-of-return regulation. The antitrust actions settled in 1956 declared that vertical integration allowed Bell to evade regulation by hiding its monopoly profits in Western Electric, an unregulated equipment supplier. The divestiture of the operating companies makes cross-subsidizing or regulatory avoidance less likely by removing the incentive of the operating companies to help Western maintain its monopoly.

The justification for the divestiture must be that any loss from breaking up the joint economies of providing local exchange and interexchange services from divestiture itself is more than offset by the benefits from increased efficiency in breaking up Bell's Long Lines monopoly in interexchange service. Because there was virtually no evidence produced to demonstrate the existence of joint economies, the justification for divestiture must lie in the presumption that AT&T did not produce proof of these joint economies because they were nonexistent, or that the economies, if they existed, were outweighed by the benefits of increased competition.[30]

Effects of Divestiture

Interstate Telecommunications—The FCC's restructuring of the telecommunications industry holds out the prospects of benefiting the public immeasurably. Although the decree did not separate Long Lines and Western Electric, enough competition among interexchange carriers will eventually develop to make this vertical relationship harmless. The FCC's decision to permit entry into intercity communications and AT&T's divestiture of its local exchanges promise an era of vigorous competition in the provision of intercity telecommunications services. Changes in policy, however, do not instantly transform a monopoly-based industry into a fully competitive one.

AT&T is not at present an efficient and skillful competitor. AT&T and its operating companies have had little experience in responding to customer needs in a timely way and will have to learn to minimize their costs if they are to survive. To illustrate their existing mentality, the closing line of a recent article by two Bell Laboratories computer scientists stated, "A good product can find its way without marketing; indeed it may be the better for having no marketing concerns to drive it."[31] If that attitude significantly influences the behavior of AT&T, its longer-run future in the market is bleak. In 1982 MCI earned more than $1 billion in revenue, but AT&T still controls over 95 percent of the interstate transmission market.[32] Moreover, interstate access to essential exchange facilities is still controlled by local monopoly telephone companies. AT&T will continue for a time to dominate long-haul communications networks, but its share is likely to diminish.

Local Service—Local service remains a monopoly, but many observers believe that other new technologies called "bypass facilities" may force competition for local service.[33] One possible form is a cable television system with switching capability, which some new cable systems already have. Cellular radio also provides a mechanism for competing with the local wireline service, rather than a lower-cost technology that might replace wireline service in the near future. (Cellular radio would replace wireline service if it were substantially cheaper and offered superior service under all circumstances with no significant drawbacks.)

Access Charges—Interstate carriers construct or lease their own intercity networks yet still must use the exchange facilities of the local monopoly telephone companies to reach the homes and offices of their subscribers. In the absence of regulation these local exchanges can charge very high tolls, discriminating against or even refusing access to others. When AT&T owned the local exchange, there was an incentive for it to favor its own interstate operations. In the telecommunications industry, this bottleneck situation created obstacles to the achievement of full competition. AT&T's efforts to impede competition were a primary reason for the divestiture of the local BOCs.

Divestiture removed the incentive for discrimination in access charges, which in turn permitted a competitive marketplace. It did this by relieving the local operating company of loyalty to Western Electric.[34] Divestiture does not remove the incentive for discrimination in services within an operating company's own LATA. Under the terms of the MFJ, the divested BOCs must provide equal access to all interstate carriers.

The MFJ has brought the policy conflict between the public utility commissions of the states (PUCs) and the Federal Communications Commission (FCC) into the foreground on the issue of access charges. The MFJ required the FCC to develop a policy to govern the access charges that AT&T and the other common carriers (OCCs) will pay the divested BOCs for delivering interstate inter-LATA calls to them and for carrying those calls to their ultimate destination. On the other hand, it is the PUCs that will hear rate cases concerning access charges for the BOCs operating in individual states.

According to the best scenario of the FCC, access charges paid by the OCCs (long-distance service competitors) and AT&T to the BOCs for "local transportation" service will gradually diminish until revenues barely cover the costs of providing the service. In turn, subscribers will gradually assume more of the costs caused by their demand for access to the telephone network.

The local operating companies hold a monopoly over long-distance carriers' access to local customers. The local operating companies will be able to extract a price for providing the necessary access. The question is who will pay the bill: the long-distance companies (who will pass their costs on to their customers indirectly) or the customers of the local operating company directly. This switch in pricing the access charges from the long-distance service competitors to their own subscribers represents reducing and eliminating the sizable charges to large, interested companies who would continue to scrutinize and use legal options when advantageous. In turn it also implies levying relatively small access charges to a large number of politically unimportant subscribers.

Today, the FCC has authorized well over 200 resale carriers to offer interstate public-switched message services. Measuring the costs of access for different carriers will be no easier for the PUCs than distinguishing the costs of Telpak from those of WATS was for the FCC. As long as the operating companies retain some monopoly power in local exchange services, they will find it attractive to discriminate on access charges. PUCs have often been supportive of such discrimination because it permits cross-subsidization between different types of customers who pay the basic monthly service charge. Operating companies will obviously try to set the highest charges for those customers with the most inelastic demand for access, i.e. those with the most limited bypass options. Despite this continuing problem area, the resale and shared use of private line services has still resulted in lower long-distance telephone rates for the average consumer.

The OCCs have protested the access process in which they are supposed to receive the same connections as AT&T, allowing users to dial 1 and get the company of their choice. Regional Bells have been reputed to favor AT&T, which automatically received the default traffic, and to be unhelpful in providing useful marketing information concerning OCCs to potential customers. Also, once the OCCs achieve equal access they immediately become subject to higher access payments because they lose a 55 percent discount from AT&T's rates and face the prospect of increases in the access payments in the future. They are also faced with increased competition from AT&T, whose rates, they say, are currently below costs.

In response to this complaint the FCC has ordered local telephone companies to use a method of assigning a long-distance carrier to consumers who do not choose one, that is not biased in favor of AT&T. Since the breakup of the Bell System, AT&T has received much of its business by default. Under the new system, local phone companies must send ballots to all subscribers in an area that is being opened up to competition, asking them to choose a long-distance service. Customers will receive the primary long-distance carrier of their choice. The local company randomly assigns customers who do not respond among long-distance carriers in the same proportion as those who do respond. AT&T will now have to work for its long-distance customers instead of having them handed to it.[35]

Financial Effects—Before the divestiture it was argued that under the AT&T monopoly all BOCs had access to capital funds at a lower cost than they would have if they had been unaffiliated companies. Thus, some financial analysts believed that divestiture would expose divergences in local rate deregulation and differences in credit quality of the local operating companies and would thereby raise the cost of debt and equity capital to the BOCs. The Bell umbrella, however, was less fact than fancy. If it had lowered the cost of capital to BOCs before divestiture, one would expect them to have lower average capital costs than the postdivestiture independent telephone companies that had no umbrella. The evidence shows that the difference in costs between BOCs and independent telephone companies before divestiture was small and statistically insignificant. So divestiture will probably not change the cost of capital appreciably to the BOCs.

The profits of the Bell System will fall if it has been earning monopoly profits, and if divestiture effectively deters this anticompetitive behavior, and/or if the Bell System has extensive economies of scale that divestiture reduced. Profits, on the other hand, will rise if the Bell System was inefficient and if divestiture eliminates the source of these inefficiencies.

Some Lessons for the Postal Service

Although the reorganization of AT&T took place only recently, the FCC has been gradually opening the telecommunications industry to competition since 1968, when the Supreme Court's *Carterfone* decision permitted the use of non-AT&T equipment in the AT&T system. The Postal Service reorganization in 1971 has not been instrumental in helping competitive changes in the market for mail service. The FCC and the Justice Department could at the very least be a helpful resource in engineering divestiture, privatization, and deregulation of the Postal Service. A simple first step would be to declare homeowners' and businesses' receptacles and post office boxes available for use in connection with any delivery system, just as any individual or business can own and use its own telephone equipment when accessing the communications services of any telephone company. There is nothing to prevent immediate action on this. Customers could then, in addition to hooking up their own equipment to telephone lines, receive material from all delivery services in their postal receptacle.[36]

In 1969 the FCC gave MCI the right to hook its long-distance network into local phone systems, and the Postal Service allows large mailers to send presorted mail through the postal system at reduced rates. The difference is that AT&T is giving access to other telephone companies and the Postal Service is accommodating only large customers.[37] To help competition until the private express statutes are repealed, the Postal Service should be required to offer its local delivery facilities to other mail delivery companies that presort and combine their mail and process it together for many smaller mailers. If this was done under favorable terms, it would represent an opening up of competition. It is now being obstructed by the private express statutes and the Postal Service.

The predivestiture Bell System, like the Postal Service, operated much like a welfare system, with the power to tax and use the proceeds for "public service" purposes. Its pricing scheme made the more profitable services to businesses (urban and long-distance traffic) subsidize the unprofitable ones to residences, particularly in local and rural areas. Also, infrequent callers subsidized their talkative neighbors. Long-distance and local rates are still under some regulation, but prices are moving in the direction of reflecting the cost of providing service, especially for long-distance service. The Postal Service is still a welfare system within which first class, urban, and some business mailers subsidize other classes of mail, rural mailers, and homeowners. The PRC has failed and continues to fail to make rates for classes of mail reflect their costs. A movement toward a price-linked-to-usage system should commence in the Postal Service just as it has with the advent of the AT&T restructuring.

In both the Postal Service and AT&T costs are higher than they need to be because of overstaffing, a problem typical of monopolies. A glimpse of the potential for efficiency in AT&T surfaced in August 1984, when the 700,000 unionized workers who went on strike were hardly noticed except for the curtailment of equipment installation. The Bell System is so highly automated that it can function well in the hands of its 300,000 management employees.

The enterprising spirit that has been bridled for decades by mindless regulation in the telephone industry is being released. How desperately the Postal Service needs this same fresh air to be breathed into it! The diversification of AT&T and efficiency changes that will take place under this new climate are painful for AT&T, as they will be for the Postal Service. Users and producers will participate in a rush of competition that will lower the price of some services and equipment, and raise the price of others. Most economists believe that telecommunications will become more productive, more efficient, and less costly as a result of divestiture and deregulation.

The divestiture of the Bell System, the biggest breakup in corporate history, will require reorienting managers. Because AT&T executives, just like Postal Service executives, have not grown up with the skills they need, they may require much retraining. Managers need to be redeployed, to be taught new skills, and to have their jobs redefined. Most of AT&T's managers, just like the postal managers, were trained to excel in a regulated monopoly that operated in an hierarchical and functional manner. It attracted to its ranks those who desired the security of a monopoly. Most managers were not equipped for competition. Some of these people have never made decisions themselves and are emotionally "scared to death." Deregulation, divestiture, and growing competition make this structure obsolete.

Postal Service managers have not inspired confidence in the face of a rapidly changing environment. There are not many visionaries in their ranks. Therefore, they have not done the kinds of things necessary to keep up with the rest of the world. Altering the Bell culture from a monopoly to a competitive enterprise, from a telephone company to an information-systems supplier, is a difficult task. Undoubtedly, a much similar task awaits postmasters and postal executives when they become free to compete.

AT&T needs to decentralize and redistribute decision-making power, disperse managers throughout the system, and encourage teamwork. These changes will bring a new way of life with uncertainty, excitement, and new management opportunities. Freedom to compete and a new emphasis on teamwork and risk-taking will liberate middle managers. In the divestiture AT&T minimized employee insecurity in organizational changes by placing the vast majority of people in the same jobs and at the same locations within the new organizations. People shortages and surpluses when experienced, however, were shared among the companies, and people followed their work when changes in location were made. Much of this experience can be helpful in making the transition for the Postal Service.

Ken Foster, an area vice president for AT&T Information Systems in New York, told people before divestiture that he was a salesman for the telephone company. They would laugh, and for good reason. The Bell System was a monopoly that provided the best telephone service in the world, their own way or not at all. Can the divested companies now learn to sell?[38] Will they be able to keep pace with MCI and Sprint, which continue to capture long-distance business through rate cuts, or Westinghouse, Duke Power, Irving Trust, and Olympia and York, which are setting up their own communications networks? The divested regional companies that in the past bought AT&T equipment made by Western Electric will also be shopping for the best buys. The verdict is not yet in, but the Postal Service cannot afford to ignore what is happening with AT&T and the communications industry because this development has important implications for the organizational direction of the Postal Service.

Notes

1. Douglas K. Adie in Joint Economic Committee, Economic Goals and Inter-governmental Policy Subcommittee, *The Future of Mail Delivery in the United States Hearings*, Subcommittee 97th Cong., 2d sess., June 18, 21, 1982, pp. 295-97.

2. The British are preparing to privatize their Post Office. In connection with this, it is being split up into four separate businesses: counter services, the National Girobank, letter delivery, and parcel delivery. The post offices themselves, which provide counter services, will be formed into a separate company and added to a U.S. bank desiring to set up offices in Britain, or given to the employees. The Girobank, which is a profitable concern, will be sold. The parcel service will be sold separately. The letter services will be formed into regional units and be sold or given to the employees. See "Privatizing the Public Sector: An Initiative for Service and Savings," *State Factor* (American Legislative Exchange Council) 12 (January 1986): 5. The National Girobank, which was established in 1968, operates through Post Offices and offers ordinary check service as well as giro transfers. With giro transfers the payer issues a direct instruction to the girobank to transfer funds from his account to that of the payee. See David W. Pearce, *The Dictionary of Modern Economics* (Cambridge: MIT Press, 1981), p. 174.

3. Many more countries are discovering that when government-provided goods and services are turned over to the private sector, quality of service improves and the price falls. Even the Socialist governments of France, Italy, Spain, and Sweden are privatizing state-owned enterprises. Margaret Thatcher in Britain has led the way in refining the process. See Peter Young and John C. Goodman, "The U.S. Lags Behind in Going Private," *Wall Street Journal*, February 20, 1986, p. 20.

4. Immediately following the breakup there was chaos in the telephone industry. The severe disruptions, however, were temporary. The new emphasis since divestiture has been directed toward meeting the needs of business rather than residential users, who faced a rate increase of about 35 percent. Any household, however, that makes more than $40 worth of long-distance calls each month saves as much on those calls as it pays in increased local calls. In the past few months consumer surveys showed an approval rating of more than 90 percent. Columbia University telecommunications Professor Eli Noam calls the advent of computerized office communications systems and the 35 to 40 percent reductions for office and residential equipment "the greatest success of deregulation so far." See Malcolm Gladwell, "Bypassing Ma Bell's Orphans," *Insight*, September 15, 1986, pp. 9, 10, 13.

5. I have relied, among other sources, on Harry M. Shooshan III, ed., *Disconnecting Bell: The Impact of the AT&T Divestiture* (New York: Pergamon Press, 1984); David S. Evans, ed., *Breaking Up Bell* (New York: North-Holland, 1982); and W. Brooke Tunstall, *Disconnecting Parties* (New York: McGraw-Hill, 1985), in writing the history of the AT&T breakup.

6. The Interstate Commerce Commission (ICC) assumed jurisdiction over limited aspects of interstate telephone service in 1910. In 1921 Congress passed legislation that authorized the ICC to approve the consolidation of telephone company holdings by acquisition, thereby immunizing the companies from antitrust laws. In 1934 federal regulation of the telephone and telegraph industry was transferred from the ICC to a new agency, the Federal Communications Commission (FCC).

7. These not-so-subtle subterfuges for procuring rate increases are not dissimilar to the shenanigans of the Postal Service in arguing for rate increases before the Postal Rate Commission today. See chapter 3 for a description of rate-making.

8. It was the untrammeled greed of AT&T in pursuing its monopoly position that

produced the reaction of the government that defended the public interest. When the government is the owner of the business, as in the case of the Postal Service, relief from this quarter is apparently not as readily forthcoming.

9. The government has responded in much the same way with respect to the Postal Service by confining its monopoly to letter mail and forbidding it to enter the electronic message transmission industry.

10. It might be asked why Carter was not protected under the 1956 consent decree. The consent decree gave customers the right to use their own equipment on their premises. The Carterfone decision, on the other hand, opened up the possibility of a competing telephone system that would compete with the existing system and be linked to the wireline telephone system at any point.

11. The post-consent-decree environment for AT&T—up to the divestiture decision of 1984—had as a fairly prominent feature the enforced separation between communications and other activities (data processing in particular). In a somewhat similar fashion the Postal Service has been and is being restrained from entering the area of the electronic transmission of data and messages. As the operational distinctions between data processing and communications became more tenuous, AT&T may have come to believe that being limited to "pure" communications did not offer a promising future. Likewise, with more and more first class communications taking place electronically, the Postal Service may believe that being limited to hard-copy message delivery does not offer a promising future and becomes more amenable to the kind of restructuring advocated in this study.

12. Many of the AT&T-related cases dealt with presumptively competitive manufacturing operations; the Postal Service monopoly has a statutory basis.

13. Precommitting investment funds involves the announcement in advance that funds will be spent to purchase equipment or facilities for expansion or upgrading of telephone service. This announcement, when made by a large corporation with huge resources, has the effect of deterring the attempt of a smaller company to make a commitment to provide service in this area.

14. In 1961, when AT&T feared its largest customers might construct their own communications networks, it filed its first Telpak tariff, which consisted of bulk quantities of private line circuits offered at substantial volume discounts. The Hi-Lo tariff went into effect in June 1974. This was another fee structure that departed from nationwide average pricing for individual private line circuits. Multi-schedule Private Line (MPL) was another private line tariff departing from nationwide average pricing for individual line circuits, put into effect in April 1976, after Hi-Lo was declared null and void by the FCC because it could not be justified from costs. DDS is dataphone digital service as contrasted with analog service, which uses a synchronous digital data coding to transmit bulk data over long-distance networks.

15. The late Warren Nutter compared the process for achieving order in an industry with the following illustration. "Suppose you have a sack of potatoes and want to make it as compact as possible. One way is to devise some scheme for measuring potatoes, put the measurements into a computer, and run a program to try to find out how to fit them together in the smallest space. Anyone familiar with advanced mathematics will recognize the enormous complexity of optimizing the solution to this problem. Another way is to give the sack a couple of shakes and let the potatoes settle by themselves." This latter process, which describes the market, mobilizes knowledge for the benefit of society more

cheaply and effectively than any conscious effort. See Douglas K. Adie, "Freedom First, Last and Always," *Modern Age* 30 (Winter 1986): 56.

16. For a review of the arguments surrounding the existence of natural monopolies, see chapter 4.

17. Price reductions used to exclude competitors have been termed "predatory pricing." The developing antitrust law of predatory pricing has, however, given such behavior a particular narrow definition: first, price is set "below cost" in order to drive out or forestall entrants; later, when the potential competition is no longer contemplating entry, price is increased.

Predatory pricing is presumptively unlawful under sec. 2 of the Sherman Act because it is not rational for a business to sell below marginal cost unless by so doing it expects to eliminate its competition and later raise its prices to monopoly levels.

The predatory pricing inquiry is therefore divisible into two parts: (1) what the defendant's marginal (or in practice, average variable) cost is, and (2) whether the defendant sold below it. In the case of AT&T, as has been the case with the Postal Service, sufficiently good data have not been submitted to determine (1).

18. John Crutcher, a postal rate commissioner, in private correspondence with me, said, "The real problem, which you share along with everyone else writing about the USPS, is old data. That problem can't be handled very well for the source of data is the USPS."

19. To compare the bullying tactics of the Postal Service see chapter 2.

20. See chapter 2 for a discussion of the Postal Service's public service mission.

21. In the Reorganization Act, Congress ruled out the redistribution of discriminatory pricing by instructing the Postal Service to charge for each class of mail according to its costs. Congress also created the PRC to monitor and prevent discriminatory pricing behavior.

22. See Friedrich A. Hayek, "The Use of Knowledge in Society," and "Economics and Knowledge," in *Individualism and Economic Order*, (Chicago: University of Chicago Press, 1963), pp. 50, 51, 79.

23. See Don C. Lavoie, "Economic Calculation and Monetary Stability," *Cato Journal* 3 (Spring 1983): 165.

24. Ibid., p. 164.

25. See Hayek, "The Use of Knowledge in Society," p. 79. Also see Ronald Coase, "The Nature of the Firm," *Economica* 4 (November 1937): 386-405.

26. Melvyn Fuss and Leonard Waverman, *The Regulation of Tele-communications in Canada*, report no. 7 (Economic Council of Canada, Ottawa, March 1981).

27. In defense of AT&T, it might be suggested that the division of regulatory responsibility between the state and federal regulatory agencies contributed to the FCC's problem in measuring AT&T's costs. There are costing difficulties in postal regulation, but interjurisdictional allocations are not among them.

28. The seven regional companies are Pacific Telesis (California and Nevada), U.S. West (Far Southwest, Pacific Northwest, and Northern Plains), Southwestern Bell Corporation (Texas and Lower Midwest), Ameritech (Upper Midwest), Nynex (New York and New England), Bell Atlantic (Middle Atlantic), and BellSouth (Southeast). The Postal Service is currently organized into a Western Region, a Central Region, an Eastern Region, a Northeastern Region, and a Southern Region. It would be quite natural to divide the Postal Service into five regional companies, a support services company, and perhaps a bulk mail company for a total of seven companies.

29. Only recently businesses in Chicago wanting to access long-distance carriers had no choice but to go through Illinois Bell. Now beneath the streets of the Loop in downtown Chicago there are two sets of telecommunications lines: one belonging to Illinois Bell and the other to Chicago Fiber Optics. Fiber Optics cables, which run between buildings, bypass the local system entirely and provide superior service for 25 to 35 percent less. More than 25 percent of New York City's top four hundred phone users are using some kind of bypass system to gain access to long-distance carriers and save considerable amounts on their phone bills. The ongoing revolution in fiber optics, satellites, and high frequency microwave relay systems makes it possible for small private corporations to compete successfully with giant phone companies. It is these smaller companies that are leading the way in innovations and bringing down the costs of communication. See Gladwell, "Bypassing Ma Bell's Orphans," p. 8.

30. The first reason is a "presumption" in the correct legal sense because AT&T was in possession of any data that might indicate the existence of these economies, and if it did not produce such data one might presume that they did not exist. A presumption (in the judicial sense) is essentially a rule of law: for instance, nonproduction of evidence by a party having control of it *legally* implies that the evidence would be adverse to the party. In the case at hand, however, for the evidence to benefit AT&T, the economies would not only have to exist clearly but be substantial enough to outweigh in a welfare sense the benefits of competition.

31. See Brian W. Kernighan and Samuel P. Morgan, "The UNIX Operating System: A Model for Software Design," *Science*, February 12, 1982, quoted in Charles L. Jackson, "Technology: The Anchor of the Bell System," in *Disconnecting Bell*, ed. Harry M. Shoohian III (New York: Pergamon Press, 1984), p. 74.

32. Since the votes for long-distance carriers in 1986, AT&T has been chosen by about 75 percent of consumers. Its market share has fallen to about 80 percent of the long-distance market. MCI and Sprint, the second- and third-place firms, were able to double their market shares to about 8 and 4 percent, respectively. See Francine Schwadel, "Calling Long Distance: User Vote Shows Strong Support for AT&T," *Wall Street Journal,* August 22, 1986, p. 17.

33. The BOCs, which are anticipating competition for their local services, have begun to petition Judge Greene for permission to expand into new and different areas of operation. Greene's concern is that the regional Bell companies will use revenue and resources from local phone company business to finance or subsidize their efforts in unregulated businesses. For this reason, Greene has prevented them from entering long-distance, manufacturing, and information services but granted requests to enter businesses outside these areas. Senator Robert Dole has recently introduced a bill to remove the responsibility for supervising the Bells from Judge Greene and give it to the FCC, which would be much more lenient in granting the Bells' requests. See Christine Winter, "Bell Rings on Phone Bout's New Round," *Chicago Tribune,* July 27, 1986, sec. 7, p. 3.

34. It might be asked, if the BOCs have been relieved of loyalty to AT&T, why do they still bill for AT&T and why do they automatically give you AT&T long distance if you do not specify another? First, if you don't specify a long-distance carrier, you will be assigned one by lot according to the proportions of those who did specify, so you are not automatically assigned to AT&T. The operating

companies bill for AT&T under a private arrangement that the other long-distance carriers might seek if they so desired.

35. See Jeanne Saddler, "Phone Concerns Must End Bias Favoring AT&T," *Wall Street Journal*, June 3, 1985, p. 10.

36. Thomas Moore, a member of President Reagan's Council of Economic Advisors and head of the administration's interagency task force on privatization, is "cooking up a plan for ending the U.S. Postal Service's monopoly on first class mail, first by allowing anyone to stuff material in private mailboxes and then by gradually eliminating the laws that created the monopoly." Moore said proposals may follow and that they may start with a plan to abolish the law that prevents anyone except the Postal Service from putting material in boxes. See Bill Neikirk, "Putting Government on the Auction Block," *Chicago Tribune*, March 18, 1986, sec. 1, pp. 1, 18.

37. It is possible to view presorting other than as a mere accommodation to large customers because of their volume. Although it is not viable unless a mailer does have larger volume, it also involves a reallocation of the postal operations from the Postal Service to a private operator (often not the mailer itself but rather an independent business—see testimony of CPUM/ARF witness Ford in Docket R84-1) who sorts what would otherwise be done by postal employees. The American Postal Workers Union understands this and opposes presort discount programs. The presort program then bears some similarity to intermediate carriers in the telephone system. Mail America, a presort mailer in Chicago, a member of the National Association of Presort Mailers, sells its own stamps for letters, collects them from its own boxes, presorts them and stamps them at the presort discount postage rate for ultimate delivery by the Postal Service. It sells its stamps for less than Postal Service first class rates and still makes a profit.

38. AT&T has transformed itself into a marketing powerhouse with television commercials featuring actor Cliff Robertson, who stresses quality and reliability. Price advantage, which is only about 15 percent, is no longer the dominant factor.

6

Labor Relations in the Postal Service

Labor costs are 84 percent of total costs for the Postal Service, an extremely high figure relative to other companies, even those in service industries. Any consideration of total costs in the Postal Service needs to focus on the labor factor. Like others who have examined the level of wages, I have consistently found Postal Service wages to be excessive by approximately one-third compared to what it would need to pay to attract and hold a competent work force, or what postal workers would get, given their experience and education, if they were employed elsewhere.[1] What has been the history of labor relations in the Postal Service? How did this inequity occur? Can we correct it? Has there been a change in the labor relations climate permitting a correction? Is there any hope for redressing the inequity of excessive wages short of wholesale restructuring? These are some of the questions that this chapter attempts to answer.

Ponder PATCO—A Watershed for Labor Relations

History may show us that President Reagan's firing of the air traffic controllers in 1981 was a watershed event that dramatically precipitated a change in the climate for labor relations in this country. Reagan's confrontation with the Professional Air Traffic Controllers Organization (PATCO) set the scene for labor relations in the airline industry, the Postal Service, the federal government, and indeed for the entire country.

Except for those representing the quasi-public postal workers, government unions are forbidden to bargain over pay and benefits. PATCO, however, was so cohesive that the Federal Aviation Administration (FAA) was reluctant to enforce its prohibition. So PATCO established its ability to negotiate by power, not law. This has not been an unusual state of affairs in labor relations, for unions have frequently and for quite a long time been able to intimidate and to commit extralegal if not illegal acts for which other individuals and groups would normally be prosecuted.[2]

The confrontation developed in the following way. In 1981 PATCO rejected the FAA's 11.4 percent pay raise—more than double the administration's offer to other federal employees. Fifteen thousand members of PATCO illegally struck to cripple the nation's air transport system. Reagan said, "The law says they cannot strike. If they strike, they quit their jobs."[3] The ultimatum was softened slightly with a forty-eight-hour grace period for strikers who changed their minds. Reagan insisted, moreover, that there would be no negotiation while the strike continued and no amnesty for strikers. So Transportation Secretary Drew Lewis, on orders from Reagan, refused to negotiate while the strike was in progress.

To everyone's surprise, not least PATCO's, the president ordered the air traffic control system to operate, and the planes began flying again. Scheduled flights were cut by 50 percent at larger airports, and Lewis and FAA director J. Lynn Helms began running the air traffic control system of twenty-five major airports and twenty-three regional control centers with skeleton crews. To staff the control towers, Helms enlisted Pentagon-trained military controllers, supervisors, and 3,000 nonstrikers. By the weekend the FAA found 1,000 more controllers at sixty small airports and began training 500 military-uniformed controllers for temporary civilian duty. Confusion and crowds disappeared as the system was soon operating at 65 percent of normal capacity, and in a week at nearly 75 percent.

When a near-collision occurred over northern New Jersey, PATCO's leader, Robert E. Poli, to arouse the public's fears, announced that chaos prevailed inside the understaffed control towers. An investigation of the incident revealed the problem to be pilot error rather than an error by the air traffic controller. This situation indicated how precarious President Reagan's course of action was. The stakes for the president in the confrontation were the integrity of his economic program, the health of the airline industry, and his bargaining posture with other federal employees, and he did not shrink from placing his reputation on the line.

After the planes were running at near-normal capacity without PATCO and it appeared that the president had turned the tide in the confrontation, he did not slacken up in his pursuit of lawbreakers. He sent out thousands of letters of dismissal and took disciplinary action against strikers who returned. He fined PATCO for violating a back-to-work order and prosecuted its leaders with vigor. Just because the crimes were labor-relations-based, the president did not wink at the legal infractions, as many politicians and jurists have done in the past, but pressed the strikers and PATCO to the full extent of the law.[4] This inflicted harm on striking workers, destroyed PATCO, and took away the aura of legitimacy from lawbreakers in labor disputes.

The rebuilding of the traffic-controller system was done without PATCO.

The planes flew, the law of the land was upheld, the public rallied to the president, and PATCO destroyed itself and became an object lesson to other government unions, including the postal unions. Helms quickly trained thousands of replacements for the strikers. Applications poured into the FAA for its school in Oklahoma City where 6,000 controllers can be trained each year. The strike also revealed that the system could operate effectively with 3,500 fewer controllers. The postal unions did not ignore this lesson (see chapter 8). The PATCO strike set a precedent for labor relations in the public sector and was a turning point with wide ramifications for postal workers. In collective bargaining, postal unions should beware of an "Inspector Callahan" who says with a wide grin in response to a strike threat, "Go ahead. Make my day."

Reactions by other union leaders were extremely muted. The United Auto Workers' Douglas Fraser correctly warned that PATCO's illegal strike could do massive damage to the labor movement because Reagan's breaking of PATCO would legitimize union breaking. How right he was in his assessment of the situation. While criticizing Reagan's tactics, Lane Kirkland, president of the AFL-CIO, refused to urge his federation's members to back PATCO.

To grasp fully the change in labor relations climate that this event has caused, it is necessary to realize what the pre-PATCO situation was. Few people believed that the insistent demands of a strong union threatening a strike in a bottleneck industry could be successfully opposed. The American people had become the captives of a self-fulfilling prophecy and the impotence of a government to enforce its laws. They had become resigned to being held hostage by American unions. Reagan, however, did what would have been unimaginable twenty years ago and what to most, even ten years ago, was unthinkable. He took on a powerful union with a stranglehold on a very technical bottleneck function at the helm of the airlines industry, and won. He destroyed the mystique of labor's power because it depended upon the acceptance on the part of the public of illegal labor union tactics. Now that the public realizes it is no longer necessary to tolerate this practice, the picture changes and such practices can no longer take place with impunity.

The turning around of this situation reminds us of the young boy who said, "The emperor has no clothes." Before these words were spoken, everyone knew what the situation was but no one dared to speak. Afterward, the situation changed drastically. Now, when the demands of labor are illegal and unreasonable, any legitimately constituted authority can move unencumbered to stop the lawbreaking. The president's successful action in this watershed event has given new courage to management in negotiations with labor unions all over the country and this has turned the tide in labor relations. Upholding a right and just law has triumphed over political expediency.

Organized labor now faces a tough time not just in the airlines industry but in many places. In the absence of bullying tactics its real character will become apparent. Union growth in office, public-employee, and service industries has slowed while employers stiffen their resistance to union demands. In 1981 unions won only 30.3 percent of all certification elections and were ousted in 74.9 percent of the cases in which decertification hearings were held. Organized labor seems committed to the status quo at a time of rapid change and lacks a sense of excitement, noble purpose, and indignation. If it is to survive, it needs leaders who can open new areas of organization and articulate new concerns.

In the past, labor was a potent voice on Capitol Hill. It was so powerful that a visit from a Washington representative of a large union was often enough to sway a congressman's vote. Unions, including postal unions, no longer have this much control and cannot take anything for granted. It is now necessary for them to demonstrate grass-roots support on every issue. Many union members now enjoy comfortable middle-class life-styles and are interested in fighting inflation rather than supporting costly social programs. Unions now have to cope with a popular president while their own influence among Democrats is eroding. For instance, despite the AFL-CIO's endorsements of Jimmy Carter and Walter Mondale, many union members voted for Reagan.

Labor Relations in the Postal Service

Moe Biller, president of the American Postal Workers Union, says that for industries having similar working conditions, the Postal Service is "the most over-supervised organization anywhere." The biggest problem in controlling costs in the Postal Service is controlling wages, both supervisory and nonsupervisory.[5] Labor costs, as a percentage of total expense, have increased from 82 percent in 1970 to 84 percent in 1986. This change has taken place during a period of rapid technological growth. I examine the problem of excessive wages in Postal Service labor relations in this section. I consider some solutions for this problem, hinging on organizational restructuring, in chapter 8.

Postmaster General William F. Bolger (replaced in January 1985 by Paul N. Carlin, who was replaced a year later by Albert V. Casey, who was replaced in August 1986 by Preston Robert Tisch, who resigned in late 1987 and was replaced in 1988 by Anthony Frank), has been called the most antilabor postmaster general in history, despite his being a thirty-seven-year postal veteran. Biller quotes Bolger as saying, "Frankly if under the law I didn't have to have unions, I wouldn't." Bolger's comment or his posture in labor contract negotiations should not have surprised Biller. Almost every executive would wish, if not say, the same thing. Dealing with labor unions has thus far consumed much time and effort but has produced few benefits for postal operations. Also, union leaders have not been above using intimidation, as indicated by the following conversation reported during contract talks on July 20, 1975:

> Reporter: How is it going?
>
> James J. La Penta (President of the Mailhandlers Union): Ask those [expletive deleted] sitting in the room down the hall [USPS room]. Jim [Rademacher], why don't you tell them about dial-a-strike?
>
> [Rademacher lifts his index finger into the air.]
>
> James H. Rademacher (President of the National Association of Letter Carriers): You've got it, I'll tell you a story. We put up this finger and told them, we can put this finger on the phone and tell them [postal employees] to be calm. Or we can put this finger on the phone and—*dial-a-strike*. [Emphasis added.][6]

Bolger's first contract talks began during an inflationary period in April 1978, when President Carter was calling for restraint in wage settlements. Bolger responded by negotiating a 6.5 percent-per-year increase with a capped cost-of-living adjustment. The rank-and-file union members were disappointed with the settlement and reacted with wildcat strikes in San Francisco and New Jersey before rejecting the contract in August. Bolger fired 200 of the striking workers, refused to renegotiate, and called for arbitration. The arbitrator gave the workers a 21.3 percent wage increase over three years as well as an uncapped cost-of-living increase.

This example reinforces the opinion that as a process for redressing the inequity of excessive postal wages arbitration offers little hope. It depends first on a strong postmaster general, such as William Bolger, which is not a common occurrence. But as indicated above, even given a postmaster general who will risk a strike and bargain hard to just hold the line on preventing further excesses, the arbitration board then may undo the results of the settlement, thus affording the postal workers a more generous arrangement. This is demoralizing to management. Three years later, as Bolger faced the next contract talks, he was dismayed by the prospects of bargaining independently with each of the four major unions. To correct this, he filed a petition with the National Labor Relations Board to define the "appropriate bargaining structure for the negotiations" in the hope that the NLRB would instruct all the postal unions to bargain together toward a universal agreement. Otherwise, Postal Service management would have to expend much more effort on labor relations with union officials and run the risk of being whipsawed.

This very reasonable petition was rejected and the negotiation process resumed seven weeks later. Before the negotiations began on June 11, 1981, Bolger boldly threatened to suspend the private express statutes if there was a strike.[7] When the talks stalled on July 14, top federal mediator Kenneth Moffet, who also worked on the air traffic controllers' contract negotiations, entered the negotiations. Labor leaders were reminding management they were operating under a no-contract, no-work mandate from members, while Bolger reminded workers in a notice enclosed in their July 17 paychecks that he would fire strikers.

The contract ratification, reached without arbitration, was in all probability influenced by President Reagan's firing of the air traffic controllers. The agreement gave the unions a strong job-security provision that barred layoffs.[8] Despite the PATCO precedent, it was not possible to redress the inequity of excessive wages under the existing labor relations system. Under the most favorable conditions it was possible only to prevent the agreement from going to arbitration, where in all probability the unions would have received more.

In preparation for the contract negotiations in 1984, the postal governors asserted that increasing competition with the private sector should be a factor in contract bargaining.[9] Bolger acknowledged that he faced increasing competition from private carriers for many classes of mail. The governors also said they wanted tighter cost control to hold back postage rate increases. Recently, rates had risen about every three years; the board wanted intervals of five years between postage rate increases.[10]

In the posturing preceding negotiations, the Postal Service contended that pay for union workers was already between 10 percent and 25 percent higher than the pay for comparable private sector jobs. Relying on the preponderance of evidence in evaluating wages of postal workers, Bolger said that in some cases postal employees' pay rates were as much as 35 percent more than comparable private sector rates.[11] Biller was angered by these statements, even though a 1983 Postal Service study showed that the postal average hourly rate of $11.80 was higher than that in the retailing, banking, and insurance industries.[12]

The first wage package offered by the Postal Service in the 1984 contract talks called for a wage freeze for current employees and a one-third reduction in starting salaries for new workers. The Postal Service also included in its offer reductions in inflation adjustments, sick pay, and other benefits. The wage offer resembled the agreements reached in the airline industry. What only a few years ago would have been ludicrous elicited a serious comment from Vincent Sombrotto, president of the Letter Carriers. In raising the possibility of a strike, he said, "If people feel that's the only option open to them, they will exercise it." Biller did not raise the possibility of illegal job action.

The reactions of postal unions to hard-line management proposals became much more subdued after the PATCO affair. Although a clearly written curb against striking has always existed, in the past this would not have been much of a deterrent. Now, however, with the memory of the more than 11,000 air traffic controllers who walked off their jobs in 1981 and were fired, many members regarded a strike as only a remote possibility.[13]

The details surrounding the negotiations at the beginning were as follows. If the postal contract expired without agreement, the law called for forty-five days of independent fact-finding, which could then be waived in some cases. Sombrotto told reporters that if a tentative contract was not negotiated by midnight July 20, 1984, he would invoke the fact-finding clause of the 1970 Postal Reorganization Act. This would extend the bargaining process for forty-five more days and allow his union members more time to decide what to do. The report of this arbitration board would then become the basis for further negotiation. If ninety days after the contract expiration the dispute remained unresolved, a three-member arbitration board would have forty-five days to make a binding contract settlement.

Under the Postal Service's second wage offer, new workers would receive a 23 percent entry pay cut. The offer would also modify the inflation adjustment and sick pay benefit. The postal unions complained that the Postal Service's economic package, which included a wage freeze, elimination of the most recent inflation adjustment, a leaner formula for future inflation adjustments, and cuts in sick pay would result in actual wage cuts.[14]

Louis Cox, younger brother of former Watergate special prosecutor Archibald Cox, in representing the Postal Service's position, told union officials that he would give them until six P.M. to respond to a final package that included a three-year wage freeze, a 20 percent drop in entry pay, and a cut in the night differential. The two major unions rejected the package, the midnight deadline expired, and negotiations collapsed. Thus the arbitration process was triggered.

Neither union nor management was enthusiastic about the prospects of arbitration because it put the fate of both parties into the hands of a disinterested third party. "Arbitration has never been a positive alternative to us," one union official said.[15] The Postal Service did not wait for the report of the first arbitration committee but, rather, notified postal unions that it would put into effect its most recent wage offer when contracts expired.[16] Indeed, it immediately put newly hired workers on a pay scale that was 20 percent less than that for current workers. (At this point Congress intervened in response to union pleas to prevent the two-tier wage scale from going into effect, a matter that will be elaborated on later.) It is important to understand the arbitration process in detail and how it has worked out to realize the futility of expecting any kind of discipline on postal wages to occur under the present organizational arrangements.

The report of the independent panel of federal arbitrators was a major blow to the Postal Service. The Postal Service had demanded a wage freeze over three years for current employees and a wage structure that would pay newly hired workers less. The arbitration report recommended that the Postal Service withdraw its demand for a two-tier pay structure. This provision struck at the heart of the Postal Service's strategy for controlling labor costs over the long term. The report of the panel seems to have run counter to the trend in labor negotiations in the country. It also recommended that the Postal Service drop its demand to cut annual cost-of-living adjustments, reduce sick pay, and modify employee classifications and benefit plans. In addition to a general pay raise of $2,000 over a three-year contract, the panel recommended approval of the union's demand for a holiday on Martin Luther King's birthday.[17]

The next step was for the Mailhandlers Union to try to negotiate a contract with the Postal Service based on the arbitrators' findings. The Postal Service obviously had no interest in pursuing this and preferred to take its chances on the findings of another arbitration panel. In the absence of a negotiated settlement, the law required another independent panel of arbitrators to study the dispute and issue a binding agreement. This was the first occasion on which the final postal labor agreements were settled by arbitration. Arbitration had been used in the past to narrow issues and to resolve one of the smaller contracts but never to settle the entire agreements.

Clark Kerr, labor economist and former chancellor of the University of California, was chairman of the final arbitration panel that partially redressed the exceedingly labor-biased report of the first arbitration panel. He gave the clerks and mail carriers a modest increase, altered the schedule, and introduced a temporary two-tier wage system for new employees. New employees would be on a separate schedule 25 percent below current schedule. Their wages, however, would catch up with the regular schedule within thirty-three months. This gave the Postal Service the principle of the two-tier wage system but without enough substance to do much good in reducing labor costs over the long run.

The two-tier schedule for new workers was part of a wage policy introducing more spread into the wage schedule itself. For beginning workers, the two-tier schedule represented lower wages. The panel exercised what it called "moderate restraint" in granting a 2.7 percent annual wage increase to workers in the middle range of the scale, not according to seniority but grade level. It raised the pay for a small number of workers at the very top of the grade scale by an average annual increase of 5 percent. The cost-of-living adjustment formulas were left unchanged. In justifying the decisions, Kerr and the final arbitration panel essentially agreed with the Postal Service analysis that starting pay for postal workers was higher than for comparable entry-level jobs in business, and that workers in the middle range were compensated only slightly more than private sector employees while postal workers at the highest level were underpaid.[18]

The other arbitration awards for other postal unions followed the same pattern. All the arbitration panels rejected the Postal Service's efforts to freeze pay for current employees, to cut starting pay permanently by as much as one-third, and to tighten the cost-of-living formula substantially. The arbitration panel gave the National Rural Letter Carriers' Association an average annual wage increase of about 2.9 percent retroactive to July 1984. New rural carriers start at a 15 percent reduction. All arbitration awards reduced starting pay for new workers but allowed them to catch up with established pay scales within three years.[19]

Despite the sobering influence of PATCO and the newfound restraint exercised by postal unions in bargaining, the effects on the outcome have been only marginal because of the arbitration process. As I predicted in 1977, unions are quickly learning how to use this process to their advantage to obtain better contract terms for their members.[20]

To date there is little option but to conclude that arbitration is ineffective in redressing the inequity of excessive wages and to suggest that nothing short of wholesale restructuring will suffice.

Congressional Intervention in Recent Postal Service Labor-Management Relations

In the years preceding the postal reorganization, Frederick Kappel was the chief executive officer of AT&T. Many people viewed AT&T as being similar to the Post Office in many respects. For example, both were approximately the same size, both were in the communications business, and both enjoyed similar monopolies in their markets. The important difference between them was that the Post Office was a government department, with all the difficulties of functioning in a highly politicized environment, and AT&T was still a private corporation, even though heavily regulated. AT&T functioned as a model that many hoped the Post Office would be able to emulate if only it could operate free from political influences. The advantages of depoliticizing were frequently noted and elaborated.

President Lyndon Johnson chose Kappel to direct the commission that came to be named after him. The commission's study of the Post Office culminated in a report entitled "Towards Postal Excellence" a five-volume work with contributions from a myriad of government officials, labor leaders, postal executives, private consulting firms, mail users, and others. Out of the report came the policy recommendations leading to the Reorganization Act of 1970, which was supposed to have severed the political umbilical cord that joined the Post Office to Congress and the executive branch. Policymakers hoped that reorganization would liberate the Postal Service to pursue efficient managerial techniques without the oversight and hindrance of Congress and the executive branch.

Reaching an agreement between the various interested constituents was not an easy process. Congress and the executive branch were eager to shed the perennial problems of postal wage setting and policy-making. These tasks were viewed as a burden. Political patronage was an advantage to politicians, but they were willing to give this up for the prospects of gradually reduced taxpayer subsidies and for a reduction in the problems and headaches of being called to settle internal postal matters between labor, management, and postal patrons.

The postal executives had much to gain in reorganization. They were willing to settle for reduced subsidies from Congress in return for autonomy in conducting normal managerial functions, particularly in dealing with labor-management questions. Although postal executives would have preferred to set postal rates themselves with no interference, Congress gave regulatory authority over postal rates to the Postal Rate Commission (PRC). Postal executives reluctantly accepted this provision because it was an improvement over past dealings with Congress and the executive branch. It was the postal workers and labor leaders who were most reluctant to support the reorganization. In times past they had been eminently successful in using their political power at even the district level to reward their friends and punish their enemies. Through this political intimidation they were able to wrest above-market salaries from the appropriate congressional committees. In the reorganization they were expected to give up their accustomed political manner of influencing wage settlements and to play out the role of seeking the welfare of their members through negotiation and the other provisions stated in the Reorganization Act. To gain their political support, they were offered an exceptionally high wage increase.

Many have argued that the Reorganization Act did not accomplish its objectives. It failed to give managers enough motivation to pursue the risk of bringing efficiency measures into the operations of the reorganized Postal Service. In very recent years the climate of public opinion has favored those Postal Service managers who tried to hold the line against the demands for wage increases by postal unions. The Postal Service, especially under the direction of Postmaster General William F. Bolger, tried to capitalize on this in recent union management negotiations. The changing climate and increased public awareness has enabled the Postal Service to take a much more aggressive position in bargaining.

As noted earlier, the Postal Service, under Bolger, imposed a two-tier structure for postal employee wages when negotiations broke down. Current employees remained on the same schedule they had been on, and new employees were brought into the Postal Service on a schedule that was 23 percent lower. This bold policy attempt, if continued, would have greatly reduced the excessive postal wages, placed by most researchers in excess of one-third above market rates for comparable work in the private sector.

However, in the process stipulated under reorganization, a panel of arbitrators dealt with matters that were unresolved in the negotiation. The formation of the panel was as follows: management chose one panel member, labor leaders another, and the two together chose the final member. In the past and in other industries this selection process has worked to the benefit of labor.[21]

Before the arbitrators submitted their report in the 1984 negotiations, a serious breach of the process occurred when members of Congress violated the basic spirit of reorganization and harkened to the desperate pleas of labor leaders. The leaders in turn reneged on the basic terms of the agreement underlying reorganization. Congress responded to union pleas in a most shortsighted manner by imposing the following ultimatum on postal managers: If they did not abolish the two-tier wage schedule, Congress would refuse to continue its subsidies to the Postal Service.[22]

In effect, congressional intervention of this kind brought the Postal Service back into the political arena from which it tried to escape in the reorganization, and seriously hampered the postal managers' ability to function. Although the conditions created in the Postal Service as a result of reorganization are far from ideal, and although it may be helpful to consider new organizational forms, this heavy-handed and coercive mode of operation by Congress in influencing the Postal Service was detrimental, inappropriate, and demoralizing to postal executives.

The postal executives unwisely knuckled under to congressional pressure and eliminated the two-tier wage structure.[23] The two-tier wage structure has brought about economies recently in the airline industry. Rather than reacting fearfully to Congress, postal executives should have recognized this event as an opportunity to renounce congressional subsidies and to seek further economies within the Postal Service by taking whatever actions were needed, including the raising of rates, to bring their costs in line with revenues. Perhaps they could have bargained even harder for decreases in the wage schedule and sped the process toward independence from the federal government.

Notes

1. See note 22, chapter 1, for references. The results of my work are contained in Douglas K. Adie, *An Evaluation of Postal Service Wage Rates* (Washington, D.C.: American Enterprise Institute, 1977.

2. See William H. Hutt, *The Strike-Threat System*, (Rochelle, N.Y.: Arlington House, 1973). Also Douglas K. Adie, "Compulsory Unionism in the Public Sector: Some Economic Issues," in *Compulsory Unionism in the Public Sector, Symposium Proceedings, April 6, 1979* (Chicago, National Right to Work Committee), pp. 33-46.

3. Many states have laws forbidding strikes by public employees; the Ferguson Act in Ohio was one. Public employee unions struck and the provisions of the law were not enforced because they were believed unenforceable. These laws in some states were changed for this reason.

4. See Hutt, *The Strike-Threat System*.

5. Kathleen Conkey, *The Postal Precipice, Can the U.S. Postal Service Be Saved?* (Washington, D.C.: Center for the Study of Responsive Laws, 1983), pp. 112, 384.

6. Ibid., p. 146.

7. Former Postmaster General Albert Casey seriously considered a partial repeal of the private express statutes in the "Manhattan corridor" that would permit complete competition in delivery of first class mail in that region. Congress has never delegated the power to repeal the private express statutes; the wording in the 1960 draft of the recodified postal laws, however, allowed the governors to make such an interpretation. See George L. Priest, "The History of the Postal Monopoly in the United States," *Journal of Law and Economics* 18 (April 1975): 79 n.228, for a legislative history of this. In response to a question from Senator Symms, Bolger said, "We have, under our administrative authority, suspended the Private Express Statutes and when there is a need we would continue to do that." See Joint Economic Committee, Economic Goals and Intergovernmental Policy Subcommittee, *The Future of Mail Delivery in the United States*, 97th Cong., 2d sess., June 18, 21, 1982, p. 164.

8. Conkey, *The Postal Precipice*, p. 110.

9. Bob Williams, "Biller Holding His Fire, For Now," *Federal Times*, April 30, 1984, p. 7.

10. Leonard M. Apcar, "Postal Service Talks to Begin Tomorrow; Fight Seen Over Call for Wage Rollbacks," *Wall Street Journal*, April 23, 1984, p. 6.

11. See note 22, chapter 1.

12. Williams, "Better Holding His Fire, For Now."

13. Apcar, "Postal Service Talks to Begin Tomorrow"; James Warren, "Postal Talks Land in Junk Mail Pile," *Chicago Tribune*, July 22, 1984, sec. 1, p. 3.

14. Cathy Trost, "Postal Unions Break Off Contract Talks, Demand Discussion of Wages, Benefits," *Wall Street Journal*, July 18, 1984, p. 27.

15. Warren, "Postal Talks Land in Junk Mail Pile."

16. *Wall Street Journal*, July 26, 1984, p. 1.

17. Leonard M. Apcar, "Postal Union Wages Should Be Boosted, Arbitrators Decide," *Wall Street Journal*, September 20, 1984, p. 24.

18. Leonard M. Apcar, "Postal Ruling Is Designed to Realign Pay," *Wall Street Journal*, Dec. 26, 1984, p. 2. This characterization is essentially correct if it is simply stated that workers in the middle range are compensated more than private sector employees.
19. Leonard M. Apcar, "Postal Workers' Contracts Follow Two Earlier Pacts," *Wall Street Journal*, January 8, 1985, p. 7.
20. Adie, *An Evaluation of Postal Service Wage Rates*, pp. 41, 62-63. The process by which the binding arbitration board is selected is as follows: the Federal Mediation and Conciliation Service submits a list of "neutral and impartial persons" to labor and management representatives from which each chooses one representative. The two representatives so selected choose a third person to serve as chairperson. This process in the past has worked out in such a way as to favor labor.
21. See Adie, *An Evaluation of Postal Service Wage Rates*, pp. 41, 50, 62.
22. In my opinion postal managers should have maintained the two-tier structure and accepted abolition of the subsidy. They could have made whatever cost-cutting adjustments they found necessary to compensate for the loss of subsidy. The managers, however, did not buck Congress. Under 39 U.S.C. sec. 3627 the Postal Service would have had the right to adjust the preferred rates upward to recapture lost income because the greatest part of the subsidies in 1984 and since has consisted of subsidies to (preferred-rate) mailers.
23. The two-tier wage structure was reintroduced by the second arbitration panel but only in a temporary version.

7

Privatization

The Early Canadian Experience

To denationalize is to transfer control of some activity or business from the public sector to the private sector after the government has nationalized it (transferred it previously from the private sector to the public sector). To privatize is to pass control of an activity or business to the private sector by an issue of stock, whether it was ever private before. The distribution of the shares of the British Columbia Investment Corporation (BCIC), March-May 1977, is an example of an early full-scale privatization.[1] It is instructive to consider this privatization experience because of what we can learn from it in structuring the privatization of the U.S. Postal Service.

In this case, nationalization preceded privatization. The province of British Columbia began purchasing corporate assets in December 1972 from the private sector. Premier David Barrett purchased Columbia Cellulose, a medium-size, money-losing forest products company for approximately $70 million (Canadian). His socialist New Democratic Party (NDP) government also purchased Plateau Mills, Ltd., a sawmill, for $7 million; Kootenay Forest Products, Ltd., for $9 million; and in January 1974, Westcoast Transmission, a natural gas transmission company, for $25.5 million. After acquiring these companies the provisional government regarded them as publicly owned just as the U.S. government regards the Postal Service.

Most people hold the accepted view that we, individual members of the general public, own public corporations. This, of course, is erroneous because there is no evidence of ownership. No one has any of the property rights usually associated with ownership, such as shares, rights to receive specific benefits or exercise control over the specific enterprises, or rights to buy and sell shares. When we use the term *public ownership*, then, we are not just committing a linguistic error but using a misnomer.

117

In addition, the fact of "public ownership," not just the use of the term, perpetuates irresponsibility on the part of the average citizen by turning him or her into a "free rider" with respect to the exercise of his or her ownership rights. It does this by alienating citizens from the functions normally attributed to owners. This is the problem that lies at the root of the accountability problem in the Postal Service and other government corporations. Under present channels of communication and control there is no adequate legitimate channel for the public to force the Postal Service to change its ways and become profitable.

To say that nobody owns public enterprises is an accurate description of the state of public ownership, for no one has tradeable shares. On the other hand, public servants, managers, or politicians effectively control public corporations by exercising the right to appropriate any financial residual that the operation might produce. Although managers cannot legally appropriate for themselves the residual in money or goods-in-kind, they can appropriate the residual as higher wages and salaries for everyone, more generous benefits, and a reduction of effort on the part of the managers or employees. (This description helps to explain the excessive wages of postal employees and many of the inefficiencies in postal operations.)

Congress has assigned the rights to control and monitor the U.S. Postal Service to the House Post Office and Civil Service Committee, the White House, the Board of Governors, postal executives and managers, the PRC, and the Government Accounting Office. Because the self-interest of bureaucrats is so clearly connected to the size of a public corporation's budget, William Niskanen, former member of the president's Council of Economic Advisers and currently chairman of the Cato Institute, has suggested that the proximate goal of a public corporation is budget maximization. In consequence, the Postal Service will overproduce total output, utilize more resources than it ought to, and so misuse resources. The net value to society of output produced by a government enterprise is most likely to be less than that produced under private enterprise. The difference between the value of output produced under private enterprise, such as private postal companies, and the value of output produced by a government enterprise, such as the Postal Service, both using the same resources, is social cost. The social cost of the U.S. Postal Service is about $14 billion annually.[2] What does society receive for this social cost? Society receives a change in the distribution of goods and services.

In the past economists used theory to argue that a monopoly with increasing returns to scale and/or externalities in the private market will not produce "allocative efficiency" and "distributional equity." The policy implication of this was that because the government had the responsibility for meeting these requirements, it would do so through direct or indirect control and/or ownership. In response to this line of reasoning, other economists used the theory of nonmarket failure to demonstrate that within a government enterprise there is no consistent mechanism for the achievement of allocative efficiency and distributional equity. This, naturally, undermined the original reason for giving the ownership and/or control over production of a good or service to a government enterprise. In fact, according to the theory of nonmarket failure, the policies of nationalization and regulation are more likely to be counterproductive in achieving the desired "allocative efficiency" and "distributional equity." The reason for this is that a democratic government's internal mechanism can lead to even greater problems of inappropriate production levels and even less attractive distributions of economic benefits than what occurs spontaneously in the private sector.[3]

In this book I have discussed all of the defects of a nationalized or government-owned and -operated enterprise mentioned above, namely, lack of accountability, inefficiency of operations, excessive wages, salaries and benefits for employees and managers, misappropriation of resources, excessive output, loss in net value to society, and a maldistribution of economic benefits. All are present to some degree or other with the Postal Service. Regulators seem to be recognizing this fact, and it is this recognition that is producing the change in climate in this country favoring deregulation and privatization.[4]

When the Social Credit Party, which is much more conservative than the NDP, took power in British Columbia, it did not ignore this accumulation of private business in the government and the accompanying inefficiencies but sought to return these businesses to the private sector. The new premier, William R. (Bill) Bennett, began the process by asking Austin Taylor, then vice-president of the brokerage firm McLeod, Young, Wier, Ltd., to set up a task force under the code name "Project West" to develop the privatization process.

The provincial government conducted the privatization in the following manner. In March 1977 it reported that a holding company, British Columbia Resources Investment Corporation (BCRIC), would issue shares to be distributed by the entire financial community. The government excluded foreign shareholders from the distribution, restricted the shareholdings of individual investors and institutions, and retained some shares for itself. It might be advisable for the federal government to issue shares of a divested Postal Service through a holding company much like BCRIC. Should the privatization of the Postal Service be conducted this way, knowing the details of the process by which BCRIC was formed and how it operated with the financial community in the distribution of shares would be helpful in the working out of the process of privatization for the Postal Service's divested companies.

According to the initial plan, the government was to sell the assets to

BCRIC for a fair market price, and the holding company was then to issue shares to the public at reasonable market value. Although it is difficult to price shares of any enterprise, it is even harder for a public enterprise. If BCRIC sold shares too cheaply, the loss would accrue directly to the people. If BCRIC priced the shares too high, all the shares would not sell and the offering would be a failure. To solve this problem, Gordon Gibson (provincial MLA and Liberal Party leader in August 1977) and Milton Friedman (Nobel Prize-winning economist) recommended *giving* the shares away.[5] This approach to pricing shares is particularly applicable to government-owned enterprises and guarantees that a transfer of ownership will take place.

Giving shares away, however, is not the only mechanism for accomplishing a transfer. The British, as we will examine later in this chapter, have sold their shares with considerable success. Premier Bennett, however, adopted the Friedman solution. On January 11, 1979, he announced that each Canadian citizen or applicant living in British Columbia for one year, aged sixteen to sixty-five, would receive five free shares in BCRIC, "probably worth $50 in total." Applications would begin in March and be completed before June 15, with shares available for distribution on August 6. At the same time British Columbians could buy up to 5,000 shares at $6 per share. One hundred shares would be needed to become a registered owner. The provincial government hoped that this distribution scheme would be a success. Giving the stock away at least eliminated the risk inherent in the most important decision, the pricing of shares, and helped to insure the success of the distribution.

Eighty-six percent of eligible British Columbians responded to the offer of shares in BCRIC—that is, 2 million applied for free shares. In addition to the free shares, BCRIC also raised $487.5 million from 170,000 purchasers, with a distribution cost of only $38 to $42 million. The first day the stock opened for trading it closed at the encouraging price of $6.10 per share. Overall, most observers considered this property rights transferral scheme a success. Many regarded the experience as a model for a more general privatization of other government-owned businesses. More specific to postal policy, consideration of the details of the BCRIC distribution could be an important part of the planning for a transfer of ownership of the divested Postal Service companies.

In Canada Barbara McDougall, minister for privatization, and her aide Ian Sadinsky are actively considering prospects for privatizing certain crown corporations. In the last two years approximately $2 billion (Canadian) has been raised through the privatization of TeleGlobe Canada (an international communications company), Fishery Products International, Ltd., Canada Development Corp. (a holding company), De Haviland Aircraft (sold to Boeing), and Canadair. In addition the trucking and hotel divisions of the Canadian National Railway have also been privatized and others are under review. Petro-Canada and Air Canada are still active candidates for privatization although nothing has been done yet. In addition El Dorado Nuclear, Radio Chemical Canada (a division of Atomic Energy Canada), and National C Products (a fish company) are on the drawing board with the small companies: Nanisivik Mines, Ltd., Pecheries, Canada, and Northern Transportation Co., Ltd. The Ministry for Privatization is planning to raise between $5 and 6 billion (Canadian) from privatization projects under consideration within the next few years.

There is no good reason that potentially divestable companies in the United States, and the Postal Service in particular, should not be scrutinized in a similar way. To be a good candidate, a company needs to provide a marketable product or service that will produce revenue and be capable of surviving commercially. The Postal Service should be able to meet these criteria.

It is helpful to the privatization process for a public corporation to have an appropriate public image. The board of directors and senior management can achieve this by maintaining a high business profile and publicizing their decision-making ability and activities. A divested Postal Service would need to do much in this area to turn around the public's perception of ineptitude that has developed over many years. The Postal Service needs a new image based not so much on shallow public relations techniques as on proven performance. In this regard, the exhibition of genuine talent on the part of the new board of directors is essential.

The Heritage Foundation has advocated two types of partial privatization in the postal industry.[6] The first would encourage the development of the already existing private electronic mail systems, overnight carriers, and envelope delivery services. Repealing the private express statutes would effectively accomplish the change.[7] This type of privatization will work and should be the centerpiece of any reorganizational effort. By itself it gives the Postal Service under its present organizational form little or no chance of surviving.

Postal Rate Commissioner John Crutcher advocates a second type of privatization, which is better called contracting out. Crutcher points out that under the current legal framework, the Postal Service would operate more efficiently if it contracted out to private companies many large segments of its operations, such as rural delivery.[8] Although this would no doubt save the Postal Service from pressing up against its budget constraint, would it contribute to long-run overall efficiency? I doubt very much that the Postal Service would use the gains from these efficiency measures in any other way than it has in the past, namely, to increase salaries and operate less efficiently in other areas. Under its present organizational form a spur to operate efficiently is absent. If it were to receive gains from contracting out there is no incentive for it to pass those gains on to customers in the form of lower rates, or to taxpayers in the form of lower transfers from the federal government.

Both forms of partial privatization represent improvements over the existing situation. Both plans fall short of what is attainable under divestiture, privatization, and deregulation. The first type of privatization reduces to repeal of the private express statutes and is a necessary ingredient in any reorganizational scheme. By itself, it leaves the Postal Service as a government corporation with all the problems this entails, and is the better of the two partial privatization proposals. The second solution, relying heavily on contractual services, would in all likelihood lead to a more efficient operation than there is at present. However, we cannot assume that there is an appropriate incentive for the managers to use the savings from contracting out in the public's interest. The second, while providing some temporary savings to the Postal Service, does not offer much promise for the future. In addition, it sets up contractors who will have a vested interest in preserving the status quo. This will make any real change to private ownership more difficult. Full privatization and deregulation will avoid these problems.

The British Experience

In Britain nationalized industries operate with the lowest productivity levels, highest wage scales, and greatest number of strikes. John Egan, chairman of Jaguar Cars, Ltd. a nationalized industry for most of the 1970s, agreed that Jaguars were "lemons." The Series 3 sedan "completely lacked quality and reliability." One of the woodworkers at Jaguar said that the cars made in the 1970s were disasters. Although parts of all types were plagued with defects, the paint jobs were truly abysmal. Tom Bryant, executive editor of *Road and Track* magazine, recalls that when he wanted to test a Jaguar XJ-6 in 1979 he had to ask for five cars before he got one that would run right.

It was not the fault of the workers. They were dissatisfied with the work they were doing but were unable to put the time and effort into doing the job right. Managers kept saying, "It'll do, it'll do." Clearly, it didn't do.[9] Jaguar, which was forced to operate in a very competitive automobile market, lost its good reputation and almost lost its business. The Postal Service, of course, has been able to avoid the vulnerability of Jaguar because it still has a monopoly position.

The Jaguar car certainly lacked quality, but the company was also inefficiently run. Egan said, "We often had two men on the floor for every one that was 'needed' while we had one-fourth of the engineers we needed." Revenues were spent on the wrong priorities. The description of the operations of Jaguar, although perhaps a little extreme, is not atypical of a government-owned enterprise.

In 1980, when Egan slashed the work force from 10,500 to 7,000 and doubled the number of engineers, the union wanted to strike. In anticipation of privatization, Egan explained that if workers did not perform their jobs well, they would lose them to German competitors. With the threat of competition at their backs and the prospects of no more government bailouts after privatization, the union backed him. Jaguar began rigorously testing its parts, raised output to 3.4 cars per employee per year, and received an "absolutely trouble-free" report on the first test car for *Road and Track* magazine.

The case of Jaguar is only one experience of British privatization. Margaret Thatcher, the conservative prime minister of Great Britain, is a strong advocate of getting the government out of business. By the end of July 1987, the British government had sold over $30 billions' worth of state assets and planned to continue selling at the rate of $5 billion per year.

The British government recently sold the telephone company to private investors. The government was going to sell British Airways on February 14, 1985, for $700-800 million. A lawsuit brought against British Airways by receivers for the bankrupt Laker Airways delayed the transaction. The suit was settled in Washington, D.C., in July 1985. British Air paid $32.5 million in the settlement, of which Freddie Laker was offered—and he accepted—$8 million. The government raised $4.75 billion per year by selling businesses, including British Airways, Rolls-Royce (auto manufacturer), British Petroleum, Cable and Wireless, British Gas, Telecom, BL, Ltd. (airplane engines), and its spare-parts manufacturer, Unipart. These companies operate British airports, British National Bus Company, British Steel Corporation, and Short Brothers and Harland, an aerospace firm in Belfast, Northern Ireland.

Other companies the government plans to sell are British Steel, the electric utility, the rails, and the post office.

Many have noticed that a number of companies have improved performances dramatically since they were sold. The results have been increased revenue, higher profits, increased investment, and eventually more jobs.

John Moore, financial secretary to the treasury, says the British government's efforts to spread ownership of shares constitutes an important strand of its policy. In his opinion the bane of society has been the illusory barriers between employers and employees, between management and workers, and between "them" and "us." Because in his opinion the barriers undermine British economic life, he desires to break them down by spreading wealth. This is one of the stated objectives of the government in privatizing British Telecom (according to Nigel Lawson, chancellor of the Exchequer). A goal has been to create a new and healthier social order by giving more people a stake in business.[10]

The above British strategy contrasts with the Canadian experience cited earlier. With regard to the Postal Service, a major point emerges for considering these two approaches, namely, giving the shares away versus selling them at below market prices. The United States government will need to give some thought to its social policy objectives before devising a procedure for distributing shares of the divested Postal Service companies. The Canadians and British have tried different policies; each has positive and negative features. Consideration of both should greatly help the choice of a distribution strategy for the Postal Service. A third strategy, of course, is to try to sell them at the price the market will bear.

Before the sale of Telecom raised $4.69 billion for the British government, institutional investors owned 75 percent of all shares and there were only 1.34 million private investors. The number of individuals owning stock probably doubled after the sale. Nearly 2.3 million people or 5 percent of the adult population bought shares and most of them were probably first-time stock owners.

The phone company union urged its members to reject the offer of British Telecom stock, but more than 90 percent of its members ignored the union's advice and took the opportunity to become capitalist shareholders. From all companies sold to date, more than 500,000 employees acquired shares in the formerly government-owned companies for which they work. Overall, 90 percent of employees working for companies that were privatized opted for share ownership in the companies. In two companies stock purchase participation reached 95 percent.

This experience suggests a strategy to help gain the cooperation of Postal Service workers and managers in the divestiture, privatization, and deregulation. In addition, their stock ownership might motivate employees to work harder and cooperate with management initiatives in the divested companies after restructuring. When employees have a stake in the continuing performance of the company they work for, they have a pecuniary incentive to pull together during the changes that will make letter delivery efficient. There is probably enough motivation without this, but it might help to make the Postal Service companies more viable financially and consequently more salable.

The British social policy of spreading ownership around the general population has been successful, but not as successful as it first appeared. Recent studies have suggested that many small holders sell out quickly to big investors. For instance, after the government sold Jaguar Cars, Ltd. in the summer of 1984, 125,000 people held stock; within two months the number was 50,000. Such shrinkage certainly does not affect the success of distributing shares of a government-owned business to the public, yet might frustrate the policy of spreading ownership to the general population if the purchasers of the initial distribution were first-time equity owners. On the other hand, the policy is not necessarily frustrated if, having owned shares, the sellers purchase some other shares later.

When the government grossly underprices issues, small investors will typically take quick profits, as should be expected. For instance, investors in Amersham International, a small radio-isotope company, were able to sell at a one-third profit within twenty-four hours of obtaining their shares. With Enterprise Oil, however, the government set the price too high. Underwriters were stuck with unsold stock that the government had to buy back. Obviously, the company was not effectively transferred to the private sector. This is the worst kind of failure that can occur in share distribution. It nullifies the attempt to privatize and makes future efforts more difficult. The Canadian process with BCRIC avoids this disappointing result. To reiterate the above point, the United States government needs to weigh all these concerns before it devises its plans to privatize the Postal Service.

In distributing the shares of British Telecom, the government underpriced the shares. Indeed, the shares soon traded at nearly double the initial offering price. In this case, however, the investors were given an incentive to hold their shares by a promised reduction in their phone bills or bonus shares if they held their shares for three years. Early indications are that most buyers are holding their shares. This device represents another form of incentive to encourage widespread and continued stockholding. Perhaps a creative alternative such as this one should be adopted in the distribution of Postal Service stock.

Other countries either have followed or plan to follow the British lead in privatizing telephone and telegraph service, airlines, bus service, public housing, and social security. Japan has sold its state-owned Nippon Telephone and Telegraph Company and its airlines. Malaysia has partially privatized its airlines and some of its toll roads, and its telephone and telegraph service is listed for privatization. Thailand plans to privatize its telephone and telegraph, and bus services; Bangladesh and South Korea, their telephone and telegraph, and airline industries. Bangladesh has privatized its textile industry and is privatizing banking. Sri Lanka has already privatized its telephone and telegraph, and bus services. Mexico has a plan to privatize its telephone and telegraph service but has not been pursuing it enthusiastically. Singapore has privatized, Turkey is privatizing, and Spain has a plan for privatizing their airlines. Cuba and China are privatizing their public housing. Chile has privatized its social security system, and India has a proposal to privatize toll roads and highways.[11]

West Germany is injecting private capital into its state-owned companies and banks, and Italy and Canada are planning to sell state holdings to private owners. Countries all over the world, even socialist countries, are discovering that the government can turn its enterprises over to the private sector, which will operate them at lower cost with improved service. Although many countries are benefiting from transfers of ownership from the public to the private sector, the U.S. government is extremely slow to adopt such a policy. This must seem especially puzzling because many regard the United States as the champion of the private sector, and the current president and administration are supposedly committed to free enterprise principles.

In 1970 Congress believed that the provision of postal service was more compatible with a business organization than a government department. In accordance with this, it created in the Postal Service reorganization a structure that resembled a business. The chief reason for doing this was that postal revenues came chiefly from customers. Congress forgot to provide for adequate motivation and control in 1970. The experience of the past eighteen years has impressed these shortcomings on us and this book represents an attempt to document them. The same features that argued for a business structure in 1970 now argue for privatization.

The current problems in the Postal Service were predictable. They have resulted primarily from the organizational form of the Postal Service. At present we have the opportunity to expand the restructuring under a new climate that has emerged since 1970. The Heritage Foundation suggests, "The long term future of the Postal Service should be reexamined. In a competitive age in which the telephone, not the post, provides essential communication, it is unclear why there should be a publicly owned and supported national document delivery company."[12]

Privatization of the Postal Service may seem radical, but it was not that far removed from the minds of those who reorganized the Postal Service in 1970. The Kappel Commission did not see the independent postal corporation as a final step in the organizational transition but more as a halfway house between a public mail service and a private profit-making business: "*The possibility remains of private ownership at some future time*, if such a transfer were then considered to be feasible and in the public interest" (emphasis added).[13] In light of the growing experience with successful divestiture, privatization, and deregulation, the time may well be soon.

Testifying before a congressional committee in 1969, Frederick Kappel justified what he had done by saying, "If I could, I'd make it [the post office] a private enterprise and I would create a private corporation to run the postal service and the country would be better off financially. But I can't get from here to there. But we are trying to retain the efficiencies of a corporation and create minimal controls from Congress."[14] Unable to move all the way to a private business in one swoop, Kappel sought to make the postal corporation a provisional step toward that end. Kathleen Conkey says, "Congress should have had little doubt that to Frederick Kappel, postal excellence meant private ownership of postal operations."[15] His vision was clear and correct. It remains for us to actualize it in the present milieu.

The answer we are suggesting is a response to a question that has been asked with respect to the Postal Service over most of its history. Who should move the mail, a government-owned postal organization or private industry? Many European countries formed government-owned postal, telephone, and telegraph agencies. Others believed private industry could do a better job. Which system has performed better? The new Postal Service's first three postmaster generals after reorganization, Winton Blount, Elmer T. Klassen, and Benjamin Bailar, seemed to share the belief that it is inherently better for private industry than for a government agency to move the mails.[16] In defense of private industry, Bailar argued against any Postal Service role in electronic communications. "I felt that way while I was in office and said so. My contention was that if private business was able and willing . . . [and] if electronic mail is a needed public service and I think it is, I think it ought to be left to the private sector."[17]

Bailar raised the uncomfortable question of whether the Postal Service is an anachronism:

> This is not a very popular posture for a head of a federal agency to take. The unions didn't like it and frankly a lot of people on Capital Hill didn't like it. . . . I think the Postal Service would benefit from a substantial restructuring of its service down to the level that public needs require because even a government agency is not immune to conventional economic pressures. Now a government agency is slower to respond to those stimuli than a business but sooner or later they'll have to respond to them.[18]

Looked at from a different standpoint, but not without some justification, James LaPenta, president of the Mailhandlers Union, suggests that the reorganization and its first leaders were part of a deliberate effort to sabotage the Post Office. He said, "I've been on public record that it was a conspiracy, I'm not talking about an illegal conspiracy, but it was a God damned political conspiracy to wreck the Postal Service."[19]

Perhaps a summary of objections to privatization with answers would be helpful. For instance, could mailers trust an array of private companies with the privacy of their personal letters and the security of their business correspondence, valuables, and money? The answer is that they could trust them as much as they trust AT&T with the privacy of their telephone conversations, or UPS or Federal Express with their parcels and express mail.

Who would be responsible for making connections between the various companies carrying the mail? The companies themselves would make connections by means of contracts and arrangements among themselves without the care or concern of customers, just as long-distance telephone calls go through two or three exchanges before reaching the destination party without any hassle for the original caller. It is in the financial interest of all private businesses handling mail to coordinate their efforts.

Who would forward mail? The primary company that a customer designated to make his or her local deliveries. Which private companies would deal with foreign postal systems? Whichever ones offered a foreign delivery service to local customers.[20]

And so the questions will be answered. The crucial principle behind each answer, as in the past in so many other business situations, is that the market usually develops satisfactory solutions.

Notes

1. See M. L. McMillan, K. H. Norrie, T. M. Ohashi, T. P. Roth, and Z. A. Spindler, *Privatization: Theory and Practice. Distributing Shares in Private and Public Enterprises* (Vancouver, B.C.: Fraser Institute, 1980), pp. 3-107. The following description of the Canadian privatization experience is based on this source.
2. See Madison Pirie, *Dismantling the State* (Dallas: National Center for Policy Analysis, 1985), pp. 8-53. Pirie says that costs of production (in U.S. private industry) are 40 percent lower than in the public sector. He also says that when the activities are contracted out, although the responsibility for the provision of services remains with the governments, immediate savings are normally in the range of 20 to 40 percent. The addition of the fact that postal employees are one-third overpaid suggests that a 50 percent saving from privatization would not be unreasonable. See also Robert Poole, "Privatization from the Bottom Up," in *Privatization* ed. John C. Goodman (Dallas: National Center for Policy Analysis, 1985), pp. 66-67. Poole says that private air traffic controllers can do their job for *half the cost* of the publicly managed air traffic controllers.
3. Zane A. Spindler and others, "'Bricking-Up' Government Bureaus and Crown Corporations," in T. M. Ohashi, T. P. Roth, Z. A. Spindler, M. L. McMillan, and K. H. Norrie, *Privatization: Theory and Practice. Distributing Shares In Private and Public Enterprises* (Vancouver, B.C.: Fraser Institute, 1980), p. 155.
4. Kenneth Sturzenacker, a private postal consultant, recently indicated that there was almost universal support among the supervisory-level postal service employees present at a conference in Phoenix for some measure of privatization, including outright sale of post office operations to the private sector. The postmasters perceive that the greatest opposition to change will come, as we had

suspected, from lower-level postal employees, rural constituents, and members of Congress.

5. See Milton Friedman, *Newsweek*, December 27, 1976, and Milton Friedman, *Friedman on Galbraith and on Curing the British Disease* (Vancouver, B.C.: Fraser Institute, 1977), p. 51.

6. Heritage Foundation, "Privatization: A Strategy for Cutting Federal Spending," *Backgrounder*, December 7, 1983, p. 9.

7. Robert Poole, "Is This Any Way to Run a Postal Service? No," *Wall Street Journal*, October 11, 1982.

8. John Crutcher, "The Privatization of the Postal Service," *Washington Times*, June 2, 1983.

9. Erik Colonius, "Jaguar Climbs Back to Prosperity," *Wall Street Journal*, July 18, 1984.

10. Ray Mosely, "Britain Marketing Capitalism: Thatcher's 'Privatization' Revolution," *Chicago Tribune*, December 23, 1984, sec. 7, pp. 1-2.

11. See Peter Young and John C. Goodman, "U.S. Lags Behind in Going Private," *Wall Street Journal*, February 20, 1986, p. 20. Two good short books describing and analyzing the British experience in privatizing are Pirie, *Dismantling the State*, and Goodman, *Privatization*. I have updated information on these countries with the help of Stuart Butler, John Goodman, Peter Young, and John Tepper Marlin.

12. Heritage Foundation, *Mandate for Leadership*, project team report for the U.S. Postal Service and Postal Rate Commission (draft, 1980), pp. 22-23, 30. More recently the Heritage Foundation advocates that the USPS be converted into an umbrella organization responsible for postal service. It recommends, "Many of the actual services . . . be provided by private sector contractors on a competitive basis . . . USPS would . . . turn over operation of its collection, sorting, transportation, and distribution functions to private firms on a contract basis." See Carlos E. Bonilla, "Postal System," in *Agenda 1983: A Mandate for Leadership Report*, ed. Richard N. Holwill (Washington, D.C.: Heritage Foundation, 1983), p. 353.

13. President's Commission on Postal Organization, *Towards Postal Excellence* (Washington, D.C.: Government Printing Office, 1968), vol. 5, p. 2.

14. U.S. Congress, House, *Post Office Reorganization* (Part I), Hearings before the Committee on Post Office and Civil Service, Serial No. 91-3, 1969, p. 277.

15. Kathleen Conkey, *The Postal Precipice, Can the U.S. Postal Service be Saved?* (Washington, D.C.: Center for the Study of Responsive Laws, 1983), p. 45.

16. Ibid., p. 104.

17. Ibid., p. 455. Phone interview with Benjamin Bailar, November 17, 1981.

18. Benjamin Bailar, "Postal Service-Political Birthright or Economic Choice?" (speech to the Economic Club of Detroit, March 8, 1976), in Committee on Postal Service and Civil Service, 94th Cong., 2d sess., *Problems of the U.S. Postal Service: A Compendium of Studies, Articles, and Statements on the U.S. Postal Service* (Washington, D.C.: U.S. Government Printing Office, March 1976), p. 172. Senate, *Problems of the U.S. Postal Service, A Compendium of Studies, Articles and Statements on the U.S. Postal Service* (March 1976), p. 172.

19. Conkey, *The Postal Precipice*, p. 105. Interviews with James LaPenta, January 1981.

20. We are proposing that private postal companies be given discretion to deal

directly with foreign governments and postal administrations, even though in the field of overseas airlines the Civil Aeronautics Board, before its sun had set, awarded overseas routes, and the secretary of transportation has done so since. In both cases, the president, in the exercise of his foreign relations powers, may override or alter the decisions on noneconomic grounds. Despite this precedent for governmental intervention in the allocation of overseas airline routes, former postmaster general William F. Bolger said; We have, under our administrative authority, suspended the Private Express Statutes and when there is a need we would continue to do that.

In the international field, we only control international mail that goes over post roads and post routes in the domestic United States. We do not have any control of the mail until it hits our shores. After it leaves our shores we just don't have any control.

In general, I don't think we have the Private Express Statutes applying to the international mails category. See Joint Economic Committee, Economic Goals and Intergovernmental Policy Subcommittee. *The Future of Mail Delivery in the United States*, 97th Cong., 2d sess., June 18, 21, 1982, p. 164.

8

Organizational Choices

In 1970 Congress reorganized the Post Office into the U.S. Postal Service, with its Board of Governors appointed by the president and confirmed by the Senate. It retained its postal monopoly but Congress no longer regulates it. Wages and benefits are now set through collective bargaining or arbitration, as described in chapter 6. Further, management now has sole responsibility for decisions concerning new facilities, operations, and personnel policies.

Congress established the Postal Rate Commission (PRC) as part of the reorganization to review rate increase proposals. The PRC has no subpoena power and receives only the information the Postal Service deems necessary.[1] It has no authority to question management decisions or to reject rate proposals but, rather, can only make recommendations. The PRC passes its recommendations to the Board of Governors, which may approve them, allow them under protest, or reject them.[2] If the board allows under protest or rejects a given recommendation, it goes back to the PRC for resubmission. The governors can modify a resubmitted recommendation with a unanimous vote. As long as the governors are unanimous, the Postal Service can set its own rates with virtually no congressional oversight and no PRC control.[3]

Shielded from Congress, not regulated by the PRC, and not being accountable to shareholders, the Postal Service has become a monopolistic, independent public corporation. In short, the reorganization has failed. The public corporation has frustrated rather than helped responsibility and accountability in the Postal Service. The Postal Service has no real accountability.

As examples of behavior in the Postal Service without accountability, Murray Comarow, former senior assistant postmaster general for customer service, recalled that "Klassen [a former postmaster general] was under attack by everyone. He didn't have a friend in the world and he bought friends. He gave the unions everything they wanted."[4] Benjamin Bailar, a later postmaster general, was even more generous in the 1975 negotiations than Klassen.

As an explanation for the lack of accountability, former PRC chairman A. Lee Fritschler suggested:

> It's a monopoly, the unions are tough, the public does not look over their shoulder. It's a classical monopoly situation and it's not successfully regulated. . . . You're not going to find [postal] workers cutting their pay back the way the automotive workers are going to have to. The auto workers know that either they cut back or they don't have a job. The handwriting is clearly on the wall. That's not going to happen in monopoly industries.[5]

Fritschler believed that tighter regulatory control would remedy the situation. He said, "I think a monopoly like the USPS should be controlled by a quasi-judicial body, just as you control the phone company. I find that analogy a very fitting one."[6] This statement, made before the divestiture of AT&T, was too optimistic. The regulatory history of AT&T demonstrated that because regulatory boards could not control it, divestiture and deregulation was the only solution. Fritschler's view illustrates how older views on natural monopolies can describe the problem accurately but not see the obvious solution.

As regulation ultimately failed in the case of AT&T, so it is failing in the Postal Service. Without altering the present organizational structure, there are only a few alternatives for increasing postal accountability. For instance, Congress could increase the surveillance powers of one or more of the following: the president, the Board of Governors, the Congress, and/or the PRC. This kind of tinkering, however, is merely reconfiguring the regulatory powers and in all probability would be ineffective.

Morris K. Udall (D-Ariz.), a member of the House Post Office Committee, compared the operations of AT&T with the U.S. mail service and concluded that although "the phone service is keeping pace with current technological advancements, the mail is still operating basically as we operated one hundred years ago." Udall said, "I want to make very clear, I do not blame postal employees. I think we have fine dedicated people working for us. I do not blame those who have undertaken to manage it in the past. I blame *the system*."[7]

It is now clear that only the free market operating without the interference of the private express statutes can provide responsibility and accountability. Changes in accounting and evaluative procedures, which are needed, are not enough to motivate managers to perform efficiently. Like it or not, the free market solution appears through the process of elimination to be the only policy with any prospect for success.

There are many ways to implement free market solutions. The present study analyzes in detail a single, clean and clear alternative: a privately owned, divested, deregulated company created out of the USPS operating in a free market. Like Winston Churchill's evaluation of democracy, even though such a postal system may appear flawed to some, there just may not be a better real alternative.[8]

Deregulation

Deregulation is a shorthand word that stands not only for the relaxation and removal of regulations but also for the development of patterns of reform that rely on market forces to serve customers. When considering deregulation in many different fields, one sees elements common to all the controversies surrounding the role of special interest groups and the public interest. For instance, some regulated firms that declare they defend the public interest from irresponsible new entrants argue against deregulation. (Businesspeople desire to avoid the unpredictability of market forces accompanying competition.) They argue against deregulation to avoid competition and preserve their interests, which were created inadvertently by regulation itself.

In the view of Roger Noll and Bruce Owen, there ought to be a presumption in favor of competitive market approaches for achieving effective social control of business because competition encourages the most efficient adaptations to change.[9] Arguments for deregulating our economy are gaining adherents because economic and technological conditions are changing so rapidly. Despite the real advantage to the public from deregulation, it is still difficult to gain political support for it because the benefits to the public from competition are diffused. On the other hand, where regulation has raised barriers to entry, it has a ready-made constituency. Because deregulation suffers from lack of political support, Noll and Owen suggest that economists adopt a predisposition for it. They also believe that the advocates of continued deviation from the competitive model be made to bear the burden of proof for their position.

Deregulation of the postal system involves two separate issues. The first is repeal of the private express statutes, which have for many years hindered or prevented private companies from delivering private correspondence in competition with the Postal Service. The hallmark of any deregulation program, irrespective of the ultimate disposition of the USPS, is opening up the market to private competition.

There are many ways the Postal Service could be reorganized. I advance one specific structure as a starting point for debate, although other models could also succeed. The differences between them are much less important than repeal of the private express statutes. Without repeal, there can be no true postal reform. As an argument favoring repeal, Milton Friedman has written that if the postal monopoly were abolished, a vigorous private industry would arise, containing thousands of firms, employing tens of thousands of workers.[10]

There are two implications of repeal of the private express statutes. The first is the abolition of the PRC; the second is the removal of all prohibitions against the Postal Service entering new business areas, including telecommunications. After repeal the PRC should be abolished because its function of regulating postal rates is no longer needed. Also, it would only be fair to the deregulated Postal Service to remove the prohibition against its entering the market for telecommunications, although removal is not necessarily implied by repeal. The privilege could accompany privatization and divestiture, which are the other major elements of the restructuring.

Former postmaster general Bolger said that he wanted regulatory restrictions removed if the private express statutes were repealed—and rightly so. The USPS could then compete on equal footing with private business without the burden of its public service image. It might then offer a nationwide electronic mail service by combining its post office facilities in every town with its ability to reach every American through hard-copy delivery.

Although not in the original Postal Reorganization Act, the Postal Regulatory Commission (PRC) was added by Congress to protect the public interest. Its abolition is probably undesirable as long as the Postal Service retains its monopoly on the delivery of first class mail in the private express statutes. The PRC is necessary if not to oversee rates at least to slow down the process of rate increases. Without monopoly, however, the marketplace would easily restrain the Postal Service's desire to raise rates.

The postal monopoly makes it impossible for postal managers to control labor costs. Lack of competition deprives them of the necessity to press for economical wage settlements. Under competition the Postal Service would not be able to pass along increased costs to its users without suffering severe deterioration of volume and market share.[11] This would almost certainly constrain postal workers' wage demands.

Private businesses have argued against allowing the USPS to enter the market for electronic message transmission service[12] for the following reasons:

- The USPS might use its monopoly on first class mail to subsidize electronic message service and drive out private carriers.[13]
- The Postal Service might use its monopoly on first class mail to the disadvantage of firms that competed with them for other services.
- The USPS might try to extend the private express statutes to legally monopolize electronic transmission services.[14]

Despite the self-interested motivations of the proponents of these arguments, they have validity under the private express statutes. I recommend that the USPS be kept out of electronic transfers until it is privatized in some form and deregulated and the private express statutes are repealed. This makes the specific restructuring of the Postal Service advocated in this book, as well as repeal of the private express statutes, prerequisite to the Postal Service's entrance into the electronic mail services market.

Labor leaders have lobbied for the broadest role for the USPS in electronics and have been critical of postal managers for their preference for raising revenues through higher postal rates, which reduce business, rather than through larger congressional appropriations. James J. LaPenta, Jr., president of the Mailhandlers Union, said "The third largest workforce in the United States . . . is going to be devastated by our emerging national policy on telecommunications."[15] Understandably, LaPenta would like to see the Postal Service enter the telecommunications industry. Under existing circumstances this would give it an undeserved advantage, possibly putting private companies out of business, not due to their inefficiencies but as a result of unfair play. Policy should look out for postal workers, but it should also look out for workers in the private sector who might lose their jobs if the Postal Service were given free rein in the telecommunications industry while it still had a monopoly under the private express statutes.

We should confine the USPS to producing its existing services for its declining market until Congress repeals the private express statutes and privatizes the USPS. In the absence of any action the Postal Service revenue base will erode, prices will rise and eventually drive away business, leaving high overhead and diminishing volume. Barring increased government subsidies or borrowing to cover deficits, the USPS will have to increase efficiency or reduce quality of service. A reduction in quality of service will reduce its business volume further. At some point the USPS will shrink.[16]

My 1982 congressional testimony considered some of the details connected with deregulation. Without lengthy discussion I proposed that all individual post boxes be unshackled to receive materials from all delivery systems. This is equivalent to open access in the local telephone system. The existing prohibition is simply an inconvenience and an obstruction that serves no useful function except to help preserve the vested interest of the postal monopoly.[17]

Divestiture

The second critical aspect of a deregulation program is the reorganization of the Postal Service. One alternative would be to simply strip it of its subsidies and tax breaks, allowing it to compete with private industry. There is, however, no reason to preserve a hybrid creature like the quasi-public Postal Service; indeed, its mere existence would forever tempt Congress to intervene again in the postal market.

Another deregulation possibility would be to dismantle USPS, selling off its assets to private firms. This approach probably would disrupt mail service, something that would be politically unthinkable, however short-lived the inconvenience.

Or Congress could follow the model of Conrail, turning USPS into a private company by selling shares to the public. Doing so would minimize the attempt of government officials or public policy analysts to construct artificially what they believe the market should look like. But privatizing USPS in this fashion would also place potential competitors at a significant disadvantage initially.

Finally, the Postal Service could be privatized and then broken up. Such a divestiture could essentially be modeled after the breakup of AT&T, with USPS divided into a bulk mail delivery company, a centralized mail clearinghouse service company, and five regional mail delivery companies.

It might first be asked why there should be a separate bulk mail company, or why bulk mail should be handled separately from other kinds of mail. Most people probably think that bulk mail is collected at one local post office and sent directly to another local post office together with first class mail. Quite to the contrary. Except for passing through the local post office where packages are collected, bulk mail is already handled separately from flat mail after it is received. (The technology at present makes it more efficient to handle it separately.)

In March 1971 Postmaster General Winton Blount announced the building of the National Bulk Mail System. In five years Postmaster General Klassen built a system around twenty-one major and twelve auxiliary regional facilities at a cost of nearly $2 billion. Each Bulk Mail Center is in a centralized location and is equipped with expensive and elaborate machinery for processing all bulk mail originating in or coming into its area. The Postal Service sorts and processes all bulk mail including parcels, circulars, advertisements, and some magazines at these centers. This processing and delivery system already uses facilities that are separate from those used for first class mail. The bulk mail network failed to recapture the lost parcel post business. (The Postal Service now has only some 25 percent of the package business and may eventually be eliminated from this field.) Another company might be able to run the business at a profit and at least deserves the opportunity. The bulk mail facilities could and should be sold as a separate unit as soon as possible.

For purposes of administration, the Postal Service has already divided the country geographically into five regions: Western, Central Eastern, Northeastern, and Southern (see figure 8.1). The regions could easily be served by five Postal Operating Companies (POCs)—similar to the Bell Operating Companies (BOCs) created through the breakup of AT&T— each providing local delivery service.[18] It would be quite natural and not involve much reorganization to divest the Postal Service into these divisions. After divestiture the Postal Service would be five regional companies, a centralized support services and clearinghouse company, and perhaps a bulk mail company for a total of seven companies.

In preparation for privatization in Britain, the government is dividing the Post Office into four separate businesses: counter services, the National Girobank, letter delivery, and parcel delivery. The government will sell the Girobank, a profitable concern. It will also sell the parcel delivery separately. The government plans to place all the local post offices, which provide counter services, into a separate company; it believes the company would be an attractive acquisition for a U.S. bank that desires to set up offices in Britain.[19] Otherwise, the government might give the company to the company's employees. Further the government will divide the letter pickup, handling, and delivery services into regional units and sell or give them to their employees. Alternative plans afford the government latitude and leverage in gaining the political support of constituencies for its privatization policy.

Why should the Postal Service be divided into regional delivery systems, a support services company, and a bulk mail company? Is it not the monopoly nature rather than the national reach of the Postal Service that is the problem? The experience of AT&T has taught us that it is both the monopoly nature and the national reach and overall size that are problems. At present it is the monopoly of the Postal Service that is the problem because other firms are forbidden to enter the market for first class mail and the Postal Service must charge uniform rates for all the services it offers, in all markets. In effect, the Postal Service while receiving monopoly protection is restrained from the destructive consequences of predatory price competition with smaller firms. With repeal of the private express statutes there will no longer be such a restraint and the Postal Service is likely to behave more like AT&T.

How did AT&T behave? AT&T controlled over 85 percent of local telephone service but did not have a monopoly over all local service. How did it treat its smaller competitors? It refused to interconnect with them; it charged exorbitant rates for interconnecting; it intimidated them by threatening to withdraw interconnect privileges if they connected with any other company. AT&T preannounced its investment plans to forestall competitors from entering the area it was planning to service. If AT&T had

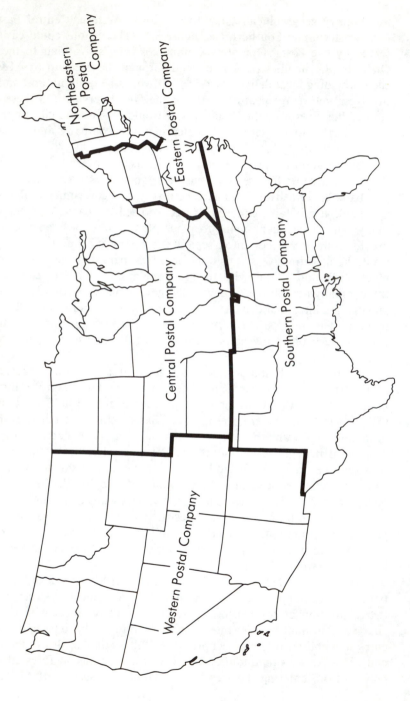

FIGURE 8.1
Postal Operating Companies

been a smaller, regional company, doing so would not have had the same intimidating effect. In all probability, a single national U.S. Postal Service would be in a position to wield the same power that AT&T wielded before divestiture.

By using different tariff schedules, AT&T delayed the use of new technology and the entrance of competitors. Because AT&T was so large, it could charge rates below average cost for a limited line of service for a long time. By doing this, AT&T drove almost any company it wanted to compete with out of business. AT&T also had the resources to engage in protracted legal processes without being affected financially; this is not true for smaller companies. Because of its size, AT&T could also manipulate the regulatory system for its own advantage. It was the size of AT&T, not just its monopoly status, that compounded the problem. A single national postal service could wield the same amount of influence as AT&T, but smaller regional companies would not pose such a threat.

Small, new-entrant local firms would have a much better chance of surviving if they can interconnect easily with a larger company. They would have a better chance of doing this if they can deal with a clearinghouse or five regional companies, rather than one national company. Also they would have a better chance of surviving if they are competing with one of a number of regional companies rather than a single national unified Postal Service.

From the standpoint of the POCs, divestiture would simplify their labor relations problems. Instead of having to deal with all workers represented together, each of the regional companies would conduct its own labor relations with its own employees and their representatives. Some of the POCs may even be able to reduce the scope of collective bargaining within their operations. Work stoppages in one region need not affect services in any of the others. Strikes would not necessarily be catastrophic; they would merely give competitive local companies an opportunity to increase their market shares.

Would jurisdictional and factional struggles at the employer-employee levels increase under a privatized, divested, and deregulated Postal Service? Because employers will conduct their own labor negotiations, more effort will be devoted to working out labor arrangements. Also, each of the employers will have more freedom to work out its own labor relations for its labor force. Different regional companies may or may not be represented by unions. (Unions will probably represent most workers in most companies.) Although divestiture, privatization, and deregulation will lead to more negotiating activity, there may or may not be more intense struggles.

Up to the present the labor struggles in the Postal Service have not been very intense, but this has not been without cost. To avoid conflict, management has capitulated to many union demands. There has been no incentive for it to do otherwise. Giving in has only required raising first class postage a few cents, which under the monopoly for first class mail and the low elasticity of demand did not reduce mail volume much.

Under the privatized postal system, unions where they exist will have the right to strike and will be covered by the same National Labor Relations Board rules that apply to all other private companies. Employers will have more freedom to negotiate and will negotiate only for their own companies. The important difference will be that management will have an incentive to negotiate diligently because the residual profit can be appropriated.

Both unions and management in each company will have a strong incentive to avoid strikes, work stoppages, slowdowns, or any diminution in service for the following reason: any of these disruptions will cause customers to shift their purchases of document delivery services to other competing carriers who, under repeal of the private express statutes, will be eager to take advantage of the situation. Resuming work may not necessarily bring back lost business and so might result in a permanent loss of business and consequent layoffs. If workers want job security and employers want to retain market share, they will not just prevent work stoppages, they will work together to improve reliability of service.

The no-strike proviso will be abolished under the privatized postal service. The unions have not really respected this proviso. They have threatened to strike and conducted strikes when it suited their purposes. Since the air controllers' strike, however, references to the strike have disappeared from postal unions' rhetoric, not because postal unions respect the law but because they fear the consequences. Abolition of the no-strike proviso under the privatized postal service should not spell disaster for the delivery of written communications because of competition generated by the repeal of the private express statutes.[20]

Under the privatized postal system local or regional shutdowns will not destabilize the whole system as much as they do today. Now when there is a strike or shutdown in a local or regional area, mail is not delivered to or picked up from the area. As disconcerting as this is, it is not the source of the problem. The source is the private express statutes that prevent other companies from stepping into the gap and offering the same service. Under the privatized, divested, and deregulated regional postal system, regional shutdowns will merely take one local carrier out of the picture temporarily. Other local and regional carriers, which will compete for postal business alongside privatized postal service companies, can and will pick up the slack. This is one of the reasons for repealing the statutes. It ameliorates otherwise difficult situations.

With divestiture, the Postal Service Investment Corporation can privatize the regional postal delivery companies one at a time. This will reduce the risk of pricing the stock issue too high or too low. The market will price the first issue. The price of issues already trading will guide the pricing of new issues sold to the public.

The question might be raised whether five is the optimal number of regional companies. Eugene B. Dalton, president of the National League of Postmasters, said in a slightly different context, "If I were Postmaster General . . . the first thing I would do is reestablish at least ten regions versus five, do away with three levels of management and save money, like when we had fifteen regions."[21] This kind of restructuring would obviate the need for the three management levels of the five regional offices, the district offices, and the SCMs (Sectional Center Managers). Dalton's remark suggests that a larger number of regional companies than five might be optimal. To resolve this question will take a detailed study of the equipment, technology, and operations.

The task of structuring the divestiture is to construct the POCs in such a way as to induce an evolution toward an efficient use of technology and equipment. Just as the technology is not expected to remain constant over time, neither would the initial restructuring. After the Postal Service is privatized, further restructuring would take place voluntarily through mergers, acquisitions, and sales of divisions. Key in determining the size and location of the POCs in the original restructuring is the efficient use of existing technology and equipment. This was a fundamental consideration in creating the BOCs in the AT&T divestiture, and it should be so in the divestiture of the Postal Service, too.

To be relevant, the restructuring should consider not just the technology being employed in the Postal Service but also the technology that is available. Although it has not been done under the Postal Service, mail handling is capable of being upgraded from mechanization to automation. It requires, however, a nine-digit ZIP or other extended code, Optical Character Readers (OCRs), and Bar Code Readers (BCRs).[22] OCRs read ZIPs with nine digits and print a bar code on the letter at the first station. Less expensive and reliable BCRs process mail at every other station, alleviating the need for postal workers to sort mail or memorize carrier route schemes. If the letter has only the five-digit code, this takes it to a post office where clerks (who memorize schemes) must sort for carriers. The remaining digits, when present, enable the post office to sort mail mechanically down to the carrier and section of a city block. The process can reduce the Postal Service's dependence on labor and has relevance for the size and structure of the divested organizational units.

How can we ensure that postal facilities and equipment will be used

under a privatized and divested postal service without creating new inefficiencies? In the longer run, when there has been sufficient time for adjustment, the new market for postal services will adjust to changes in
technology and consumers' needs and wants, and will encourage the technological changes that will make the production of postal services more
efficient than it has ever been under the not-for-profit nationalized monopoly that currently exists. This is one reason that it is important for the
economic environment to allow the new organizations to adjust to technology over the longer term.

In the short run the economic problem centers on the most efficient use
of existing equipment and facilities. So, in the divestiture of the Postal
Service, if the organizational divisions and the allocation of equipment and
facilities among regional companies and the clearinghouse company do
not "match," it will be possible to create new inefficiencies. This potential
eventuality is why it is important, as Judge Greene discussed in the AT&T
divestiture, to divest the Postal Service into regional companies and allocate existing equipment and facilities among them in an "optimal" way,
that is, in terms of efficiency.

Rather than describe in detail what the optimal distribution of equipment and facilities among privatized and divested companies would be, I
will instead describe a process by which it could be discovered. First, because the Postal Service is already divided into five regional divisions, this
is a good reason for divesting it into five companies along the same geographical lines. An allocation of equipment and facilities to the regions
that now control them would be the status quo allocation. It is unlikely to
introduce new inefficiencies that would not be more than compensated for
under the new incentive system of the privatized business organization.
The status quo allocation, however, might not be the most efficient. If after
an intensive review of operations it appears that the allocation could be
improved, it might be advisable to allocate accounting dollars to the regions on the basis of the capital equipment they currently control and
allow them to bid at an auction conducted by the clearinghouse for the
equipment and facilities they desire. This would allow the regional companies the opportunity to reassess their operations and try to adjust the
mix of capital equipment and facilities they control and use, if a change
appeared advantageous.

If the Postal Service were divested into regional operating companies
how would the fragmented system work? The companies could provide
complete delivery between any two points within their region (see figure
8.2). Private haulers could compete to handle the transport of mail between the local delivery areas within a POC's region. Alternatively, POCs
could provide this service themselves.

FIGURE 8.2
Local and Long Distance Delivery Schematics

Local Delivery, One Company

Long-Distance Delivery, One Company

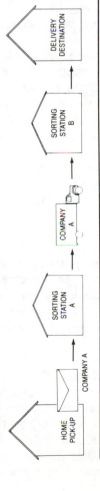

Long-Distance Delivery, Two or More Companies

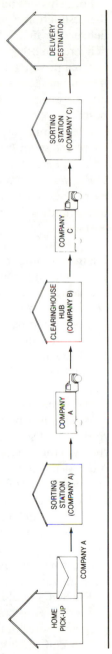

For deliveries outside its region, a POC would have to transport mail to the destination region and have an arrangement with the company there to deliver the mail. Alternatively, a POC could also transport mail to be delivered in other regions to a clearinghouse hub. If a regional POC established a private relationship between itself and another regional company, it could have a carrier deliver its outgoing mail directly. Such transportation between regions could be purchased from carriers on a competitive basis.

Even though the BOCs still have a monopoly in the provision of local telephone service, the increasing use of two-way cable and mobile cellular units will erode it. When Congress repeals the private express statutes, the POCs would face competition for first class mail immediately because entry does not require a large investment of capital and there exist many opportunities for providing better service more efficiently and at a lower cost.

If a regional company used a clearinghouse company instead of delivering mail to other regions directly, it would exchange bags between regional companies at the hub location. Private regional companies could belong to the clearinghouse, which would establish rates for delivery on a bulk basis within regions. Companies that sent more mail out of their regions to other regions would pay for the difference. Companies that received more mail for their regions than they gave to the clearinghouse would receive payment for delivering it. The clearinghouse would also be responsible for setting delivery standards for its members, establishing rates, and arranging for timely exchanges and exchange facilities at the hub, which would be the center of its operations.

Would the coordination of these activities be an obstacle to smooth regular mail service? Despite disaggregation in the provision of service in the banking (check-clearing), transportation, health, and now telephone industries, agreements between firms have always provided the required coordination. At first customers typically experience some difficulties from lack of coordination, but an underlying financial incentive quickly encourages the participants to work them out. There would probably be differences in the intrastate and interstate mail delivery services. Additional flexibility would arise because the POCs would have complete autonomy in contracting with mail haulers. Although much latitude would exist for experimentation, competition would shape the ultimate arrangements.

The POCs would provide local delivery service (like a city bus company). For instance, to complete a delivery to a destination within the specified geographic area of the POC, a postal consumer uses only a service provided by the POC or a competitor serving that area. As in the transportation industry but not the telephone industry, the consumer, after repeal of the private express statutes, would likely have alternatives to the POCs for local delivery service in urban and rural areas. The POC might be quite large, perhaps encompassing entire states or more (see figure 8.1).

As a result of a Postal Service breakup into regional companies, carriage of mail from one point to another, like transportation of people from one place to another, might require the services of two companies and the clearinghouse, or if delivered directly, just two companies (see diagram 8.2). To make an interstate mail delivery, a consumer would use the local delivery service of either a POC or a competitor. His or her mail would then reach the facilities of the interstate delivery system of the Postal Service or one of its competitors. The Postal Service or one of its competitors would make the delivery to a delivery station in another POC. From that point, the POC or a competitor serving the area would make the delivery to the designated address. However, for postal deliveries between points in the same postal operating area, the POC might, at least in many instances in the beginning, be the only "intra-POC" carrier.

Consumers would purchase an entire "trip" from the POC or one of its competitors to which it would give letters, although several carriers might cooperate in a long-distance mail delivery. The price of mail delivery would then include the local delivery costs paid by the POC (or its competitor) to the other regional delivery firm operating in the geographical area of the mail's destination address. This is not very much different from many deliveries today. For instance, mail is collected by private contractors operating local post offices. It is handed over to the Postal System, which sorts and bags it for transportation. Interarea transportation is often provided by an independent contractor who delivers the mail to another local post office, where it can be delivered again by an independent contractor.

Judge Harold Greene commented on the effectiveness of the world's largest corporate divestiture policy solution.[23] He said, "There have been a few more problems than I expected—but none of them are of such magnitude that I have changed my mind about the breakup being in the public interest."[24] Greene said there has been some pretty fierce competition in long-distance service, which led to rate reductions. He also noted there has been a proliferation of new, sophisticated equipment, which he believes is only the beginning of things to come. As a final defense of divestiture he said, "We have to remember we're in the information age; it's the key service in our economy today, and telecommunications is the key component in the information revolution. I don't have any doubt that competition will give us more sophisticated, cheaper, more adaptable tools for the information age than would be produced in a regulated monopoly."

The financial strength of the local BOCs relative to AT&T surprised Judge Greene. He had believed that AT&T would have more difficulty adjusting. AT&T realized it was no longer a public utility and acquired marketing, advertising, and sales skills. To help the operating companies, Greene provided them with less bureaucracy, the lucrative Yellow Pages, the Bell logo, and the right to sell equipment. It might be prudent to provide the divested regional POCs with the same kind of packaging to aid their financial viability. To restructure the Postal System in this way, it would be desirable to balance the benefits between regions and other companies so as to enhance overall efficiency.

Having dealt with the different parts of the Postal Service over long years, the POCs might have the tendency to maintain those same relationships, especially if a postal service company provides a clearinghouse function between regional delivery companies. In fact, Greene was concerned lest the eight companies on paper start acting with the coordination of one. But this fear is proving groundless as the locals are increasingly exerting their independence. In the postal divestiture, one might have similar concerns. However, because each regional POC would be a separate profit center responsible to its board of directors and ultimately its shareholders, it would form relationships that would contribute to its profitability.

The repeal of the private express statutes should alleviate any concern over rising postal rates resembling the recent increases in local telephone rates associated with divestiture. In fact, Judge Greene sees no justification for these increases and believes that blaming the need for rate increases on divestiture, as some of the BOCs have done, is just an excuse. The access charges paid by the long-distance carriers to local companies have made up whatever shortfall the local companies experienced from elimination of the cross-subsidies between long-distance and local service. According to the judge, this is the only divestiture-related reason to increase rates.

In any case, competition in local delivery, which will take place immediately, should be enough to keep local delivery rates in line. In short, state Public Utilities Commissions (PUCs) would not need to regulate rates for local postal delivery service at all.[25]

Judge Greene has been preventing the BOCs, which are still monopolies, from diversifying into other lines of business with the capital they accumulate as a result of their provision of local telephone service. The problem is that if they squander the capital they earn through the provision of monopoly local telephone services on speculative business ventures, it is their customers who end up paying for it through regulated rate hikes. The BOCs, however, say they desire to diversify for protection from the imminent threat of bypass in their local areas from new technologies that will yield their monopolies less profits. Greene believes that the local monopolies have grossly exaggerated the imminent danger to their profitability. Would a similar concern be applicable to the postal industry? Probably not, because competition in local delivery after repeal of the private express statutes would make such a scenario unlikely.

Design for Privatization

Albert V. Casey, who became postmaster general in January 1986, appointed ten task forces to investigate and recommend changes to reduce costs and improve service. The groups were expected to report in the summer of 1986 and recommend a form of "privatization," but no information on their proposals was released. No one expects the groups to recommend general privatization, turning over the ownership and control of the Postal Service to the private sector, but only an extension of subcontracting services to private businesses. The USPS already contracts approximately 10,500 routes. The Heritage Foundation has recommended that the Postal Service subcontract to private businesses another 7,000 rural routes and small post offices. It is likely that the Postal Service recommendations will follow this line.[26]

Unfortunately, the probable change will not bring the long-awaited helpful effects to taxpayers or postal patrons. If handled properly, it will produce only short-term savings for the Postal Service. The next question is whether the savings will result in lower public subsidies, a reduction in tax concessions, or lower postage rates. Any of these changes are highly unlikely over a protracted period because there is no incentive for the Postal Service to pass along its savings to any of its constituencies. What is more likely is that the Postal Service will spend the savings for salary increases, subsidies for other inefficient operations (increased employment), or even graft or kickbacks.[27]

The key element in privatization is the transfer of ownership and control from the public to the private sector. For the sake of discussion, we can divide the act of privatizing into assessment of operational potential in the private sector, choice of disposal methods, identification of potential private purchasers and operators, and determination of the amount to be raised.[28]

Assessment of Operational Potential in Private Sector

An assessment of the operational potential of the Postal Service in the private sector should answer the following questions. First, is the Postal Service currently a profit-making or a loss-generating endeavor in the public sector? Second, would privatization generate greater profit-making potential for the Postal Service? Third, what is the profit potential of a privatized Postal Service?

The Postal Service is not at present a profit-making business, even with its nontax, monopoly status and the favorable borrowing rate it pays on the government-guaranteed bonds it issues. In defense of the Postal Service one could argue that the law restricts it from earning a profit. More important, the Postal Service also has no incentive to do so because it is not possible to appropriate the profit legally.[29] The incentive and motivational system within the Postal Service does not adequately reward employees and/or managers for improving the efficiency of their operations, if it rewards them at all.

There is tremendous opportunity for making profits in the Postal Service if it were privatized. Under current regulations, if revenues remained the same, costs could possibly be reduced by 50 percent. To do this, one could cut the current wage rates of postal workers by at least one-third without impeding the ability to staff positions, and save over one-third of labor costs because postal workers are overpaid by this amount. Because labor costs are over 85 percent of total costs, this alone would result in a cut in total costs of 28 percent. There is also plenty of room to cut labor costs through mechanization, reorganization of functions, liberalizing work rules, and introducing incentive systems into the wage and salary scales instead of the severe compression that exists in the scale now. A merit system rather than a seniority system would also provide more incentive for efficiency.

An inspection of the operations of UPS, Federal Express, or Roadway Package System (a parcel delivery company started by Roadway Services, Inc.) would suggest other strategies for cutting costs. UPS, a privately held company, had a profit of $567.6 million in 1985 on revenue of $7.69 billion.[30] The nation's largest package deliverer achieved its rank by paying close attention to detail and closely scrutinizing its 152,000 highly paid unionized employees through meticulous human engineering. The company's drivers are all Teamsters and earn $15 an hour. With overtime, many earn $35,000 to $40,000 per year. In return UPS seeks maximum output from them.

How does UPS achieve worker efficiency? More than 1,000 industrial engineers use time study techniques to set standards for many closely supervised tasks. For instance, drivers are instructed to walk to a customer's door at the brisk pace of three feet per second and to knock first lest seconds be lost searching for the doorbell. The operational procedures of UPS are continually tested in its markets by the dynamics of competition. It has successfully battled the Postal Service for its parcel delivery and is now entering the market for overnight delivery against Federal Express, which currently enjoys revenues of about $2.0 billion per year and an annual growth rate of between 25 and 40 percent. It will also face Purolator

Courier, Airborne Freight, Emery WorldWide Air Freight, and others in this market.

While UPS is challenging others in the overnight delivery market, UPS itself is being challenged in its own package delivery market by an upstart company called Roadway Services, Inc., with an entirely different mode of operation. Roadway cuts its labor expenses by using independent drivers who own their own trucks. Roadway increases productivity by reducing labor through automation. Its package hubs use bar codes, laser scanners, computers, and special mechanical devises to sort packages; UPS is still very labor intensive in these functions. Roadway, a very small regional company that operates only in the East, will lose about $14 million on revenues of $70 million. If it grows as expected, its financial picture could brighten considerably.

There are lessons that can be learned by assessing the activities of these competitive firms. For instance, UPS and Federal Express contract out very few of their operating activities. It is only in comparison with its current mode of operation as a rigid bureaucratic, publicly owned business that contracting out represents efficiency gains for the Postal Service. For a private profit-making business (as the Postal Service should become when privatized, divested, and deregulated), tightly controlled delivery cycles require the minute-to-minute coordination that is less possible with substantial contracting out.[31]

Federal Express and UPS both transport their mail through national hubs. UPS has its hub in Nashville, through which it routes its next-day air service and much of its second-day service. The Postal Service could use an air hub at an airport in Memphis, Nashville, St. Louis, or Athens, Ohio, to reship bulk lots of mail. It could then provide one- or two-day mail service between the approximately 560 postal sectional centers. There would be no sorting of individual letters at the hub except for bulk containers. All sorting would be confined to sending and receiving sectional centers. Where volumes warranted, mail might move directly between centers rather than through the hub.

There does not appear to be any reason that the Postal Service could not participate in the efficiency changes taking place within this industry except for the fact that it is not subject to the dynamics of competition. Repealing the private express statutes and privatizing the Postal Service would throw open the market for first class mail to all the innovative techniques being employed by firms in the mail transport industry and also free the Postal Service to participate and compete for other aspects of the message transmission business. Adoption of all the other cost-saving techniques, whether increased mechanization or the more efficient utilization of labor, should produce savings of at least another 22 percent to make total savings of approximately 50 percent.

The Postal Service is very inefficient now and still manages, in an occasional good year, not to operate at a deficit. Although it enjoys special benefits now, the Postal Service has remarkable promise to be profitable if privatized under the best arrangement, even when it loses its special benefits and competes in its market without the protection of the private express statutes. Of course, repealing the private express statutes is the critical consideration for assessing profit potential because it would permit any firm to compete with the privatized postal service for any aspect of its business.

The proposal in this book suggests divesting the Postal Service into five regional companies but does not constrain other private delivery companies to regional operations, nor should the divestiture be viewed necessarily as defining the industrial organization in perpetuity. After three to five years' experience, divestiture could be reviewed with a view to permitting some of the regional Postal Service companies to merge if they desire. The companies desiring to merge could be any combination of former Postal Service regional divisions and private companies. Competition, however, would eventually reduce the profit potential for the divested privatized postal service companies. The reorganization of resources caused by competition would increase efficiency.

Choice of Disposal Methods

The Postal Service could be privatized in several ways, including being divested into five regional companies, a service-clearinghouse company, and a bulk mail company. The parcel post now operates independently of the USPS's main postal service and so could be sold separately. The five regional POCs could be sold independently, and one at a time, by stock offerings. Blocks of stock might be sold to interested businesses, unions, employees, and the general public.

The experience in disposing of public enterprises in Canada and Great Britain was discussed in chapter 7. The Canadian experience was the best for insuring that the government would no longer be involved. It also transferred the value of the enterprises to the members of the public evenly. The government, however, was able to retain none of the value for itself. In the BCRIC experience this was not needed as a motivational factor to provide an incentive for implementing the privatization policy. If the political climate in the United States would tolerate this form of privatization, it would be most equitable.

In the United States, privatization at the national level has the possibility of being implemented, among other reasons, as a means whereby the federal government could raise revenues to reduce the deficit to stay within Gramm-Rudman targets. Using privatization for this purpose excludes following the Canadian experience and suggests that a variety of British privatization might be more appropriate. To succeed, it may be desirable to divorce the privatization process from Congress by placing responsibility for its devising in a separate corporation so details can be worked out and negotiated if necessary. The experience with Conrail has demonstrated that the delays caused by congressional involvement can reduce the value of the deal.[32]

In the sale of Conrail the Senate discussed such things as who would be the best guarantor of Conrail's financial strength and service and how it could be sold in a way that would maximize its chances of survival without further federal support. These are obviously not the right questions to be asking. When the government sells an enterprise, it should simply state that the new firm is on its own and has no prospect of receiving any special federal support. The best guarantee of a company's financial strength and service is the degree of competitiveness in the market it serves and its ability to adjust to changing market conditions, not the financial characteristics of its owners.

The question that should be asked is, how can we maximize the return from the sale of the enterprise so as to save taxpayers' resources? It can best be answered by a careful inspection of the technical and financial aspects of the privatization carried out by a corporation that is charged with the responsibility of conducting the privatization in the public interest.

The British government hired a financial adviser, N. M. Rothschild & Sons, Ltd., to help it privatize British Gas in the biggest share issue ever. The government sold 4.15 billion shares for $1.92 each to raise $7.96 billion. Between 40 and 64 percent of the shares are allocated to individuals in the United Kingdom, with the remainder going to U.K. institutions and foreign investors. As a special incentive, individual investors had the choice of accepting either vouchers for the payment of gas bills or one free bonus share for every ten purchased, provided they are held for three years. Share prices immediately rose 30 percent when they began trading.[33] Similar specifics could be worked out for a sale of Postal Service stock to the public by a corporation charged with the responsibility of privatizing the Postal Service.

Identification of Potential Private Purchasers and Operators

It might be advisable to form a government corporation called the U.S. Postal Investment Corporation (USPIC), like the British Columbia Resources Investment Corporation (BCRIC) in Canada, to handle the privatization. Before selling stock, USPIC would appoint temporary boards of directors for each of the divested companies. After the stock is sold, large stockholders would nominate regular directors and all stockholders would elect them. The board is then responsible for hiring and firing top management, which in turn is responsible for operating the company.

Who might the purchasers be? The possibilities include (a) parties who currently have an interest in the existing operation either as contractors, or employees or employee unions; (b) pre-identified private sector corporations or individuals with whom acquisition would be a matter of negotiation; (c) private individuals, companies, or corporations who might make a tender offer or bid at auction; and (d) the investing public through an issue of stock. USPS might employ one or more investment bankers to solicit bids for large blocks of stocks.

The British have structured their public offering of shares to give preference to individual British investors. They have desired to have the shares distributed as widely as possible so as to bring more individuals into the ownership of large companies. They have also given incentives for stockholders in Britain to hold their shares for a few years. In pricing they have aimed at prices 20 to 30 percent below the initial trading price so purchasers will know they have received value for their payment. They have used the increase in value to make shares available in differing amounts to employees, managers, and so forth, so as to buy their cooperation in the privatization. Subject to these qualifications, they have still tried to maximize the revenue the government raises for itself from the stock offering so as to decrease the financial pressures on the national treasury.

Determination of Amount to Be Raised

Where the price of the postal company is a matter of negotiation or bid at auction, the answer is obvious. The highest bidder will determine the price. If USPIC sells the postal company to the general public, investment bankers can undertake an underwriting or aid USPIC on a best-efforts basis. If the stock issue is sold by an underwriting, investment bankers will bid for the right to be underwriters. Included in the bid will be the price they guarantee for the entire block of shares and the amount they receive as a fee for the service. In this case the price for the company will be the highest competitive bid among the underwriters. If the divested companies issue shares and "go public" one at a time, the reception of the first issue would guide underwriters as they bid for subsequent issues for the remaining companies.

It is critical for USPIC to evaluate the price of the company before the sale, where investment bankers sell the stock issue on a best-efforts basis. In this case USPIC after consultation with investment bankers determines the price and number of shares. Investment bankers do not guarantee the results of the sale, as they would if they operated as underwriters. The bankers sell the issue on a best-efforts basis for a commission that is less than the commission plus fee for an underwriting. The government bears the risk for pricing the issue correctly and ends up with the shares not sold. The difference between best efforts and underwriting is who bears the risk for insuring the proceeds from the stock sale. In the first case it is USPIC; in the second it is the lead underwriter.

How does one determine the amount of proceeds that USPIC can realistically expect to realize through privatization? The earnings potential would be an important consideration that will limit the upper bound of what the government can hope to get for the Postal Service. As a lower bound it is important to know the liquidation value of the Postal Service's assets. This can be estimated by examining the balance sheet for the USPS, which evaluates the Postal Service's assets at market value.

The U.S. Postal Service balance sheet, as of September 30, 1986, is summarized by table 8.1.[34] The balance sheet lists the assets, liabilities, and net worth. The total assets include current assets and fixed assets. Current assets are cash, government securities, and receivables. Fixed assets are tangible, relatively long term, and used in the delivery of mail; they include land, buildings, machinery, equipment, and vehicles. Fixed assets are usually valued on the balance sheet at historical cost, although their replacement value, if not their market value, can be several times such valuation. For the downtown locations of post offices purchased many years ago, the understatement of value is greatest. Government accounting procedures do not necessarily identify realistic current values of these assets. The value of postal assets listed here does not include such intangibles as monopoly status, earnings potential, or goodwill.

Before privatization Postal Service property and assets should be inventoried completely and evaluated at market prices. The inventory list should include all property owned by the Postal Service, such as land, buildings, service locations, leasehold property, easement options, mineral reserves, water, and forestry land and timber; operational property such as power stations, warehouses, machinery, mobile equipment, rolling stock, fixtures, and fittings; and nonoperational properties, including investments and pension funds. In the balance sheet of the Postal Service for September 30, 1986, the USPS reported only $362 million for net worth. But the real estate (land and buildings), which is evaluated at an original cost of $5.37 billion, is in all probability worth several times this amount, even after the deduction of depreciation. A proper inventory study would evaluate the

TABLE 8.1
United States Postal Service Balance Sheet
September 30, 1986 (Dollars in Millions)

Assets	Reported	Modifications	Amended
Cash	$ 129	$	$ 129
Government securities	3,823		3,823
Receivables, net	543		543
Supplies, advances and prepayments	164		164
Total current assets	4,659		4,659
Other Assets	19		19
Fixed Assets at Cost:			
Land	687	1,200	1,200
Buildings	4,683	8,500	8,500
Equipment	2,993		2,993
Less allowances for depreciation	(2,774)		(2,774)
Net real estate, eqpt.	5,589		9,919
Construction in progress	1,360	750	750
Leasehold improvements, net	145		145
Net fixed assets	7,094		10,814
Deferred retirement costs	18,043		18,043
TOTAL ASSETS	$29,815		$33,535
Liabilities and net worth			
Current liabilities	4,847		4,847
Long-term debt, non-current portion	3,093		3,093
Other liabilities			
Retirement benefits	17,630	8,500	8,500
Employees' accum. leave	815		815
Workers' comp. claims	3,048		3,048
Other	20		20
Total other liabilities	21,513		12,383
Total liabilities	29,452		20,323
Net worth	362		13,212
TOTAL LIABILITIES AND NET WORTH	$29,815		$33,535

Source: *Annual Report of the Postmaster General 1986*, pp. 14-15.

assets in this category at market value. For the present, however, it is reasonable to increase the value of land and buildings by a factor of slightly less than two.

In the liabilities section of the balance sheet, all but $3.235 billion of the Postal Service's liabilities is *interest-free*. (The Postal Service must pay interest on $3.093 billion of long-term debt and a small portion of its current liabilities, namely, the current portion of its long-term debt of $142 million.) This, of course, frees the Postal Service to pursue other objectives besides servicing its debt and other liabilities. The current liabilities that do not require debt service are outstanding postal money orders ($361 million), compensation and employee benefits ($1.77 billion), amounts payable to other U.S. government agencies ($106 million), other accounts payable and accrued expenses ($836 million), deferred revenue ($614 million), and estimated prepaid postage ($1.02 billion). These current liabilities represent an attractive, below-cost way of financing postal activities. The other liabilities, which cover employee retirement, leave, and workers' compensation benefits, amount to $21.5 billion and also do not require debt servicing.

Although at this stage of planning it is not possible to put firm numbers on this privatization restructuring, I have nevertheless constructed a sample Financing Structure for Postal Privatization in table 8.2. The table shows under "Uses of Funds" and "Sources of Funds" how USPIC would raise and spend dollars if the entire Postal Service were privatized as a single business entity. Before privatization USPIC should conduct an inventory and asset valuation study for each of the divested companies. Table 8.2 is viewed as a sample planning document for USPIC, the corporation that handles the privatization. From the "Uses of Funds," we begin with the total assets at current value, namely $33.535 billion. To allow for the effects of the repeal of the private express statutes on profitability, we discount the price by $10 billion. After this decrease, the value of the operations is still $23.54 billion. All liabilities ($20.32 billion from amended column of table 8.1) with the exception of $3.235 billion of federal financing add up to $17.09 billion. These are subtracted from the $23.54 billion to arrive at the $6.45 billion purchase price. The success of a stock offering will be the final arbiter, but it is my opinion that there is so much room left for efficiency changes that the postal business can be made immensely profitable even under repeal of the private express statutes.

We add to this $6.45 billion purchase price another $4 billion, which is the estimated amount it would take to bring about the needed changes in equipment and structure involved in privatization. Severance and contract termination costs of $750 million are also added in to arrive at $11.20 billion.

TABLE 8.2
Financing Structure for Postal Privatization
(dollars in millions)

Uses of Funds:	
Purchase of assets at current value, based on amended balance sheet restated as of 9-30-86	$33,535
Purchase price discount (assumed)	10,000
Less assumption of all liabilities except $3.235 billion of federal financing (probably not assumable)	17,088
Net purchase price of operating assets	6,447
Prospective capital outlays, funded by the privatization transaction, to begin operating as a private business	4,000
Severance and contract termination costs	750
Total uses of funds	11,197
Sources of Funds:	
Proceeds from liquidation of excess fixed assets	3,000
Sale of stock to USPS employees and to a postal ESOP (assumed to average $3,000 per employee)	2,250
Sale of stock and debt to institutions and to the general public	5,947
Total sources of funds	$11,197

Source: Table 8.1, U.S. Postal Service Balance Sheet.

There is a need for funds of $11.20 billion. Selling excess fixed assets unneeded in the private operation of the Postal Service Companies would yield about $3.0 billion. This figure would include all bulk mail handling centers involved in parcel post delivery. USPS employees and the Postal Employees Stock Ownership Plan (ESOP) might purchase stock at a discount, if this is necessary to insure their cooperation and provide them an incentive to work constructively and efficiently. USPIC would raise $2.25 billion from this source if, on the average, each employee purchases $3,000 worth of stock. USPIC will sell the remaining stock and possibly the debt, valued at $5.947 billion, to the public. These figures are very tentative but represent a model for discussing the issues involved in privatizing the Postal Service.[35]

Recommendations and Proposals

The Postal Service is a bureaucracy that no one controls. It pays its employees whatever it wills and piles up debt without effective limit. In the search for a source of discipline for the Postal Service, Congress gave up trying to handle wages and rate-making in the reorganization; the PRC has failed because it lacks any real power; the courts have failed because they cannot make business decisions. Repeal of the private express statutes is the market solution. Unless Congress commits utter folly by placing electronic transfers under the statutes, market forces constitute the only viable alternative left.

Home computers with print capability connected by telephone can divert first class mail. Consumers will pay more of their bills with computers connected by telecommunications. It is only a matter of time before increasing postal rates and the widespread availability of lower-cost technological alternatives diverts enough first class business from the Postal Service to make it an anachronism. Barring a reversal of this process, which is not currently on the horizon, the public will escape from the Postal Service problem, but the cost will be the demise of the Postal Service. In this book I have outlined a divestiture alternative that gives a privatized and deregulated Postal Service a future and a hope.

It will take positive constructive policy to turn this situation around and give the Postal Service a chance. Instead of waiting for the situation to worsen, events to overtake us, and much folly to be perpetrated, Congress should take a series of actions that will lead to the repeal of the private express statutes, divestiture, and privatization of the Postal Service. The following five steps toward privatization and competition should be considered:

1. Create a new corporation, the United States Postal Investment Corporation (USPIC), to conduct the divestiture, privatization, and deregulation. It would have supervisory authority over both the PRC and the USPS.

USPIC would organize the USPS into seven or more separate units, assign assets and personnel, and appoint management and a temporary board of directors. It could sell the parcel post business and other assets as soon as possible. USPIC would negotiate with investment bankers and schedule stock and bond distribution for the divested companies.

2. USPIC, under authority from Congress, should curtail certain rights and privileges that the Postal Service enjoys because it is a government-owned corporation, which include the following:
   • Eliminate the Postal Service's right to borrow through the Treasury.

Up to the present the Postal Service has borrowed in excess of $5 billion through the Treasury.[36] This represents liabilities to the U.S. taxpayers. USPIC should immediately cut off this source of funds to make the discipline effective, to protect taxpayers, and to put potential lenders on notice that the U.S. Treasury does not guarantee Postal Service debt instruments.

- Eliminate the Postal Service's right of eminent domain.

This is an antiquated right that does not belong to private business, and should not belong to the Postal Service. USPIC should end it immediately.[37]

- Phase out congressional appropriations. Congress presumably remunerates the Postal Service only for services that it gives. As I suggested in chapter 3, the government should contract with someone else to provide these services if it desires to continue them and cease all financial payments to the Postal Service. USPIC should supervise the contracts with Congress for the Postal Service, phase them out, and supervise a cessation of the services provided by the Postal Service under the terms of the contracts.
- Phase in taxes at all levels. Each of the POCs should begin calculating the tax consequences of its actions so it can organize its activities in the way that would benefit it most. Each of the POCs should become cognizant of, and begin paying, taxes at all levels as soon as practicable.
3. USPIC could initiate internal business policies with the Postal Service in preparation for privatization and deregulation, such as the following:
   - Prohibit the Postal Service's entrance into electronic transfers until after privatization. Extending the postal monopoly over electronic transfers would be disastrous for the communications business. Allowing the Postal Service to subsidize electronic transfers would slow down the growth of legitimate cost-efficient firms. Prohibiting the Postal Service from subsidizing electronic transfers while allowing it to provide the service would be impossible to monitor and discipline adequately under present circumstances. After complete restructuring, the POCs could compete on the same basis as any other business.
   - Encourage the provision of auxiliary services to other communications companies, such as extending the presort program.
   - Cease entering into new contracts for services with private companies. Rewrite existing contracts in terms applicable to POCs for short terms only.

At present the Postal Service contracts with private carriers to transport mail, with entrepreneurs to run postal stations, and with star carriers to deliver mail. Contracting out is an efficient policy, but only when compared to internal bureaucratic operations. Compared to all the alternatives open to a private POC, it is not an efficient policy alternative. POCs should have maximum freedom for making contracts and organizing their affairs internally.

- Allow the POCs to accumulate surpluses and profits if any. This is necessary to prepare the POCs to operate competitively in the private sector.
4. Repeal the private express statutes. This is the most important discipline to the efficient operation of the Postal Service, whether privately or publicly owned, and must be the hallmark of postal policy changes. Congress should repeal the statutes. Barring that, the Postal Service could suspend the statutes.
5. Privatize the Postal Service and eliminate the PRC. USPIC would be responsible for constructing a detailed plan and timetable for the sequence of operations involved in this policy. Some steps in this process have been suggested in this book.

Where to from Here?

In 1980 the communications equipment industry spent 5.2 percent of its net sales on research and development; the office, computing, and accounting machines industry spent 10 percent. In 1981, the Postal Service spent 0.1 percent of its total sales on research and development (see table 8.3). The research and development program of the Postal Service lacks support of top management, adequate funding, and competent scientists and engineers. Under the present organizational structure this may not be a bad strategy because it does not put public money at risk.[38] But the defect places the Postal Service at a substantial disadvantage in its ability to adapt to changing circumstances and should be corrected by the postal policy of divestiture, privatization, and deregulation.

Concerning the Postal Service's entrance into electronic communications, William Bolger said, "This thing will never be clarified until the Act of 1934 is updated and the role of the Postal Service is made clear. We will not make major investments until public policy has been pronounced."[39] For years there have been various bills to update the Communications Act of 1934 and set policy for new communications services. Most have concentrated on deregulating the industry, with particular emphasis on restructuring AT&T so other companies might compete with it and vice versa. Now that Judge Greene has clarified this, Congress could give the same attention to the postal industry, and it could culminate in an equally helpful arrangement. Why not start in the same place and in the same manner with the Postal Service? Judge Greene, in a suit brought by the

TABLE 8.3
Spending on Research and Development

Year	Industry	Percentage of Total Sales
1980	Communications equipment	5.2
1980	Office computing and accounting machines	10.0
1985	IBM	3.8
	AT&T	3.9
	ITT	9.1
	General Electric	3.8
	Eastman Kodak	9.2
	Digital Equipment	10.7
	3M	6.5
	Sperry	8.8
	Honeywell	6.8
1981	Postal Service	0.1

Source: Kathleen Conkey, *The Postal Precipice, Can the U.S. Postal Service Be Saved?* (Washington, D.C.: Center for the Study of Responsive Laws, 1983), pp. 385-86; *Wall Street Journal*, November 10, 1986, p. 5D.

Justice Department, took the initiative to handle the many details of restructuring. He could do the same for the Postal Service.

Suits are not new to government departments. The Department of Commerce and the Department of Justice jointly filed a statement before the PRC saying the Postal Service should not offer E-COM. The Justice Department then sued the Postal Service to keep it out of E-COM. Congressman Charles Wilson (D-Calif.) offered a unique explanation for the USPS delay in entering electronic communications during hearings before the House subcommittee. He said, "Actually, up until the time Mr. Bolger became Postmaster General, many of us feared that there was an ulterior motive afoot amongst his predecessors to destroy the system so that AT&T could take it over."[40]

By refusing to offer the Postal Service real direction in electronic mail, Congress has pushed the USPS further behind its competitors. The problem is reminiscent of the early history of the telegraph, when several postmasters general urged government control of the new technology and Congress failed to respond. Control quickly slipped away until it was too late for Congress to act. The telecommunications industry is counting on a repeat performance. This is the time for Congress to act and straighten out the market for postal service.

The urgency of the problem has been highlighted by union leader James J. LaPenta, who said that policymakers ought to focus on "what kind of transition are you going to have as this country enters into the electronic age? There's got to be an orderly transition. . . . The nation's third largest work force with 650,000 workers is going to be affected. The impact of 650,000 workers out of a job in a matter of years is a problem that has to be faced."[41]

Daniel Oliver, chairman of the Federal Trade Commission, says the Postal Service is an inefficient federal monopoly and should end.[42] To bring this about, the Private Express Statutes, which are the barrier to the entry of competitors, should be repealed. The statutes give the Postal Service the legal right to shut down competing first class letter delivery services, which it has done repeatedly to preserve its revenues. The objective of repealing the statutes is to increase the liberty of U.S. citizens to enter the business of delivering first class mail, and to use competing mail delivery services.

In addition, the Postal Service should be divided (in the manner of American Telephone & Telegraph Company) into five regional operating companies, a parcel post company, and a support services clearinghouse company. One large company would have the same influence as AT&T did before its breakup; smaller regional firms would be more conducive to effective competition.

The seven companies should be sold independently and one at a time through stock offerings. Blocks of stock might be sold to interested businesses, employees, and the general public. Stock should be sold to postal employees at a 15 to 20 percent discount to encourage their support of privatization. Sales of stock to employees of Great Britain's National Freight Company and British Telecommunications illustrate the benefit of this approach in gaining public support for privatization.

Diversification, say, in telecommunications or any other type of business that the Postal Service cannot now enter, should become possible for all the privatized companies. It represents the best insurance for the survival of the institution and the preservation of jobs. Under privatization, management will have freedom to pursue other profitable endeavors, and unions will receive the freedom to strike. In response to residents of rural areas who fear that they may suffer cutbacks in service or large increases in rates, Rep. Philip Crane (R-Ill.) points out, "The Postal Service already employs 4,800 private contractors to deliver mail in rural areas. These private carriers save up to two-thirds the usual delivery costs and still make a profit."[43]

In the change to a privatized, divested, and deregulated postal system what will happen to the symbolic elements of a national postal service? Could some of these elements be preserved in a denationalized environment? Such things as the name, eagle, other logos, slogans, and history could be passed on to the clearinghouse, bulk mail company, and regional companies. In this way the divested and privatized companies would retain some of their previous identity in the breakup along with their labor forces, management, equipment, and facilities. These symbols of affiliation might be an aid to them in their competition with emerging private delivery companies. In this way some of the traditions of the Post Office/Postal Service would continue. There is no guarantee that a document delivery service system such as the postal system we know will be needed in the twenty-first century.[44] For this reason, the privatized companies should be free to change their functions and services as market conditions and technology warrant.

Preston R. Tisch, a former Mondale supporter who served as postmaster general from August 1986 to spring 1988, indicated recently in a letter to FTC chairman Dan Oliver that he is wedded to the outworn and discredited concept of raising the Postal Service up by its bootstraps through "better management." He asserts that allowing private companies to compete against the Postal Service "will not stir us to do any better."[45] History has shown that management techniques and strong leadership at best have only a slight transitory effect while competition produces real and beneficial changes. Let's give competition a chance.

Notes

1. The commission can use sec. 3642(c)(2) to extract information not provided by the USPS. It has done this (in Docket MC78-1) and been upheld on court review. In addition, sec. 3642(b) empowers the PRC to make rules "for . . . (3) discovery both from the Postal Service and the parties to the proceedings." This it has also done. See also 39 CFR sec. 3001.28, 3001.54(s), 3001.56, 3001.64(i), and 3001.66.

   The USPS's unwillingness to make its data available to others has prevented a thorough examination of the efficiency of postal operations. A Department of Justice report declared, "There is no credible and reliable evidence at hand that would permit public policy makers to reach an informed judgment regarding the need, if any, to retain the private express statutes." See United States Department of Justice, *Changing the Private Express Laws* (1977), p. 27. Even the PRC has difficulty getting relevant data from the USPS. See Postal Rate Commission, Docket R80-1, Appendices to Opinion and Recommended Decision, vol. 2, February 19, 1981, Appendix E, pp. 1-5. The unavailability of data has not been limited to prices alone. The PRC said, "The USPS had clearly and consistently refused to provide the Commission any information on any substantive issue in the remanded ECOM docket." See *United States of America* vs. *United States Postal Service*, December 30, 1981, p. 9.

   Commissioner John W. Crutcher's experience inclines him to believe that the data we all get from the Postal Service "is usually of more interest for historical purpose than any other" (private correspondence).

2. The statute empowers the PRC to set rates to enable the Postal Service to break even "under honest, efficient, and economical management" (39 U.S.C. sec. 3521). Thus the PRC may not recommend, nor the governors adopt, rates reflecting management choices not meeting the quoted standard. The PRC may

and does question management choices. For example, see PRC MC78-3 (1979); management's design for the E-COM system was revised based on the evidence adduced at PRC hearings. Given the fate of E-COM, the revisions were obviously insufficient.

3. 39 U.S.C., sec. 3625(d) reads: "... with the unanimous written concurrence of all of the Governors then holding office, the Governors may modify any such further recommended decision ... if the Governors expressly find that (1) such modification is in accord with the record and the policies of this chapter, and (2) the rates recommended by the Commission are not adequate to provide sufficient total revenues so that total estimated income and appropriations will equal as nearly as practicable estimated total costs."

Dissatisfied parties are permitted to take the Postal Service governors to court. In *Time Inc., v. U.S. Postal Service*, 685 S.F. 2d 760 (2d Civ. 1982), the court made it plain that the governors' modification authority depends entirely on their responsibility for overall break-even, and that the specific rates recommended by the commission are not modifiable on other grounds. Because the Postal Service has continued to receive rate increases while being grossly inefficient, rates have been set to enable the Postal Service to break even, but not under efficient and economical management.

4. Kathleen Conkey, *The Postal Precipice: Can the U.S. Postal Service Be Saved?* (Washington, D.C.: Center for the Study of Responsive Law, 1983), pp. 149-50.

5. Ibid., p. 265.

6. Ibid., p. 264.

7. Ibid., pp. 48-49; House, *Post Office Reorganization*, pt. 1, pp. 5-8.

8. A democracy requires the losers in an election to go along with the winners, but the market allows everyone to vote with his or her dollars for whatever goods and services he or she desires. It metes out to all according to the number of dollar votes cast. In this respect it is much more efficient than a democracy in distributing to individuals according to what they desire, subject, of course, to their budget constraints.

9. Roger B. Noll and Bruce M. Owen, eds., *The Political Economy of Deregulation. Interest Groups in the Regulatory Process* (Washington, D.C.: American Enterprise Institute, 1983), preface and p. 161.

10. Milton and Rose Friedman, *Free to Choose* (New York: Harcourt Brace Jovanovich, 1980), pp. 288, 294.

11. It might be suggested that early predatory pricing supported by the deep pockets of a gigantic unregulated Postal Service could kill off competition before it blooms. This possibility is one reason that it might make sense to divest the Postal Service into smaller companies. This organizational development would make it easier for companies to compete for a part of the postal business without having to take on a Postal Service everywhere at once.

12. In 1984 Federal Express began an electronic document delivery service called ZapMail, which could transmit a brief from New York to Phoenix in just seconds. The plan looked good on paper. Federal Express figured that satellite transmission would supplant air travel as the document delivery service of choice, especially to remote locations. Customers were not drawn by a $35- or even a $25-per-transmission charge. Frequent faulty transmissions due to technical problems did not help matters, either. Anxious to protect its image in competition with other carriers and to cut its losses, Federal Express terminated ZapMail in October 1986. It is too early to know why the attempt by

Federal Express to offer electronic mail failed. Some believe Federal Express was impatient in terminating service too early. Perhaps the service will take a different organizational form. At any rate, this service will not automatically replace document delivery. See John J. Keller and John W. Wilson, "Why ZapMail Finally Got Zapped," *Business Week*, October 13, 1986, pp. 48-49.

13. In an opinion in a postal rate case, former postal rate commissioner A. Lee Fritschler states that a large pool of monopoly revenues could easily be used by the Postal Service to compete unfairly with private enterprise, and he believed the PRC's most important responsibility was to prevent this. See Joint Economic Committee, Economic Goals and Intergovernmental Policy Subcommittee, *The Future of Mail Delivery in the United States*, 97th Cong., 2d sess., June 18, 21, 1982, p. 213.

The Postal Reorganization Act states, "... the temptation to resolve the financial problems of the Post Office by charging the lion's share of all operational costs to first class is strong: that's where the big money is." See Senate Committee on Post Office and Civil Service, *Postal Reorganization*, June 3, 1970, S. Rept. 91-912. p. 13.

14. Joel L. Fleishman, ed., *The Future of the Postal Service* (New York: Praeger, with the Aspen Institute for Humanistic Studies, 1983), p. 214.

15. U.S. Congress, House of Representatives, *Committee on Post Office and Civil Service*, U.S. House Subcommittee on Postal Personnel and Modernization, *The Postal Act of 1979*, 96th Cong., 1st sess., 1979, pp. 80-82 March 31, 1979. See Fleishman, *The Future of the Postal Service*, p. 53.

16. From the appendix, it should be noted that population growth is the most important factor affecting the demand for first class mail. Population growth might keep up the demand for first class mail even in the face of other factors that tend to reduce demand and increases in postal rates that reduce quantity demanded.

17. Joint Economic Committee, Economic Goals and Intergovernmental Policy Subcommittee, *The Future of Mail Delivery in the United States*, pp. 294-97.

18. The Post Office in Britain is being split into separate functional units and the letter services formed into regional units to ease in privatization.

19. See "Privatizing the Savings," *State Factor* (American Legislative Exchange Council) 12 (January 1986): 5.

20. Just because the Canadian postal workers (who work for the crown corporation, Canada Post) have been allowed to strike and wreak havoc with the delivery of written communications, this is no indication of how things would develop in the privatized U.S. postal system when the "no-strike" proviso is abolished. What makes the Canadian postal delivery intolerable is not the right to strike but the fact that Canada Post, a government-owned and -operated business, still retains a monopoly on the delivery of first class mail. If this barrier to entry were abolished, the right to strike would not paralyze the Canadian document delivery service either. For a discussion of the effect of union strike activity on productivity at Canada Post under the "exclusive privilege" of delivering first class mail see L. M. Read," Canada Post: A Case Study in the Correlation of Collective Will and Productivity" in *Research on Productivity of Relevance to Canada*, Donald J. Daly, ed. (Ottawa: Social Science Federation of Canada, 1983).

21. Postal Services Act of 1979, p. 117.

22. The multiline OCR is allegedly capable of reading an ordinary address and

comparing it with a data file in order to impose the correct bar code. This machine, if reliable, could make the nine-digit ZIP code superfluous.

23. In addition to presiding over the AT&T case, Judge Greene quite coincidentally was the judge in the 1981 case in which 13,000 government-employed air traffic controllers lost their jobs in an ill-fated strike. See Robb Deigh, "The Tough Judge Who Rules America's Phone Companies," *Insight*, September 15, 1985, p. 15.

24. Christine Winter, "A Ringing Defense of the AT&T Break-up," *Chicago Tribune*, October 28, 1984, sec. 7, pp. 1, 5.

25. The dual character of regulation in telephone and transportation (i.e. state versus federal or intrastate versus interstate) stems from the Constitution (Art. I, sec. 8, cl. 3), allowing Congress to "regulate Commerce . . . among the several states." The United States, however, may not regulate commerce that is wholly within a state, and a state may not regulate or unduly burden interstate commerce.

   By contrast, the clause permitting the Post Office "to establish Post Offices and post roads" is exclusive (Art I, sec. 8, cl. 7). The states cannot set up postal systems nor regulate that of the United States (*Ex parte Jackson* 96 U.S. 727, 1878; *United States* v. *Maxwell*, 137 F. Supp. 298, W.D. Mo. 1955, affirmed, 235 F. 2d 930, 8th Cir., certiorari denied, 352 U.S. 943, 1956).

   The privatized, divested, and deregulated postal system advocated in this study is still a system of "post offices and post roads" in the constitutional sense, even though private firms handle all of its business. The postal system would then be still a purely federal creation. If any regulation were to exist with respect to rates or quality of service, such regulation must be by a federal agency. It would then not be necessary to rely on competition to exclude the need for state PUC regulation; such activity would simply be unconstitutional.

   The alternative, which in my opinion is much less attractive, is for private postal businesses to be thought of as "nonpostal" in character, so that they do not form part of an establishment of "post offices and post roads." In this case, to the extent that business activity was technically intrastate, it would be subject to state regulation regardless of Congress's intention in changing the postal statutes. If private postal businesses are permitted to exist and for constitutional purposes come under the commerce clause rather than the post office clause, Congress cannot forbid the states to exercise their regulatory powers over them. The Supreme Court has treated many activities as interstate when the interstate impact was only marginal. For instance, even hotel lodging is treated as an interstate activity. Given this precedent, there is little that Congress cannot do if it wants to. (Clarification on the legal points in this footnote, as in many others, has been suggested by David Stover, chief counsel to the Postal Rate Commission. All opinions expressed, however, are my responsibility.)

26. Les Winke, "If Postal Service Gets 'Privatized,' What Will It Mean for Collectors?" *Chicago Tribune*, April 20, 1986, sec. 13, p. 37.

27. For instance, Peter Voss, a former governor of the Postal Service, pleaded guilty May 30, 1986, to accepting more than $20,000 in illegal payments from a Michigan-based public relations firm as part of a plan to steer $250 million worth of agency contracts to a Dallas-based manufacturer, Recognition Equipment, Inc. (REI). Former postmaster general Paul Carlin said in an affidavit that, beginning in January 1985, he was pressured by Voss and another postal

board governor, Ruth Peters, to make decisions favoring REI. Three forn senior agency officials were convicted earlier this year for participation in multimillion-dollar kickback and bribery scheme. Last April the governoi limited the independent Postal Inspection Service's access to tapes of closec board meetings that were and are still needed to probe the Voss scandal.

The Postal Inspection Service is also investigating possible insider trading in the stock of REI, the bidder for the mail-sorting equipment contracts. A surge in REI stock trading occurred immediately after the closed meetings of the Postal Service Board of Governors, where policy changes enhancing REI's chances of landing a lucrative contract were discussed. For example, on December 2, 1985, the day of the meeting, 19,600 shares were traded on the New York Stock Exchange, with a closing price of $12.375; on December 3 and 4, there were 111,000 and 234,600 shares, respectively, traded with a closing price on December 4 of $13.625. The day after the closed January 6 meeting, in which the board, acting on the recommendation of Voss and another governor, decided to replace Carlin with Albert V. Casey, trading of REI was 251,900 shares, with the price closing at $15.125.

A federal judge denied Carlin's request for a temporary order to stop the appointment of a new postmaster general. House Post Office Committee Chairman, William Ford (D-Mich.), suggested that the board defer a decision on a successor to Casey until the investigation of the scandal was completed; this was not done.

See Jeanne Saddler, "Postal Official Was Asked to Quit Post as Agency Tried to Deal with Scandal," *Wall Street Journal*, June 27, 1986, p. 12; Jeanne Saddler, "Ex-Postal Chief Sues Service To Get Job Back," ibid., July 1, 1986, p. 19. Bruce Ingersoll, "Postal Unit Probes Trading Activity of Firm's Stock," ibid., July 3, 1986, p. 34.

When Casey became postmaster general, he gave his old friend and Harvard Business School classmate, John T. Garrity, a no-bid contract for $900 per day to advise the Postal Service on a major reorganization, under which he was paid $156,000 over the next seven and a half months. As if this was not enough, in November 1986 Casey gave him another no-bid contract to evaluate the recommendations he made under the first contract. Up to the middle of May 1987 Garrity had received $117,000 under this contract. The current postmaster general, Preston R. Tisch, continues Garrity's $900 rate even if he works as little as one hour a day.

Senator David H. Pryor (D-Ark.), chairman of a Senate Governmental Affairs subcommittee, asked Tisch to cancel Garrity's contract. Pryor said it was "bad enough" for Garrity to be paid $156,000 in salary and $14,000 in expenses for work that was actually done by a dozen or so senior postal officials, but that it bordered "on the outrageous" for Garrity to be rehired so he can "pat himself on the back" for his earlier recommendations. See Howard Kurtz, "At USPS, a $900-a-day Consultant," *Washington Post*, May 13, 1987, p. A21.

28. The organizational breakdown for privatization used in this section was suggested to me by Lynn Scarlett of the Reason Foundation, who took it from an issue paper published by SYNCOM, a South African private-sector public policy research organization.

29. The Postal Service cannot pay profits to stockholders, and it is postal policy specified in the reorganization act not to earn a surplus. In the days of the old Post Office Department, whenever surpluses were earned, they were "con-

fiscated" in the form of lowered subsidies or lowered rates. The goal of the Postal Service is only to break even and perhaps retain a small contingency fund. A contingency fund of $537 million was authorized in a postal-rate case. See U.S. Postal Rate Commission, *Opinion and Recommended Decision: Postal Rate and Fee Increases*, Docket No. R76-1 (1975), p. 51. See also Douglas K. Adie, *An Evaluation of Postal Service Wage Rates* (Washington, D.C.: American Enterprise Institute, 1977), p. 8.

30. See Daniel Machalaba, "United Parcel Service Gets Deliveries Done by Driving Its Workers," *Wall Street Journal*, April 22, 1986, p. 1.

31. Bert Ely, "*Privatizing the Postal Service—How To Do It*" (Alexandria, Va.: Ely and Co., February 26, 1986), p. 13.

32. In 1983 the Department of Transportation and its investment adviser sought potential buyers for Conrail as a unit. It was late spring of 1984 before a serious bidder could be found. In February 1985, Secretary Elizabeth Dole recommended Norfolk Southern because it could best guarantee Conrail's financial strength and service. Twelve months after Dole's recommendation, the Senate passed legislation mandating the sale to Norfolk Southern. Eighteen months after the recommendation, Norfolk withdrew its bid, although Conrail was later privatized through a stock offering.

33. Ann Monroe, "British Gas Underwriters Use Incentive Plan to Lure U.S. Investors and Fight 'Flowback,'" *Wall Street Journal*, December 26, 1986, p. 25.

34. The following analysis of the Postal balance sheet was suggested in Ely, "Privatizing the Postal Service—How To Do It."

35. In an exchange with Thomas Gale Moore, a member of the president's Council of Economic Advisers, in testimony before the President's Commission on Privatization, January 28, 1988, I estimated that the sale of the Postal Service could conservatively raise $15 billion. Moore believed the figure would be closer to $30 billion.

36. The Postal Service borrowed $1 billion in fiscal year 1985 and has indicated that it intends to continue to borrow the same amount on a yearly basis over a five-year period.

37. Although some private businesses performing public utility functions, such as natural gas companies holding FERC certificates and hydroelectric companies licensed under the Federal Power Act, still have this right, this does not justify the Postal Service's retention of eminent domain. Perhaps it is time to question the necessity and potential misuse of power it represents in all private uses. See, for example, 15 U.S.C., sec. 717f(h) for natural gas companies holding FERC certificates and 16 U.S.C., sec. 814 for hydroelectric licensees under Federal Power Act. Also see 26 Am. Jur. 2d, Eminent Domain, sec. 20.

38. The Postal Service has had a uniformly poor record in innovating. It is doubtful whether its operations can be made substantially more efficient on an overall basis with any innovations. If some phase of the business is made more efficient through innovation or private contracting, the tendency is to "waste" the savings elsewhere in higher wages and salaries or reduced performance pressure. Because profits cannot be directly appropriated and the Postal Service is unlikely to propose rate reductions for first class mail, there is no other alternative. Former postmaster general Eric Kierans of Canada Post in 1968 attempted to mechanize operations and modernize managerial control. The Canadian Union of Postal Workers responded with a militant policy statement, which concluded by saying: "We therefore declare that unless the above reason-

able and just conditions are met by our Employer, we shall ensure that the enormously expensive and complex mechanization program in the Post Office WILL NOT SUCCEED" (emphasis in the original). Experience suggests that CUPW has kept its promise. See L. M. Read, "Canada Post: A Case Study in the Correlation of Collective Will and Productivity," p. 131.

39. William Bolger, "The Postal Community Looks at Electronic Mail and the Future" (remarks at Cavanaugh Associates Seminar, Washington, D.C., September 15, 1980). See Conkey, *The Postal Precipice*, p. 443.

40. House, Post Office and Civil Service Committee, Postal Personnel and Modernization Subcommittee, *Electronic Message Service Systems, Hearings,* January 29, February 6, 20, March 11, 20, 25, April 1, 1980, Serial No. 96-78, pp. 68-69. See Conkey, *The Postal Precipice*, p. 454.

41. Conkey, *The Postal Precipice*, p. 180.

42. See Daniel Oliver, "Saving the Post Office" (remarks before the Direct Marketing Association's Government Affairs Conference, Washington, D.C., May 15, 1987), pp. 3, 4, 6, 8.

43. *Cong. Rec.*, April 30, 1987, p. E.1670.

44. Regardless of the fate of the document delivery service market in the twenty-first century, the Postal Service has played an important role in the lives of many people and, indeed, in the life of the nation for a long time. It would be fitting and appropriate to erect a museum where Post Office and Postal Service history could be portrayed graphically, with paraphernalia, audiovisual displays, other artifacts, and perhaps even wax figures. A memorial building, housing displays, could be located in Washington, connected with the Smithsonian Institution, to help preserve and perpetuate the memory of the Post Office and Postal Service, and to engender among the general public the appreciation and respect they deserve.

The Canadian government is much ahead of its U.S. counterpart in this regard. In September 1974 it opened a modest museum in Ottawa in the Sir Alexander Campbell Building at Post Office Headquarters at Confederation Heights. The museum displays philatelic items, postal records and documents, tools, equipment, and other materials used to provide postal communication from the beginning of Canada's history. Other displays trace written communication and postal references back to ancient times. The museum houses the National Stamp Collection and collections of postage stamps of the member countries of the Universal Postal Union. The museum also serves as a symbol and reminder of the thousands of postal employees who have devoted many years of dedicated service to the Post Office in Canada.

On June 28, 1984, the National Postal Museum was opened in the Wellington Building in downtown Ottawa across the street from the Parliament buildings and close to the National Archives and the National Currency Collection, so it would be more accessible to the 25,000 members of the general public, school children, and philatelic researchers who visit the museum annually. The new location doubled the floor space to make room for approximately 250 new exhibits that trace the history of the mails from the first European settlement in New France and British North America. A postal library in the museum houses the finest collection of philatelic literature on British North America in existence. See Canada Post, *Annual Report 1980*, p. 25; *Annual Report, 1981* p. 26.

45. See Christopher Elias, "Would Privatization Make Postal Service Letter-Perfect?" *Insight,* July 6, 1987, p. 42.

Appendix: The Demand and Supply of First Class Mail Services

Where there is a presumption that a business is operating efficiently under competitive conditions, one can, by analyzing data generated from its production operations and costs, determine the scale and cost conditions of its operations.[1] Although this very important precondition for analysis is not present in regard to the Postal Service, I will nevertheless use data provided by the Postal Service to estimate what would otherwise be the parameters of the production and total cost functions for postal services. In the second part of this appendix, I estimate parameters of the demand function for first class mail service.

Because the Postal Service produces more than four classes of mail service simultaneously with the same resources, there is a problem in assigning costs to the different types of mail. I have approached this problem by using average cost estimates of the four classes of mail together with the volume of each class to calculate a first class mail equivalent volume for quantity that represents the quantity of all mail services, expressed in terms of first class equivalents and designated Q. The other variables used in estimating the parameters of the production and total cost functions are L, the quantity of labor; K, the quantity of capital; and C, the total costs. Table A.1 lists the values and description of these variables.

A Cobb-Douglas Production Function for the Postal Service

To measure production characteristics, a Cobb-Douglas production function is used, namely,

$$Q = AL^a K^b \tag{1}$$

where the sum of parameters a and b indicates the scale. That is, if the conditions for estimation prevail (i.e. the firm is operating efficiently under competitive conditions and $a + b > 1$), this indicates that there are increasing returns to scale. The parameters of function (1) can be estimated more easily with a natural log function, namely,

$$\ln Q = \ln A + a\ln L + b\ln K. \tag{2}$$

Using the data in table A.1, we estimate the parameters A, a, and b in (1) by means of a stepwise least-squares regression technique on equation (2). The estimated equation is

$$\ln Q = 1.57 + 1.46 \ln L + .0931 \ln K \tag{3}$$
$$\quad\;(.908)\;(.224)\qquad(.059)$$

adj. $R^2 = 56.1$
D-W $= 1.35$,

where the standard errors of the regression coefficients, .908, .224, and .059 are in parentheses below their respective coefficients. The t-values of *lnA*, *a*, and *b* are 1.73, 6.52, and 1.57, respectively, which indicate, through use of a one-tailed t-test, that the coefficients are significantly different from zero at the 95, 99, and 90 percent levels, respectively. The value of the adjusted R^2, 56.1, indicates that variations in L and K explain approximately half of the variability in Q. The Durbin-Watson statistic, D-W, is 1.35, and ρ, the partial first difference coefficient, is zero.

The production function relating the quantity of output to the quantity of inputs labor L and capital K can now be expressed as

$$Q = 4.81 L^{1.46}\; K^{0.0931}. \tag{4}$$

If this production function were used to describe a profit-maximizing firm operating under competitive conditions, one would use the values of the parameters $1.46 + .09 = 1.55$ to say something about the scale of operations. The fact that $1.55 > 1$ would indicate that production takes place under conditions of increasing returns to scale. This scale is consistent with that of a "natural" monopolist. Once again, however, it must be emphasized, the Postal Service does not operate efficiently under competitive conditions, and so the estimating technique used here is inappropriate for determining the scale of operations.

Total Cost Function for the Postal Service

Once again, where a firm operates efficiently under competitive conditions, the nature of its costs conditions can be analyzed by estimating the parameters of the total cost function

$$C = d Q^f, \tag{5}$$

where C is total costs, Q is the total adjusted mail volume, and d and f are

TABLE A.1
Data for Cost and Production Functions, Fiscal Years 1978-1981
(October 8, 1977-October 2, 1981) (Numbers in Millions)

Acct. Period	Labor Quantity[1] Q	Labor Hours[2] L	Labor Cost[2] LP_l	Capital Cost[3] KP_k	Total Cost[4] C
1	6906.8	87.677	897.98	156.249	1054.23
2	8111.8	88.392	921.01	159.795	1080.80
3	8383.6	100.462	1015.77	175.830	1191.60
4	6942.1	88.974	942.44	162.571	1105.01
5	6782.0	90.008	950.76	163.341	1114.10
6	7061.6	93.633	974.44	167.020	1141.46
7	6795.3	92.652	961.60	164.241	1125.84
8	6757.0	91.429	952.63	162.042	1114.67
9	6499.5	85.899	917.20	155.007	1072.21
10	6059.5	83.284	893.73	150.325	1044.05
11	6086.9	87.666	931.35	156.187	1087.54
12	6432.4	85.407	910.53	147.323	1057.85
13	6432.4	92.631	978.02	156.581	1134.60
14	7078.6	91.874	985.52	161.625	1147.14
15	6618.8	88.026	964.12	157.634	1121.76
16	8538.2	101.169	1084.14	175.955	1260.09
17	6974.9	92.259	1046.96	169.294	1216.26
18	6842.0	92.272	1018.25	169.743	1188.00
19	7302.1	92.252	1044.21	175.219	1219.43
20	7014.2	93.866	1030.55	176.018	1206.57
21	6812.7	93.328	1026.13	174.544	1200.67
22	6325.9	88.043	1003.72	171.937	1175.65
23	6559.4	86.788	986.75	169.425	1156.17
24	6444.0	89.848	1034.21	176.540	1210.75
25	7014.8	86.726	1011.14	171.792	1182.93
26	7014.8	94.317	1080.26	183.752	1264.01
27	7414.5	92.318	1074.19	197.007	1271.20
28	6847.9	88.490	1050.49	191.820	1242.31
29	9170.7	100.757	1187.79	216.059	1403.85
30	7648.1	92.616	1115.04	201.822	1316.86
31	7658.1	93.317	1131.87	203.964	1335.84
32	7728.2	96.601	1160.36	209.330	1369.69
33	7367.7	95.748	1146.84	212.279	1359.12
34	7397.9	94.347	1135.39	208.911	1344.30
35	6806.5	89.359	1126.01	204.596	1330.61
36	6928.1	87.818	1109.39	204.239	1313.63
37	7196.3	90.976	1159.65	210.360	1370.01
38	7493.0	88.087	1135.60	204.181	1339.78
39	7493.0	95.724	1214.26	226.701	1440.95
40	7864.9	93.630	1197.85	227.113	1424.97
41	7132.1	89.045	1165.61	224.264	1389.88
42	9239.8	100.204	1307.36	253.236	1560.60
43	8360.0	92.967	1236.11	238.322	1474.43

TABLE A.1 (Continued)

Acct. Period	Labor Quantity[1] Q	Labor Hours[2] L	Labor Cost[2] LP_l	Capital Cost[3] KP_k	Total Cost[4] C
44	7998.7	94.169	1244.06	240.227	1484.28
45	7859.2	96.885	1272.94	246.060	1519.00
46	6888.4	95.921	1262.95	242.928	1504.89
47	7032.0	93.970	1244.09	238.118	1482.29
48	6721.7	89.562	1228.90	236.318	1465.22
49	6577.1	88.407	1214.59	233.809	1440.40
50	6536.3	91.042	1243.16	238.189	1481.35
51	7212.4	91.457	1247.62	238.296	1485.92
52	6976.8	92.039	1253.69	238.827	1492.51

Sources: Data supplied by the Postal Service; and James C. Miller III and Roger Sherman, "Has the 1979 Act Been Fair to Mailers?" in *Perspectives on Postal Service Issues*, ed. Roger Sherman (Washington, D.C.: American Enterprise Institute, 1980), table 4.2, p. 65.

1. The quantity figures were obtained using the "Mail Volume and Revenues" reports supplied by the Postal Service, and the "Postal Service Revenue less Judge's Estimates of Attributable Costs, Difference per Piece of Mail" figures from a table in Roger Sherman, ed., *Perspectives on Postal Service Issues* (Washington, D.C.: American Enterprise Institute, 1980). The figures for average costs for the four classes of mail given in the table were for 1977, and were adjusted for subsequent years using the Consumer Price Index. Call these figures $(R-C)/V$ (revenue minus cost over volume). I got the revenue and volume figures from the revenue and volume tables, and solved to find the average cost per piece of mail for first, second, third, and fourth classes, for each accounting period. I then divided each of these four average cost figures by the average cost for first class mail, to calculate an index number for each class of mail, which was multiplied by the volume figures to get adjusted volumes for each class of mail. The sum of adjusted first, second, third, and fourth class volumes for each accounting period is the number used here for quantity.
2. Labor hours and labor cost were taken directly from the "National Payroll Hours Summary Reports" for fiscal years 1978-1981 supplied by the Postal Service. The figures used were total USPS employee wages and benefits, and total USPS employee work hours for each accounting period.
3. I obtained data for capital cost from the Postal Service Annual Reports for 1978-1981, and from "Mail Processing Equipment: Total Cost, Accumulated Depreciation, and Net Book Value" (unpublished Postal Service figures). From the annual reports I found what percentage of labor costs (total wages and benefits) all other costs were. Call this number capital cost percentage. I used the net assets figures from the mail processing equipment reports to adjust the capital cost for each fiscal year, and the percentage deviation from that mean for each accounting period in the fiscal year. I used these deviations to adjust the capital cost percentage for each accounting period. Multiplying the capital cost percentage by the labor cost, we obtained the capital cost figures used here for each accounting period.
4. Total cost is simply the sum of labor cost and capital cost.

parameters. This particular form of the function allows the estimates of the parameters to determine whether the firm operates under increasing, decreasing, or constant cost conditions. To facilitate estimation, this equation can be expressed in natural log form as

$$\ln C = \ln d + f \ln Q. \tag{6}$$

The parameters of this equation are estimated as

$$\ln C = 1.77 + 0.606 \ln Q \qquad\qquad (7)$$
$$ (1.38) \quad (.156)$$

$$\text{adj. } R^2 = 21.7$$
$$\text{D-W} = .16,$$

where the standard errors of the regression coefficients, 1.38 and .156, are in parentheses below their respective coefficients. The values of $\ln d$ and f are 1.77 and .606, respectively, and together with the standard errors indicate t-values of 1.28 and 3.89. Using a one-tailed t-test, one finds these estimates of the coefficients $\ln d$ and f are significantly different from zero at the 90 and 99 percent levels.

This total cost function can therefore be expressed as

$$C = 5.87\, Q^{0.606}. \qquad\qquad (8)$$

From this we can calculate the average cost, which is

$$\frac{C}{Q} = 5.87\, Q^{-.394}. \qquad\qquad (9)$$

If the conditions for estimation had been met, namely, that the Postal Service produced efficiently under competitive conditions, the negative coefficient of Q, $-.394$, would suggest decreasing average costs, another condition consistent with the operation of a natural monopoly.

If we could ignore the fact that the estimating technique is inappropriate for analyzing production conditions of the Postal Service, we might notice that the decreasing average cost conditions indicated by (9) and the increasing returns to scale of $1.55 > 1$, estimated from (4) are consistent with each other. Under competitive conditions they would suggest increasing returns to scale, which is a condition for a natural monopoly.

Discussion of Results

In the past, economies of scale (which the preceding uncritical analysis of the raw Postal Service data does seem to indicate because average costs are decreasing and production seems to take place under increasing returns to scale) were said to be a sufficient condition to show that a company was a natural monopoly. From the empirical work described in this appendix, it appears that technically the Postal Service seems to produce under "increasing returns to scale," or "decreasing average costs." Estimates of the coefficients of the production and cost functions, however, are irrelevant for a business that does not operate under competitive incentives to efficiency. Gross inefficiencies in management and production mean technically that the Postal Service is not operating on an isoquant. This fact makes the estimates of the coefficients of the production function useless for determining economies of scale. Consequently, one should not use estimates of the parameters of the total cost function to determine the nature of costs. A government-owned enterprise, not subject to competitive pressures or the profit motive, does not utilize resources efficiently or minimize costs, and thereby violates important assumptions for estimating coefficients of production and cost functions from data analyzed with regression techniques.

These results, therefore, do not mean that the Postal Service is necessarily a natural monopoly. To turn the discussion around, Baumol, Bailey, and Willig argued in 1977 that "scale economies are neither necessary nor sufficient for monopoly to be the least costly form of productive organization."[2] Instead, they suggested the test for a natural monopoly should be whether the firm's cost function proves to be "sub-additive," which is the case when the alleged natural monopolist firm produces all of its different outputs at less cost than would be the case with multiple firms.[3] To apply the concept of subadditivity to the Postal Service, we need to be able to allocate Postal Service costs among the various classes of mail.[4]

The X-efficiency literature is also applicable to this case and suggests that the inefficiency of a government-run monopoly such as the Postal Service is so large as to offset any economies of scale it may enjoy.[5] Competition in all postal activities would lead to lower costs because it would improve the incentives to operate efficiently.

It does little good to use the relatively modern concept of "natural monopoly," defined by Henry C. Adams around 1910, to explain the historical justification for a government monopoly that dates back almost to the founding of this country. To cast even more doubt on the use of the "natural monopoly" category to underpin policy actions, the concept of "natural monopoly" is today being discredited by economists.[6]

The Demand for First Class Mail

An examination of the demand relationship between the quantity and price for first class mail and other related variables is helpful in assessing the strength of the Postal Service monopoly on first class mail and its ability to raise revenues through rate increases. The usefulness of this analysis does not depend on the competitiveness and efficiency of the Postal Service operations, as did the technique for estimating the scale of production. To determine the effects of postal rate changes on the quantity of first class mail and total revenues, it is necessary only to be able to measure consumers' reactions to such changes contained in the demand function for first class mail. In this section of the appendix I will estimate empirically the parameters of such a function.

The law of demand states that the demand for a good or service varies inversely with its price if other variables such as income, population, the price of other goods, technology, and consumers' tastes are held constant. A change in any of these will cause the demand curve to shift, making the estimation of the relationship between the quantity demanded and its price more difficult and the results less exact. To measure this relationship, the model includes some of the variables that are not constant over time such as income, prices, and population. Because it was difficult to find adequate proxies for consumers' tastes and technological change, I omitted them from the equation.

The model used in the empirical estimation uses the quantity of first class mail handled per month as the dependent variable while the postal rate, personal income, the price of a toll telephone call, and the resident population of the United States are independent variables. The price and income figures are in 1967 dollars to account for any inflation or deflation that may have occurred over the period of analysis.

Data Transformation for Demand Estimation

The empirical estimation uses monthly data from December 1977 through November 1982. Table A.2 lists the data. The Postal Service keeps its accounting records of the volume of mail delivered in 28-day accounting periods. The data for the quantity of mail handled per month required transformation from the original 28-day accounting period to monthly form, so that they would be compatible with data for other independent variables. Because in thirteen accounting periods there are only 364 (28 days x 13), as opposed to 365 days in a normal year, the beginning and ending dates of an accounting period change from year to year. Furthermore, leap years also cause a shift in the annual start and finish dates of the accounting periods.

To convert the volume of mail—measured in millions of pieces—from accounting period to monthly form, I took the following steps: (1) I divided the quantity of first class mail per accounting period by twenty-eight—the number of days in each period—to obtain the average number of letters mailed per day for the accounting period; (2) I multiplied this figure by the number of days in each month during the accounting period to obtain a partial total of the volume handled during the month; and (3) I added

TABLE A.2
Data Used for Empirical Estimation of the Demand Function
for First Class Mail Equivalents

Month	Quantity of mail, first class equivalents Q	Real first class postage rate PR	Population POP	Real income INC	Index of long distance telephone rates TEL
12/77	5054.04	6.985	220995	873.186	53.735
1/78	4993.48	6.944	221145	869.925	53.312
2/78	4918.25	6.900	221308	872.028	52.707
3/78	4987.42	6.849	221504	876.396	52.397
4/78	4950.51	6.789	221689	880.888	52.037
5/78	5117.44	6.829	221890	879.928	51.526
6/78	5079.12	7.680	222095	880.748	51.024
7/78	4880.63	7.626	222317	887.595	50.636
8/78	4694.73*	7.583	222572	890.597	50.404
9/78	4769.78*	7.526	222794	892.022	50.050
10/78	4924.32*	7.466	223003	896.565	49.627
11/78	4972.99	7.426	223195	900.743	49.381
12/78	5099.11	7.393	223392	908.477	49.409
1/79	5068.34	7.328	223577	905.423	48.754
2/79	4982.93	7.243	223744	903.042	48.069
3/79	5214.57	7.174	223941	904.735	47.585
4/79	5208.09	7.092	224137	899.385	47.045
5/79	5118.23	7.006	224352	894.816	46.474
6/79	5148.92	6.925	224567	891.921	46.076
7/79	5216.74	6.852	224803	897.807	45.614
8/79	5043.07*	6.784	225056	896.924	45.228
9/79	5242.67*	6.714	225287	894.091	44.718
10/79	5134.87*	6.655	225509	894.765	44.389
11/79	5071.82	6.593	225732	894.154	43.934
12/79	5440.67	6.525	225938	892.649	43.475
1/80	5266.36	6.432	226127	890.480	42.560
2/80	5434.88	6.345	226300	881.768	41.498
3/80	5291.37	6.255	226505	875.396	40.909
4/80	5267.94	6.186	226686	865.155	40.474
5/80	5245.80	6.125	226955	860.637	40.159
6/80	5294.08	6.058	227156	857.431	40.206
7/80	5449.82	6.053	227363	872.680	40.577
8/80	5423.57*	6.014	227595	875.421	40.457
9/80	5076.23*	5.959	227805	878.029	40.167
10/80	5264.78*	5.908	228014	880.977	39.819
11/80	5212.88	5.855	228177	882.201	39.481
12/80	5499.34	5.805	228339	883.514	39.222
1/81	5630.91	5.758	228486	886.027	38.925
2/81	5434.88	5.699	228626	885.296	38.564
3/81	5291.37	6.035	228788	887.099	38.287

TABLE A.2 (Continued)

Month	Quantity of mail, first class equivalents Q	Real first class postage rate PR	Population POP	Real income INC	Index of long distance telephone rates TEL
4/81	5301.91	6.747	228948	884.424	37.825
5/81	5363.56	6.691	229123	884.040	37.468
6/81	5375.11	6.635	229307	887.864	38.375
7/81	5295.26	6.560	229533	889.548	38.915
8/81	5219.97	6.510	229760	887.443	39.169
9/81	5462.72	6.445	229982	888.603	39.675
10/81	5449.63	6.431	230170	890.274	39.544
11/81	5503.42	7.125	230339	887.247	39.751
12/81	5142.94	7.105	230511	884.637	40.000
1/82	5277.01	7.080	230669	887.015	39.820
2/82	5465.16	7.057	230810	889.650	40.163
3/82	5451.37	7.065	230969	891.840	40.239
4/82	5507.65	7.035	231120	890.352	39.934
5/82	5391.07	6.966	231298	883.104	39.470
6/82	5338.87	6.882	231479	885.797	39.305
7/82	5393.66	6.845	231708		
8/82	5854.76	6.831	231909		
9/82	5684.70	6.819	232114		
10/82	5462.50	6.800	232317		
11/82	5474.98	6.812	232493		

Sources: *Monthly Labor Review*, various issues; *Survey of Current Business*, various issues; U.S. Postal Service; U.S. Bureau of the Census, *Current Population Reports*, pp. 25, 926.
*-Estimated.
Note: Q, in millions of pieces, seasonally adjusted; PR, in cents; POP, in thousands; INC, in billions of dollars; TEL, an index number.

together all the partial monthly totals from the accounting periods to get the quantity of first class mail for the month. For example, accounting period six in fiscal year 1978 ran from February 25 through March 24. The volume of first class mail for the period was 4449.9 million pieces. I divided this figure by twenty-eight to give an average daily figure of 158.925 million pieces. For the period, there were four days in February and twenty-four days in March. Multiplying four days by 158.925 yields a subtotal of the quantity of mail for the four February days of 635.7 million pieces. Similarly I computed the figure for the twenty-four days in March as 3814.2 million pieces. I repeated this process for all the accounting periods adding the monthly subtotals to obtain the monthly figures.

For unknown reasons, there were no Postal Service data for accounting period twelve in fiscal years 1978, 1979, and 1980. I estimated the figures for accounting period twelve by multiplying one plus the growth rate between accounting periods eleven and twelve for the fiscal year 1977 to the data for accounting period eleven.

I seasonally adjusted the quantity of first class mail by regressing the quantity of mail per month with eleven dummy variables (January was the reference month). I added the residuals for each month to the mean of the quantity of mail for January to obtain the deseasonalized data set.

To obtain real variables—variables of constant purchasing power—I divided each variable, namely, the postal rate, personal income, and the index of telephone calls, by the Consumer Price Index (CPI) and then multiplied by 100 to obtain figures in 1967 dollars. To compute a monthly postal rate during the months when the rates changed, I used a weighted average, with the weights being the number of days at each rate.

The monthly resident population figures were reported as of the first of the month by the Bureau of the Census. These figures were used as population estimates for the previous month. For example, the resident population estimate reported for June 1, 1982, was 231,298,000; I used this number for the resident population in May 1982.

The price of a telephone call (TEL) used in this appendix is the average of the index for intrastate and interstate toll calls. The indices of prices of intrastate and interstate telephone calls were components in the CPI that referred to all urban consumers. The aggregate personal income (INC) and the index of telephone calls (TEL) were lagged four months to account for the adjustment time in people's behavior when these variables changed.

Two functional forms are used in this appendix to estimate the demand expression for first class mail, namely,

$$Q = a + b\text{PR} + c\text{POP} + d\text{INC}_{t-4} + e\text{TEL}_{t-4} \tag{10}$$

and

$$\ln Q = \ln a + b\ln\text{PR} + c\ln\text{POP} + d\ln\text{INC}_{t-4} + e\ln\text{TEL}_{t-4}, \tag{11}$$

where Q denotes the quantity of first class mail delivered per month, in millions, PR is the postal rate, POP is the resident population, INC is aggregate personal income, and TEL is the price of a toll call in index form. The subscript, $t-4$, indicates a lag of four months in the variable.

The results of estimating the relationships shown in (10) and (11) by the ordinary least squares regression method are:

$$Q = -16230.186 - 189.074PR + 0.0825POP + 3.257INC_{t-4}$$
$$(4808.21) \quad (51.00) \quad\quad (.0192) \quad\quad (1.688)$$

$$+ 25.63TEL_{t-4} \tag{12}$$
$$(13.801)$$

$$R^2 = 0.70754, \quad D\text{-}W = 1.8921$$
$$R^2 \text{ adj.} = 0.6846$$

and

$$\ln Q = -38.076 - 0.2280\ln PR + 3.449\ln POP + 0.560\ln INC_{t-4}$$
$$(10.374) \quad (.0606) \quad\quad (.827) \quad\quad (.289)$$

$$+ 0.196\ln TEL_{t-4} \tag{13}$$
$$(.115)$$

$$R^2 = 0.71113, \quad D\text{-}W = 1.8571$$
$$R^2 \text{ adj.} = 0.68848.$$

The standard errors of the regression coefficients are listed in the parentheses beneath the coefficients. R^2, the unadjusted coefficient of determination, indicates the percentage variability of the dependent variable accounted for by changes in the independent variables. The *D-W* indicates the Durbin-Watson statistic, which tests the presence of serial correlation where the partial first difference factor ρ equals zero.

The interpretation of each variable's coefficient assumes that the other variables do not change. For instance, from equation (12), a rise in the postal rate of one cent in 1967 dollars—or a rise in the postal rate of approximately three cents in current dollars—will cause a decrease in the quantity of first class mail delivered per month of 189,074 million pieces if all other variables remain constant. A rise in the resident population of the United States by 100,000 will cause the dependent variable to increase by 8.25 million pieces per month. In other words, the quantity of mail will increase by 82.5 letters per month for every net increase of one person born. The meaning of the coefficient of the income variable 3.257 indicates that an increase in income of $1 billion in 1967 dollars or a $3 billion increase in current dollars results in an increase in the amount of first class mail delivered per month of 3.257 million pieces. Finally, should the index of the real price of a telephone call rise by one unit, then the quantity of mail will increase by 25.630 million pieces per month.

Using a one-tailed t-test, we find all the coefficients of the variables in equation (12) except INC_{t-4} and TEL_{t-4} are significant at the 99 percent level; these two variables are significant at the 90 percent level. The Durbin-Watson statistic is sufficiently close to two to indicate an absence of serial correlation in the residuals of the model. Furthermore, the R^2 indicates that the regression equation explains a little less than 71 percent of the variation in the quantity of first class mail delivered each month.

The logarithmic version of the above model, estimated in equation (13), gives much the same results and in addition yields the elasticities directly. For this equation, the values in the parentheses beneath the coefficients are standard errors. Using a one-tailed t-test, we find all coefficients of the variables in equation (13) except INC_{t-4} and TEL_{t-4} are significant at the 99 percent level; these two variables are significant at the 90 percent level. The D-W statistic, the Durbin-Watson statistic, tests for the presence of serial correlation. It is 1.8571 and is sufficiently close to 2.0 to indicate an absence of serial correlation in the residuals of the model. R^2, the unadjusted coefficient of determination, indicates that the regression equation explains a little more than 71 percent of the variation in the quantity of first class mail delivered each month.

The price elasticity of demand for first class mail estimated from equation (13), -0.228, indicates that the demand is relatively inelastic.[7] This means that a 10 percent increase in the postal rate will cause the quantity of mail to decrease by only 2.28 percent. The cross elasticity of demand for first class mail with respect to the price of telephone service—a measure of sensitivity between changes in the price of telephone service and its effect on the demand for first class mail—is 0.196.[8] This indicates that a decrease in the telephone rate of approximately 10 percent will cause a fall in first class mail volume of about 2 percent. The income elasticity of 0.561 indicates that although first class mail service is normal it is not a superior service in that its rate of growth is faster than the growth of income. An increase in income of 10 percent will result in an increase in first class mail volume of only 5.6 percent. Finally, the variable that has the greatest positive impact on first class mail volume is population. The amount of first class mail purchased per month is highly sensitive to population changes. A 10 percent increase in resident population would result in an astounding 35 percent increase in first class mail volume.

This analysis of the demand facing the Postal Service for first class mail indicates that consumers are relatively unresponsive to price changes. The U.S. Postal Service, then, has considerable room to increase the postage price of a first class letter to raise revenues at least in the short run.

Notes

1. Computations for the supply and cost functions were performed for me by Lori Oeffner at Wheaton College; computations for the demand analysis were per-

formed by Barry T. Freeman and others at Ohio University. The values for the variables Q, C, K, and L and the way they were calculated are described in the notes to table A-1.

2. W. J. Baumol, E. E. Bailey, and R. D. Willig, "Weak Invisible Hand Theorems on the Sustainability of Prices in a Multiproduct Monopoly," *American Economic Review* 67 (June 1977): 350-65; W. J. Baumol, "On the Proper Cost Tests for Natural Monopoly in a Multiproduct Industry," *American Economic Review* 67 (December 1977): 809-22.

3. Baumol, "On the Proper Cost Tests," p. 809.

4. From 1926 to 1968 the Post Office Department allocated costs based on the "cost ascertainment system" (CAS), which allocated costs on the basis of some tangible measurement, such as pieces of mail, or weight of mail and/or speed of delivery. In the Postal Reorganization Act, Congress developed a new cost allocation method that states "that each class of mail or type of mail service bear the direct and indirect postal costs attributable to that class or type plus that portion of all other costs of the Postal Service reasonably assignable to such class or type." See U.S. Postal Rate Commission, *Postal Rate and Fee Increases*, R74-1, vol. 1, *Opinion and Recommended Decision* (Washington, D.C., August 1975), p. 91. The major problem now is to decide whether to determine "attributable" costs on the basis of cost or noncost criteria. Melvyn Fuss argues, "Noncost criteria must be used in any cost allocation exercise that is designed to yield a rate structure." See Melvyn A. Fuss, "Cost Allocation: How Can the Costs of Postal Services Be Determined?" in *Perspectives on Postal Service Issues*, ed. Roger Sherman (Washington, D.C.: American Enterprise Institute, 1980), p. 43.

5. See Harvey Leibenstein, "Allocative Efficiency vs. X-Efficiency," *American Economic Review* 56 (June 1966): 392-415.

6. See Thomas Hazlett, "The Curious Evolution of Natural Monopoly Theory," in *Unnatural Monopolies: The Case for Deregulating Public Utilities*, ed. Robert W. Poole, Jr., pp. 1-25, especially p. 9 (Lexington, Mass.: Lexington Books, 1985).

7. In 1976 Bernard Sobin, working for the Postal Service, computed the elasticity for first class mail as -0.232, which is very close to the estimate made here. Sobin's estimates of the elasticities for the other classes of mail were -0.544 for third class bulk circulars, -0.21 for parcel post, -0.285 for special rate fourth class, and -0.163 for second class. See U.S. Postal Rate Commission, *Postal Rate and Fee Increases*, Docket R76-1, vol. 1, *Opinion and Recommended Decision* (Washington, D.C., 1977), p. 127.

8. The existence of cross-elasticities between class of mail is part of the reason that Congress has discouraged the Postal Service from using the Inverse Elasticity Rule (IER) in setting rates. The use of the IER assumes that the cross-elasticities between the different classes of mail are zero, or nearly zero, which is unlikely to be the case. Here, in the demand function estimated in this appendix however, the cross-elasticity between first class mail and telephone service is very low. See Joel L. Fleishman, ed., *The Future of the Postal Service* (New York: Praeger, with the Aspen Institute for Humanistic Studies, 1983), pp. 230-33.

Bibliography

Adie, Douglas K. *An Evaluation of Postal Service Wage Rates*. Washington, D.C.: American Enterprise Institute, 1977.

———. "Are Corporations Indifferent to Worker Job Alienation?" In *The Attack on Corporate America: The Corporate Issues Sourcebook*, ed. M. Bruce Johnson. New York: McGraw-Hill, 1978.

———. "Compulsory Unionism in the Public Sector: Some Economic Issues." In *Compulsory Unionism in the Public Sector. Symposium Proceedings. April 6, 1979*. Chicago, National Right to Work Committee.

———. "How Have Postal Workers Fared Since the 1970 Act?" In *Perspectives on Postal Service Issues*. Washington, D.C.: American Enterprise Institute, 1980.

———. "Privatizing, Divesting and Deregulating the Postal Service." Remarks before the Annual Chapter Officers' Conference, National Association of Postmasters of the United States, Washington, D.C., February 20, 1984. Unpublished.

———. "Abolishing the Postal Monopoly: A Comment." *Cato Journal* 5 (Fall 1985): 657-61.

———. "Freedom First, Last and Always." *Modern Age* 30 (Winter 1986): 50-59.

Alter, J. "Life inside the Postal Rate Commission." *New Republic*, November 8, 1980.

American Legislative Exchange Council. "Privatizing the Public Sector: An Initiative for Service and Savings." *State Factor* 12 (January 1986).

———. "And Now, the 20-cent Letter?" *U.S. News and World Report*, May 5, 1980.

Apcar, Leonard M. "Postal Service Talks to Begin Tommorrow; Fight Seen Over Call for Wage Rollbacks." *Wall Street Journal*, April 23, 1984.

———. "Postal Union Wages Should Be Boosted, Arbitrators Decide." *Wall Street Journal*, September 20, 1984.

———. "Postal Ruling Is Designed to Realign Pay." *Wall Street Journal*, December 26, 1984.

———. "Postal Worker's Contracts Follow Two Earlier Pacts." *Wall Street Journal*, January 8, 1985.

"Around the Corner: 20-cent Stamp." *U.S. News and World Report*, October 12, 1981.

Bailar, Benjamin F. "Why Postal Rates Will Go Up Again" (interview). *U.S. News and World Report*, March 17, 1975.

———. "Easy Answers or Lasting Solutions?" (address, June 11, 1975). *Vital Speeches*, July 15, 1975.

———. "Postal Service—Political Birthright or Economic Choice?" Speech to the Economic Club of Detroit, March 8, 1976.

———. "Address by B. F. Bailar, March 8, 1976." *Vital Speeches*, April 1, 1976.

———. "Mail Service Better—But. . . ." *U.S. News and World Report*, February 14, 1977.

Bailey, Elizabeth E.; Kaplan, Daniel P.; and Graham, David R. *Deregulating the Airlines*. Cambridge: MIT Press, 1985.

Bailey, Elizabeth E., and Willig, Robert D. "Weak Invisible Hand Theorems on the Sustainability of Prices in a Multiproduct Natural Monopoly." *American Economic Review* 67 (June 1977): 350-65.

Bain, Joe. *Barriers to New Competition*. Cambridge: Harvard University Press, 1965.

Baratz, M. S. *Economics of the Postal Service*. Washington, D.C.: Public Affairs Press, 1962.

Baumol, William J. "On the Proper Cost Tests for Natural Monopoly in a Multiproduct Industry." *American Economic Review* 67 (December 1977): 807-22.

Beck, M., and others. "Unsafe Post Offices." *Newsweek*, January 21, 1980.

Berman, P. "Do We Really Need the Postal Service?" *Forbes*, June 11, 1979.

"Big Postal Snafu." *Newsweek*, April 9, 1973.

Blumenthal, Ralph. "Officials Call Postal Delays Worst Since 1980." *New York Times*, December 24, 1983.

Bolger, William F. "Postal Service" (Address, November 27, 1979). *Vital Speeches*, February 1, 1980.

———. "The Postal Community Looks at Electronic Mail and the Future." Remarks at Cavanaugh Associates Seminar, Washington, D.C., September 15, 1980.

Bostick, George H., and Collier, Earl M. "The Postal Reorganization Act: A Case Study of Regulated Industry Reform." *Virginia Law Review* (September 1972): 1030-98.

Bovard, James. "Postal Monopoly Only Fuels Inflation." *Chicago Tribune*, April 28, 1980.

———. "The Last Dinosaur: The U.S. Postal Service." *Policy Analysis* (Cato Institute), no. 47 (February 12, 1985).

Buckley, W. F. "Postal Collapse." *National Review*, December 21, 1973.

Caves, R. *Air Transport and Its Regulators: An Industry Study*. Cambridge: Harvard University Press, 1962.

Clarke, G. "Why the Postal Service Must Be Changed." *Time*, July 7, 1975.

Collier, Earl M., Jr., and Bostick, George H. "The Postal Reorganization

Act: A Case Study of Regulated Industry Reform." *Virginia Law Review* (September 1972): 1030-98.

Colonius, Erik. "Jaguar Climbs Back to Prosperity." *Wall Street Journal*, July 18, 1984.

"Conflict of Goals." *Time*, September 29, 1975.

Conkey, Kathleen. *The Postal Precipice, Can the U.S. Postal Service Be Saved?* Washington, D.C.: Center for the Study of Responsive Laws, 1983.

Copeland, J. B., and Pauly, D. "In the Black." *Newsweek*, February 21, 1977.

Crutcher, John. "The Privatization of the Postal Service." *Washington Times*, June 2, 1983.

David, I., and David, L. "Big Post Office Mess." *Good Housekeeping*, (August 1979).

"Do We Really Need Today's Postal System?" *U.S. News and World Report*, March 22, 1976.

Doerhoff, J. "The Shape of Things to Come?" *Postmasters Gazette* (April 1984).

Doubleday & Company. "Bulk-Third Class Delivery Test." March-April 1983.

Douglas, G. W., and Miller, J.C., III. *Economic Regulation of Domestic Air Transportation: Theory and Policy*. Washington, D.C.: Brookings Institution, 1974.

Eads, G. C. "Competition in the Domestic Trunk Airline Industry: Too Much or Too Little?" In *Promoting Competition in Regulated Markets*. Edited by A. Phillips. Washington, D.C.: Brookings Institution, 1975.

Edgerton, Michael. "Regional Airlines Help Keep Small Cities on the Wing." *Chicago Tribune*, June 2, 1985. Ely, Bert. "Privatizing the Postal Service—How To Do It." Alexandria, Va. Ely and Co., February 26, 1986.

Evans, David S., ed. *Breaking Up Bell. Essays on Industrial Organization and Regulation*. New York: North-Holland, 1983.

Ewing, Donald R., and Salaman, Roger K. "The Postal Crisis: The Postal Function as a Communications Service." OT Special Publication 77-13. U.S. Department of Commerce, January 1977.

Fleishman, Joel L., ed. *The Future of the Postal Service*. New York: Praeger, with the Aspen Institute for Humanistic Studies, 1983.

Friedman, Milton. *Newsweek*, December 27, 1976.

Friedman on Galbraith and on Curing the British Disease. Vancouver, B.C.: Fraser Institute, 1977.

Fuller, Wayne E. *The American Mail: Enlarger of the Common Life*. Chicago: University of Chicago Press, 1972.

Fuss, Melvyn, and Waverman, Leonard. *The Regulation of Telecommunications in Canada*. Report no. 7. Economic Council of Canada, Ottawa, March 1981.

George, Anthony, and Sherman, Roger. "Second Best Pricing Rules for the U.S. Postal Service." *Southern Economic Journal* 45 (January 1979): 685-95.

Goodman, John C., ed. *Privatization*. Dallas: National Center for Policy Analysis, 1985.

Haldi, John. *Postal Monopoly: An Assessment of the Private Express Statutes*. Washington, D.C.: American Enterprise Institute, 1974.

Hanley, J. M., and Wilson, C. H. "Letter from the Chairman." *Time*, February 6, 1978.

"Head Man's Goals for the Mail Service." *National Business*, April 1975.

Heiskell, A. "Letter from the Chairman." *Time*, January 19, 1976.

———. "Letter from the Chairman." *Time*, April 19, 1976.

Heritage Foundation. "U.S. Postal Service and Postal Rate Commission." In *Mandate for Leadership*. Washington, D.C., 1980.

———. "Privatization: A Strategy for Cutting Federal Spending." *Backgrounder*, no. 310. Washington, D.C., December 7, 1983.

Hillblom, Lawrence L., and Campbell, James I., Jr. "A Practical Guide to the United States Postal Monopoly for Businessmen Who Use Private Express Companies to Deliver Documents." Washington, D.C., 1978. Mimeographed.

"Hopes Fade for a Self-Supporting Postal Service." *Business Week*, March 24, 1975.

Horsefield, J. K. "British and American Postal Services." In *Public Enterprise*. Edited by R. Turvey. Baltimore: Penguin Books, 1968.

Hutt, William H. *The Strike-Threat System*. Rochelle, N.Y.: Arlington House, 1973.

"Improving Postal Service: Postal Reorganization Bill." *Christianity Today*, December 30, 1977.

"Inflation Stamp." *Time*, May 5, 1980.

"It's No Happy Birthday for a 3-year-Old Postal Service." *U.S. News and World Report*, July 1, 1974.

Jacob, W. "Philanthropy at the First Class Window: How Your Stamps Buy Jacques Cousteau an Asparagus Fork." *Washington Monthly*, January 1980.

Jordon, W. A. *Airline Regulation in America: Effects and Imperfections*. Baltimore: Johns Hopkins University Press, 1970.

Kempton, M. "Postal Nightmare." *Progressive*, July 1981.

Kessler, Ronald. "47 Chances for Delay." *Washington Post*, June 10, 1974.

Keyes, L. S. *Federal Control of Entry into Air Transportation*. Cambridge: Harvard University Press, 1951.

Kilpatrick, J. J. "Finding a Postal Service Solution." *Nation's Business*, March 1976.

Lambro, Donald. *The Federal Rathole: How to Save Billions by Abolishing over 1,000 Nonessential Government Agencies, Offices, Bureaus, Boards, Commissions, Councils, Committees, Administrations, and*

Other Federal Programs. New Rochelle, N.Y.: Arlington House, 1975.

Lazare, D. "For a Haphazard Job, Try the Post Office." *Progressive*, July 1981.

Levine, M. "Is Regulation Necessary? California Air Transportation and National Regulatory Policy." *Yale Law Review* 74 (July 1965).

Liebenstein, Harvey. "Allocative Efficiency vs. X-Efficiency." *American Economic Review* 56 (June 1966): 392-415.

Mayer, A.J., and others. "Gathering Mail Storm." *Newsweek*, March 22, 1976.

McLaughlin, John F. "The National Commission on Postal Service: An Opportunity to Rethink the Traditional Role of Postal Services in a Changing World." October 18, 1976. Mimeographed.

McMillan, M. L.; Norrie, K. H.; Ohashi, T. M.; Roth, T. P.; and Spindler, Z. A. *Privatization: Theory and Practice. Distributing Shares in Private and Public Enterprises.* (Vancouver, B.C.: Fraser Institute, 1980).

McWilliams, C. "Congress Plays Post Office." *Nation*, February 11, 1978.

Menasche, R. L. "Black Union Leader Battles U.S. Postal Service." *Encore*, October 1981.

Merewitz, Leonard. *The Production Function in the Public Sector: Production of Postal Services in the U.S. Post Office.* Monograph 14. Berkeley: University of California, Department of Economics, 1971.

_____. "Costs and Returns to Scale in U.S. Post Offices." *Journal of the American Statistical Association* (September 1971): 504-9.

Meyer, John R., and Oster, Clinton V., Jr. *Deregulation and the New Airline Entrepreneurs.* Cambridge: MIT Press, 1984.

Meyers, R. J. "Citizen Bailar: Proposed Citizens Rate as Sign of Collapse of the Postal Service." *New Republic*, July 23, 1977.

Miller, Fritzie. "Fritzie's Bits and Pieces." *Badger Postmaster* (March 1984): 149-55.

Miller, James C., III. "End the Postal Monopoly." *Cato Journal* 5 (Spring/ Summer 1985).

"Monopoly Is a Monopoly Is a Monopoly." *National Review*, July 6, 1973.

Mosely, Ray. "Britain Marketing Capitalism: Thatcher's 'Privatization' Revolution." *Chicago Tribune*, December 23, 1984.

Nader, R. "Price Fixing by the Postal Service." *Nation*, December 12, 1981.

Noll, Roger B., and Owen, Bruce M., eds. *The Political Economy of Deregulation. Interest Groups in the Regulatory Process.* Washington, D.C.: American Enterprise Institute, 1983.

Nutter, Warren G. *Political Economy and Freedom.* Indianapolis: Liberty Press, 1983.

Oliver, M. "Albert Testifies in Support of Postal Reform Bill." *Publisher's Weekly*, April 2, 1979.

Ott, J. "Threat to Mail Revenue Arises." *Aviation Week and Space Technology*, March 22, 1982.

"Our Frail Mail." *Senior Scholastic*, December 14, 1978.

Panzat, John C., and Willig, Robert D. "Free Entry and the Sustainability of Natural Monopoly." *Bell Journal of Economics* 8 (Spring 1977): 1-20.

"Parcel of Grief for the Postal Talks." *Business Week*, April 20, 1981.

"Patience." *Newsweek*, December 23, 1974.

Perloff, Jeffrey M., and Wachter, Michael L. "An Evaluation of U.S. Postal Service Wages." University of Pennsylvania Discussion Paper. July 15, 1981.

Pirie, Madsen. *Dismantling the State*. Dallas: National Center for Policy Analysis, 1985.

"*Planned Postal Deficits*." Press release. Cambridge, Mass.: Association of Private Postal Systems, Inc., 1981.

Poole, Robert. "Is This Any Way to Run a Postal Service? No." *Wall Street Journal*, October 11, 1982.

_____. ed. *Unnatural Monopolies. The Case for Deregulating Public Utilities*. Lexington, Mass.: Lexington Books, 1985.

"Post Office Buys a Little Time." *Business Week*, August 4, 1975.

"Postal Disservice." *Commonwealth*, October 24, 1975.

"Postal Hike—and More Subsidy, Too." *U.S. News and World Report*, September 22, 1975.

"Postal Nightmare: Plan of S. Wenner." *Time*, June 16, 1975.

"Postal Pact Weighted in Favor of Productivity." *Business Week*, August 3, 1981.

Postal Reorganization Act of 1970. Public Law 91-375. 84 Stat. 719. (August 12, 1970), 39 U.S. Code.

"Postal Service Feels the Sting of Competition: Private Mail Deliveries." *U.S. News and World Report*, March 22, 1976.

"Postal Service May Close Its Electronic Mail Service." *Wall Street Journal*, June 7, 1985.

President's Commission on Postal Organization. *Towards Postal Excellence*. vols. Washington, D.C.: Government Printing Office, 1968.

Priest, George L. "The History of the Postal Monopoly in the United States." *Journal of Law and Economics* 18 (April 1975): 33-80.

Ragsdale, W. "Why Even More Rate Increases Won't Solve the Postal Mess." *U.S. News and World Report*, December 29, 1975.

"Rescuing the Postal System." *Commonwealth*, June 18, 1976.

"Return to Sender; Failure of the U.S. Post Office." *Nation*, March 22, 1975.

"Review of *An Evaluation of Postal Service Wage Rates*." *Industrial and Labor Relations Review* (October 1978): 122-23.

Rohlfs, Jeffrey. "A Theory of Interdependent Demand for Communications Service." *Bell Journal of Economics and Management Science* 5 (Spring 1974): 16-37.

Saddler, Jeanne. "Phone Concerns Must End Bias Favoring AT&T." *Wall Street Journal*, June 3, 1985.

Saks, J. B. "House Overwhelmingly Passes Postal Reorganization Bill: Senate Unlikely to Act." *Publisher's Weekly*, September 17, 1979.

Sarna, J. D. "Some Tips for the Postmaster." *Nation*, July 5, 1975.

Scherschel, P. M. "Why the Postal Service Faces a Bleak Future." *U.S. News and World Report*, December 1, 1980, p. 39.

"Search for Deliverance." *Time*, March 15, 1976.

Senior, Ian. *Liberating the Letter, A Proposal to Privatize the Post Office.* London: Institute of Economic Affairs, 1983.

Shooshan, Harry M., III, ed. *Disconnecting Bell. The Impact of the AT&T Divestiture.* New York: Pergamon Press, 1984.

Simon, P. "Unmessing the Post Office." *New Republic*, April 10, 1976.

Smith, Sharon P. "Comments of the Council on Wage and Price Stability Concerning the Private Express Statutes." U.S. Postal Rate Commission, Docket R76-4, January 16, 1976.

_____. "Are Postal Workers Over- or Underpaid?" *Industrial Relations* 15 (May 1976): 168-76.

_____. *Equal Pay in the Public Sector: Fact or Fantasy?* Research Report 122, Industrial Relations Section. Princeton University, 1977.

Sorkin, Alan L. *The Economics of the Postal System.* Lexington, Mass.: Lexington Books, 1980.

Spence, Michael. "Product Selection, Fixed Costs, and Monopolistic Competition." *Review of Economic Studies* 43 (June 1976): 217-35.

Spindler, Zane A., and others. "Bricking-Up Government Bureaus and Crown Corporations." In *Privatization: Theory and Practice. Distributing Shares in Private and Public Enterprises.* Vancouver B.C.: Fraser Institute, 1980.

Spooner, Lysander. *The Unconstitutionality of the Laws of Congress Prohibiting Private Mails.* 1844.

"Stamp-licking Era May Soon Dry Up." *Nation's Business*, April 1981.

"Stamping Out Rate Increases." *Newsweek*, November 16, 1981.

Stevenson, Rodney E. "Postal Pricing Problems and Production Functions." Ph.D. diss., Michigan State University, 1973.

_____. "The Pricing of Postal Services." In *New Dimensions in Public Utility Pricing.* Edited by Harry M. Trebbing. East Lansing: Michigan State University Press, 1976.

"Still Trying to Make the Post Office Work." *Business Week*, March 21, 1977.

"Third Class Service, First Class Rates." *New Republic*, January 24, 1976.

"This Month's Feature: Congress and the Postal Service Controversy." *Congressional Digest*, November 1976.

"This Year's Stamps: 15 cents, 18 cents, now 20 cents." *U.S. News and World Report*, October 12, 1981, p. 8.

Tierney, John T. *Postal Reorganization: Managing the Public's Business.* Boston, Mass.: Auburn House, 1981.

Trost, Cathy. "Postal Unions Break Off Contract Talks, Demand Discussion of Wages, Benefits." *Wall Street Journal*, July 18, 1984.

Tunstall, W. Brooke. *Disconnecting Parties. Managing the Bell System Break-Up: An Inside View*. New York: McGraw-Hill, 1985.

Tuthill, M. "U.S. Postal Service: a Monopoly Trying to Beat the Competition." *Nation's Business*, May 1979.

U.K. National Board for Prices and Incomes. *Post Office Charges*. HMSO, March 1968.

U.S. Bureau of Finance and Administration. *Summary Report of Cost System Task Force on Incremental Costs*. U.S. Post Office Department. Washington, D.C., May 1970.

U.S. _____, Joint Economic Committee. Economic Goals and Intergovernmental Policy Subcommittee. *The Future of Mail Delivery in the United States*. 97th Cong., 2d sess., June 18, 21, 1982.

U.S. Congress. House. *Postal Reorganization Report Together with Supplemental and Additional Views*. 96th Cong., 1st sess., May 8, 1979. H. Rept. 96-126.

_____. Government Operations Committee. *INTELPOST: A Postal Service Failure in International Electronic Mail*. April 11, 1984.

U.S. Congress. House. Post Office and Civil Service Committee. *Proceedings*. March 15, 1977.

_____. *Report on H.R. 7700: Postal Reorganization Act Amendments of 1977*. November 1977.

_____. March 31, 1979.

_____. Postal Personnel and Modernization Subcommittee. *Electronic Message Service Systems, Hearings*. January 29, February 6, 20, March 11, 20, 25, April 1, 1980. H. Rept. 96-78.

U.S. Congress. House. Post Office and Civil Service Committee. Postal Service Subcommittee. *Operation and Organization of the Postal Rate Commission, Hearings*. January 29, 30, 1974. Serial 93-43.

_____. *Hearings on H.R. 2445: Postal Reorganization Act Amendments of 1975*. 94th Cong., 1st sess., February 1975.

_____. *Hearings on Cutbacks in Postal Service*. 94th Cong., 2d sess., May 1976.

U.S. Senate. *Problems of the U.S. Postal Service. A Compendium of Studies, Articles and Statements on the U.S. Postal Service*. March 1976.

_____. Judiciary Committee. *Oversight of Civil Aeronautics Board Practices and Procedures*. Washington, D.C: Government Printing Office, 1975.

U.S. Senate. Post Office and Civil Service Committee. *Postal Reorganization*. June 3, 1970. S. Rept. 91-912.

_____. *Investigation of the Postal Service*. 93d Cong., 2d sess., March 1974. S. Rept. 95-727.

_____. *Hearings on S. 2844: Postal Amendments*. 94th Cong., 2d sess., April 20, 1976.

U.S. Senate. Government Affairs Committee. Energy, Nuclear Proliferation, and Federal Services Subcommittee. *Postal Service Amend-*

ments Acts of 1978: Report to Accompany H.H. 7700. 95th Cong., 2d sess., September 13, 1978. S. Rept. 95-1191.

U.S. Department of Justice. *Changing the Private Express Statutes: Competitive Alternatives and the U.S. Postal Service.* Washington, D.C.: Government Printing Office, January 1977.

U.S. General Accounting Office. *System for Measuring Mail Delivery Performance—Its Accuracy and Limits.* Washington, D.C.: Government Printing Office, October 17, 1975.

———. *Comparison of Collectively Bargained and Administratively Set Pay Rates for Federal Employees.* July 2, 1982.

U.S. Office of Personnel Management. *Reforming Federal Pay. An Evaluation of More Realistic Pay Alternatives.* December 1984.

U.S. Postal Rate Commission. "Comments of the Council on Wage and Price Stability Concerning the Private Express Statutes." Docket RM76-4. January 16, 1976.

———. "Comments on Proposed Restrictions on Private Carriage of Letters." Interstate Commerce Commission. August 23, 1973. Legal memorandum of the assistant general counsel, Litigation Division.

———. "Concerning the Role of the Postal Rate Commission in the Exercise of the Legal Controls over the Private Carriage of Mail and the Postal Monopoly." Docket MC73-1. July 31, 1974.

———. "Concurring Opinion of Commissioner A. Lee Fritschler." In *Opinion and Recommended Decision Upon Reconsideration.* June 4, 1981.

———. Docket MC73-1.

———. Docket R77-1.

———. Docket R78-1.

———. *Mail Classification Schedule.* Legal memorandum of the assistant general counsel, Litigation Division. "Concerning the Role of the Postal Rate Commission in the Exercise of Controls Over the Private Carriage of Mail and the Postal Monopoly." July 31, 1974. Filed in Docket MC73-1. 1973.

———. *Postal Rate and Fee Increases: Opinion and Recommended Decision.* Docket R71-1. 1971.

U.S. Postal Service. *Annual Reports of the Postmaster General.* 1970-1985.

———. *Origin-Destination Information System Quarterly Report.* Washington, D.C.: Fall 1979; Summer 1982.

———. Research and Analysis Branch Office of Commercial Marketing Customer Services Department. *Competitors and Competition of the U.S. Postal Service.* Vol. 15. December 1981.

———. *The Necessity for Change.* Staff study 1075. Rept. ed. U.S. Congress. House. Committee on Post Office and Civil Service. 94th Cong., 2d sess., December 1976.

———. "Private Express Statutes—Exclusive Right of the U.S.P.S. to Deliver Letters." Press release.

"U.S. Postal Service: Troubled Giant Heading for Change." *U.S. News and World Report*, April 25, 1977.

Wagner, S. "Long and Short Term Help Sought for Postal Service." *Publisher's Weekly*, February 9, 1976.

_____. "AAP Acts on Four Fronts Dealing with Postal Matters." *Publisher's Weekly*, January 17, 1977.

_____. "Congress Begins Hearings on Postal Recommendations." *Publisher's Weekly*, May 16, 1977.

_____. "Leo Albert Indicts Postal Policy Before Senate Group." *Publisher's Weekly*, July 24, 1978.

Warren, James. "Postal Talks Land in Junk Mail Pile." *Chicago Tribune*, July 22, 1984.

Wattles, George M. "The Rates and Costs of the United States Postal Service." *Journal of Law and Economics* 16 (April 1973): 89-117.

Wenner, Seymour, Chief Administrative Law Judge in U.S. Postal Rate Commission. *Chief Examiner's Initial Decision on Postal Rate and Fee Increases*. February 3, 1972. Postal Rate and Fees Increase. 1971. Docket R71-1.

"What's Wrong with the Mails?" *U.S. News and World Report*, April 25, 1977.

"Why People Are Sore at the Postal Service." *U.S. News and World Report*, March 15, 1976.

"Why the Post Office Can't Break Even." *Business Week*, March 29, 1976.

"Why Will It Cost More for Less Postal Service." *Business Week*, April 21, 1980.

William, Bob. Postal Scene. "Expectations Too Great." *Federal Times*, April 9, 1984.

_____. "Biller Holding His Fire, For Now." *Federal Times*, April 30, 1984.

Winter, Christine. "A Ringing Defense of the AT&T Break-Up." *Chicago Tribune*, October 28, 1984.

Wood, Fred B., and others. "USPS and the Communications Revolution: Impacts, Options, and Issues." Report prepared by the Program of Policy Studies in Science and Technology. George Washington University. Washington, D.C., March 5, 1977.

Young, Peter, and Goodman, John C. "The U.S. Lags Behind in Going Private." *Wall Street Journal*, February 20, 1986.

Index